D1440726

EMERSON CENTENARY ESSAYS

Edited by
Joel Myerson

1982

SOUTHERN ILLINOIS UNIVERSITY PRESS
Carbondale and Edwardsville

Library of Congress Cataloging in Publication Data

Main entry under title:

Emerson centenary essays.

   Includes bibliographical references and index.
   Contents: The moonless night / Evelyn Barish—
"Christ crucified" / Wesley T. Mott—Emerson's
foreground / Jerome Loving—[etc.]
   1. Emerson, Ralph Waldo, 1803–82—Addresses,
essays, lectures. 2. Authors, American—19th century—
Biography—Addresses, essays, lectures. I. Myerson, Joel.
PS1631.E53   814'.3   81-18516
ISBN 0-8093-1023-6   AACR2

Contents

Preface

One hundred years after Ralph Waldo Emerson's death in Concord on 27 April 1882, it seems appropriate to offer a volume of essays assessing his life and writings. We are now in an excellent position to do this because of the quantity and quality of previously unpublished manuscript material made available in the last twenty years.[1] The eleven essays here presented, along with new documentary and manuscript material soon to be made available, should provide a fresh starting point for studies of Emerson as man and writer.[2]

The essays in this volume offer exciting new interpretations of important periods in Emerson's life and significant evaluations of his major works. The first four essays trace Emerson's development through the publication in 1841 of his first series of *Essays*. Evelyn Barish presents new evidence concerning Emerson's early illness and discusses how his decision to deal with sickness influenced his philosophy. Emerson's ministerial vocation is examined by Wesley T. Mott, who shows the importance of the sermon "Christ Crucified" to Emerson's intellectual development. Jerome Loving follows Emerson as he goes from minister to author and shows how a change in vocation and a change in philosophical outlook went hand in hand. How Emerson then developed a sense of himself as a professional author is the subject of Glen M. Johnson's essay.

The important period from 1841 to 1844, which saw the publication of *The Method of Nature* and both volumes of *Essays,* is dealt with in the next three essays. David Robinson examines *The Method of Nature* as marking a crucial point in Emerson's life. Essays by Richard Lee Francis and David W. Hill show Emerson searching for a persona in *Essays: Second Series* and evaluate the significance of his eventual authorial voice.

The next three essays range widely in subject matter. Sanford E. Marovitz surveys and evaluates Emerson's long-time interest in Shakespeare. The response of the periodical press to *English Traits* is discussed by Robert E. Burkholder. Ronald A. Sudol shows how Emerson's reaction to technology is embodied in his poem "The Adirondacs."

A general essay completes the volume. Merton M. Sealts, Jr., provides an apt closing statement as he reminds us that Emerson was, in precept and in life, a teacher.

One other essay was originally accepted for publication in this volume but, because of limitations of space, had to be excluded: Charles W. Mignon's "'Classic Art': Emerson's Pragmatic Criticism." It will appear in *Studies in the American Renaissance 1983*.

The following abbreviations are used throughout this volume:

CW   *The Collected Works of Ralph Waldo Emerson*. Edited by Alfred R. Ferguson et al. 2 vols. to date. Cambridge, Mass.: Harvard University Press, 1971–.

CEC   *The Correspondence of Emerson and Carlyle*. Edited by Joseph Slater. New York: Columbia University Press, 1964.

EL   *The Early Lectures of Ralph Waldo Emerson*. Edited by Stephen E. Whicher, Robert E. Spiller, and Wallace E. Williams. 3 vols. Cambridge, Mass.: Harvard University Press, 1959–72.

J   *Journals of Ralph Waldo Emerson*. Edited by Edward Waldo Emerson and Waldo Emerson Forbes. 10 vols. Boston: Houghton Mifflin, 1909–14.

JMN   *The Journals and Miscellaneous Notebooks of Ralph Waldo Emerson*. Edited by William H. Gilman et al. 14 vols. to date. Cambridge, Mass.: Harvard University Press, 1960–.

L   *The Letters of Ralph Waldo Emerson*. Edited by Ralph L. Rusk. 6 vols. New York: Columbia University Press, 1939.

Life   Ralph L. Rusk, *The Life of Ralph Waldo Emerson*. New York: Scribners, 1949.

W   *The Complete Works of Ralph Waldo Emerson*. Edited by Edward Waldo Emerson. 12 vols. The Centenary Edition. Boston: Houghton Mifflin, 1903–4.

YES   *Young Emerson Speaks*. Edited by Arthur C. McGiffert, Jr. Boston: Houghton Mifflin, 1938.

Columbia, South Carolina   JOEL MYERSON
October 1981

Notes on Contributors

EVELYN BARISH is Professor of English at the College of Staten Island, City University of New York.

ROBERT E. BURKHOLDER is Assistant Professor of English at the Pennsylvania State University at Wilkes-Barre. For four years he was Editorial Assistant for *Studies in the American Renaissance.* He has published a checklist of Emerson in *First Printings of American Authors* and biographical sketches of Richard Henry Dana and F. B. Sanborn in *The American Renaissance in New England.* Currently, he is working with Joel Myerson on *Critical Essays on Ralph Waldo Emerson* and *Ralph Waldo Emerson: An Annotated Secondary Bibliography,* both of which will appear in 1983.

RICHARD LEE FRANCIS is Associate Professor of English at Western Washington University.

DAVID W. HILL, Associate Professor of English and chairman of the department at the State University of New York College at Oswego, is co-editor (with Linda Allardt and Ruth Bennett) of volume 15 of *The Journals and Miscellaneous Notebooks of Ralph Waldo Emerson.* He is now co-editing volume 2 of Emerson's poetry notebooks for the *Additional Notebooks of Ralph Waldo Emeson.* He has written on English composition and has essays in progress on Hawthorne and Twain, as well as Emerson.

GLEN M. JOHNSON is Associate Professor of English at the Catholic University of America. He is editor of volumes in series of Emerson's *Journals and Miscellaneous Notebooks, Collected Works,* and *Additional Notebooks.* He has published critical articles Emerson and on American fiction, popular literature, and film.

JEROME LOVING is Professor of English at Texas A&M University, where he has taught since 1973. He has served as a Fulbright lecturer to the Soviet Union and twice as a National Endowment for the Humanities fellow. In addition to numerous articles in scholarly journals, he has published *Civil War Letters of George Washington Whitman* and *Walt Whitman's Champion: William Douglas O'Connor*. His book on Emerson and Whitman will appear in 1982.

SANFORD E. MAROVITZ served four years in the U.S. Air Force, after which he earned a B.A. degree from Lake Forest College and M.A. and Ph.D. degrees from Duke University. He has taught at Temple University, the University of Athens in Greece (under the Fulbright Program), and Shimane University in Japan (as Visiting Professor). He is now Professor of English and Director of Graduate Studies at Kent State University. American literature is his major field of study, within which he holds particular interests in Jewish-American fiction, Western writing, and the literature of the American Renaissance. Professor Marovitz has published widely in professional journals and collected volumes of criticism; he is co-editor of *Artful Thunder,* a Festschrift in honor of Howard P. Vincent. Presently collaborating with Clarence Gohdes on the fifth edition of *A Bibliographical Guide to the Study of the Literature of the U.S.A,* Professor Marovitz is also slowly progressing on a study of the literary influence of Shakespeare and Hawthorne on Melville's fiction of the early 1850s, from a facet of which "Emerson's Shakespeare" was developed.

WESLEY T. MOTT is Editor of Publications for the University of Wisconsin Small Business Development Center in Madison. Formerly Director of the Division of Liberal Arts at Thomas College, he holds a Ph.D. degree from Boston University. His articles have appeared in such journals as *New England Journal of Business & Economics, Phylon, Thoreau Journal Quarterly,* and *American Literature*.

JOEL MYERSON is Professor of English at the University of South Carolina and editor of the annual, *Studies in the American Renaissance.* His books include *The American Renaissance in New England* (editor), *Antebellum Writers in New York and the South* (editor), *Brook*

Farm: An Annotated Bibliography and Resources Guide, Margaret Fuller: An Annotated Secondary Bibliography, Margaret Fuller: A Descriptive Bibliography, The New England Transcendentalists and the "Dial": A History of the Magazine and Its Contributors, and, currently in press, *Critical Essays on American Transcendentalism* (editor with Philip F. Gura), *Critical Essays on Ralph Waldo Emerson* (editor with Robert E. Burkholder), *Ralph Waldo Emerson: An Annotated Secondary Bibliography* (with Burkholder), *Ralph Waldo Emerson: A Descriptive Bibliography, Theodore Parker: A Descriptive Bibliography,* and *The Transcendentalists: A Review of Research and Criticism* (editor). He is presently working on a descriptive bibliography of Emily Dickinson, after which he will seriously consider borrowing an ax and looking for an uninhabited pond in eastern Massachusetts.

DAVID ROBINSON is Assistant Professor of English and Director of American Studies at Oregon State University. He has published articles on Emerson and other Transcendentalists in *Harvard Theological Review, Journal of the History of Ideas, Philological Quarterly, PMLA,* and *Studies in the American Renaissance.* In 1979–80 he was a fellow of the National Endowment for the Humanities. Professor Robinson has recently completed a book-length study of Emerson's early career as a preacher and lecturer and is currently writing a history of American Unitarianism.

MERTON M. SEALTS, JR., Henry A. Pochmann Professor of English at the University of Wisconsin-Madison, holds degrees from the College of Wooster (B.A., D.Litt.) and Yale (Ph.D.); before going to Madison in 1965, he taught at the University of Missouri, Wellesley College, and Lawrence College/University. He has edited volumes 5 and 10 of the *Journals and Miscellaneous Notebooks of Ralph Waldo Emerson* and, with the late Alfred R. Ferguson, *Emerson's "Nature": Origin, Growth, Meaning,* which Southern Illinois University Press published in a revised and enlarged second edition in 1979. Professor Sealts's *Emerson on the Scholar* is in progress.

RONALD A. SUDOL is an Assistant Professor at Oakland University. He has received degrees from St. Michael's College (B.A.), Brown University (M.A.), and the State University of New York at Stony

Brook (Ph.D.). A past fellow of the National Endowment for the Humanities, he has published articles on literature and composition in *Christianity and Literature, College Composition and Communication, ESQ: A Journal of the American Renaissance,* and *Quarterly Journal of Speech.*

Emerson Centenary Essays

The Moonless Night
Emerson's Crisis of Health, 1825–1827

EVELYN BARISH

"Sickness is the answer each time when
we are inclined to doubt our right to *our*
task."—Nietzsche to Overbeck, November 1877

In January 1825, struggling through an ongoing vocational and personal
crisis, Emerson, while reflecting on his ancestors, himself, and his ambitions, wrote in his journal: "The kind Aunt whose cares instructed my
youth (and whom may God reward), told me oft the virtues of her and
mine ancestors. . . . But the dead sleep in their moonless night; my
business is with the living" (*JMN,* 2:316). The last is a haunting sentence, but it is as much wish as fact, the twenty-one-year-old Emerson
and his immediate family having long been shadowed by the fatality of
that moonless night. Within two months of this rejection of the dead past
and his wish to turn toward "the living," Emerson, then beginning his
formal study for the ministry, the calling of all his ancestors but one for
which he felt himself unfit, suddenly and inexplicably partially lost his
sight (see *JMN,* 2:241; *Life,* p. 111). Treated for this and partly recovered, he returned to Harvard Divinity School a year later, but almost at
once became so crippled by rheumatism that he could not walk from his
room to the library (see *L,* 1:166–67). Then, eight months later, after
receiving his license to preach, a lung ailment advanced so rapidly that
less than six weeks after licensing, on 25 November 1826, he sailed from
Boston on a southern voyage, possibly—like so many others—never to
return (*Life,* p. 119). He was then twenty-three, poverty-stricken, and
proceeding on borrowed money, but this trip was the last hope, such
voyages being taken primarily when death threatened: many died in spite
of them—Emerson in fact had two younger brothers, each of whom
sailed south separately in search of health in the next few years; neither
found it, and each died before his thirtieth year.

1

What Emerson's illnesses were, however, and how he recovered from them are questions Emerson's biographers, from early to late, have not asked. Oliver Wendell Holmes set the tone: "In 1826, after three years' study, he was 'approbated to preach' by the Middlesex Association of Ministers. His health obliging him to seek a southern climate, he went in the following winter to South Carolina and Florida."[1] In the mid-twentieth century, Ralph L. Rusk followed the same pattern, saying only that "Waldo Emerson himself was now alarmed by new symptoms of disease, this time in his lungs" (*Life*, p. 119). Whether he had bronchitis, catarrh, or some other illness is left obscure, and this obscurity has left him open both to vague conjecture and to ill-grounded criticism as a valetudinarian.

I wish here to reconstruct the details of his sicknesses and their etiology so that their relation to each other and a true picture of his condition may become clear, showing finally how he emerged from this crisis stronger and healthier in many ways than before. His illnesses had psychogenic as well as physiological roots, and inevitably some material touching on Emerson's emotional reactions to experience will be mentioned, but as much as possible I shall leave these matters for subsequent discussion, concentrating on the medical history, illumination of which must be a precondition to any serious reconsideration of Emerson's development and achievement.

Some brief family history is in order, for although mortality rates were high, the Emersons had suffered more of the grimness of death than the average. Ralph was not his parents' second child, as we might assume from William being his only elder brother, but actually their fourth, two having already died by the time he was four. Of eight siblings, only two, he and William, lived to have children of their own. Phebe, a girl, had lived only two years, while John Clarke, the firstborn son, died in 1807 at the age of eight of tuberculosis after a lingering illness which we can follow in Ruth Emerson's painful letters as she gives instructions for the "milk diet" and other care of the child who had to be sent away to live with relatives in Maine.[2] The diet and fresh air were in general prescription for consumption then.[3] The remaining children were also on a milk diet, we learn from a family history.[4] John Clarke's father tragically soon followed him; already very sick in 1809, William Emerson, Sr., expired in 1811, suffering from both stomach cancer and tuberculosis (*Life*, pp. 28–29). He was forty-two.

Significantly for his later development, Emerson did not grieve for this death, but their mother, a woman known for her dignity and hard work, who had borne eight children in fifteen years of marriage, may not have encouraged open expressions of grief; Ralph was surprised and grateful when she showed affection.[5] Poverty and hard work followed his father's death, as Ruth Emerson struggled to support her family by running a boarding house. Her only surviving daughter soon died at age three, while she and her five sons, one of them mentally retarded, worked for their guests, inhabiting on at least one occasion the basement of one of the houses they rented (*L,* 1:19). She was frequently helped by the coresidence of her sister-in-law, Mary Moody Emerson, the "kind Aunt" referred to above, an intellectual, eccentric "genius" in her nephew's opinion, greatly influential on him and, not incidentally, considerably more than half in love with easeful death: she used in later years to ride about Concord wrapped in her shroud, he reported—in fact, she wore several out this way and replaced them (*W,* 10:428–29). By the age of fourteen the boys began to earn their livings by teaching school while attending Harvard, Ralph assisting William in a task he much disliked, his shyness being intensified by William's specializing in schools for young ladies.

Propelled by these two women, as well as by their own work, scholarships, and charity, all four boys were graduated from Harvard, Ralph—by then called Waldo—in the class of 1821. Rather withdrawn, he had been an indifferent student, although ambitious of prizes, wishing only to write; he wanted fame also, but there was no immediate way to live except by keeping school, an occupation that grew more and more galling. However, he represented the seventh generation of American Emersons, and every direct male ancestor before him had been a minister. His family, especially his aunt, whose religion mingled Calvinism and Romanticism in a strong brew, expected the seventh generation to carry on the traditions:[6] William attempted it, and in 1823 went to Germany to study at the fount of the new biblical researches, little knowing that he was approaching the source of what was to become notorious as "German rationalism." When he returned a year and a half later, he had lost his orthodox faith and turned instead to the law (*Life,* p. 113). That profession was out of the question for Waldo, who in 1824, full of misgivings, nameless anxieties, and fears that he had not temperament and perhaps not the beliefs for his calling, yet driven by ambition, decided to enter Harvard Divinity School, in the hope that having donned the "form" of devotion, the "substance" would come later (*JMN,* 2:241).

For a year he studied privately with the liberal-minded Dr. Channing, but in mid-February 1825, he took the decisive, expensive step of matriculating at Harvard Divinity School: at this point his medical history essentially commences. Almost no childhood diseases are reported for him except for illness following a case of worms at age two, a skin eruption at age six, and what appears to have been a bad cold at age thirteen, for which he was confined for twelve days or more and a "blister" was prescribed (*Life*, p. 19; *L*, 1:21). The brevity of the list suggests some strength, given his environment. Within a few weeks of his entry into Divinity School, however, he later reported, he "lost the use of [his] eye for study" (*Life*, p. 111). Apparently still able to see somewhat, he continued teaching, but between March and September he had an undefined "operation" and left Cambridge. He then opened a new school but soon had a second operation performed on the other eye by "his" doctor, Reynolds, who we may assume had also performed the first. From this time "he began gradually to regain his sight in spite of his having to continue teaching." No further references to these operations occur, though his eyes were occasionally weak thereafter. In December, Waldo closed the Chelmsford school and opened another close to Boston; immediately "lameness attributed to rheumatism" arose—a significant fact which will be returned to below (*Life*, p. 115).

We have only one reference to Emerson's doctor, but if it were possible to learn who he was and what procedure he followed, such information might indicate the nature of the illness as well. Fortunately, we can learn a good deal about him and ophthalmological medicine at the time and can adduce the nature of the procedure he used with some hope of accuracy. Edward Reynolds (1793–1881), one of the founders of American ophthalmic medicine, a kindly "giant of a man," was born in Boston ten years before his patient and trained there under John Collins Warren before moving to England, then in the forefront of medical knowledge. He studied in London under Drs. Abernethy, Astley Cooper, and Travers for some three years, also briefly working in Paris. He especially valued the lectures by Benjamin Travers, who wrote a book, *Diseases of the Eye*.[7] In London he attended the lectures of the famous Sir William Lawrence and was "carefully taught . . . to perform ophthalmic operations. . . . He acquired a preference for surgery and especially for ophthalmic surgery." On his return to Boston he became known for having been the first American to perform a double cataract operation at one sitting, an "entirely successful" one which had the added distinction of being performed on his own sixty-year-old father. Having "formed the foundation for a reputation [as] . . . the leading surgeon in diseases of the eye in Boston and throughout New England," he went on in 1824 to become cofounder of the Massachusetts Charitable Eye and Ear Infirmary, which continues today as the Massachusetts Eye and Ear Infirmary.[8] That this Reynolds was Emerson's doctor there can be virtually no doubt, according to an expert on Reynolds and medicine in Boston in that era, given the small size of the city, and we can safely assume that, with his recent training in London where he had met and observed at work the best of the English surgeons, themselves part of a very small professional world, Reynolds in 1825 "knew all there was to know" about eyes and eye surgery.[9]

Determining the nature of the procedure practiced on Emerson may be less difficult than at first would appear, for eye surgery at that time was fairly primitive, and the process of elimination can lead us to reasonable conclusions. The book by Reynolds's chief teacher—as well as other sources—confirms the fact that there were essentially only three types of intraocular procedures common at the time, all but one of which were major: iridectomy, sometimes called artificial pupil (in which a bound iris is freed by excising a portion of it), cataract removal, and the enucleation (extraction) of the eye itself.[10] We may rule all these out, both because they were major operations of which we would have heard much more than a passing reference, and also because they do not fit Emerson's reported symptoms. There was another procedure, however, sufficiently simple to justify the casual tone of the reference to his "operation," likely of success, fitting what we know of Emerson's condition, and almost certainly known to Reynolds. Introduced in London within the decade, it had met with marked success, finding its way as "Mr. Wardrop's procedure" into a well-known textbook by 1826 as a treatment for *ophthalmia rheumatica,* and still in use on the Continent, J. V. Solomon reported, in the 1860s.[11] This was an operation to "evacuate the aqueous humor of the eye," so named by its originator James Wardrop in 1813, and in 1819, in a second article, even more strongly recommended by him for a condition he described as "rheumatic inflammation" of the eye.[12] The procedure itself was essentially simply the puncture of the cornea (now called ophthalmo-paracentesis) by a cataract knife, couching needle, or other instrument which must be slightly turned to permit the aqueous humor to drain; otherwise the fibers of the cornea would close the wound at once. James Wardrop, as the author of two important books and numerous articles in addition to being one of George IV's medical attendants, was one of the best-known English doctors of his day.[13] He held that the process was minor and should be repeated as often as necessary, especially as it was not painful unless the eye were inflamed, being in fact "merely the first step in the section of the cornea, made in extracting the cataract."[14] He offered seventeen case histories, all successful, to buttress his argument, stressing that in no case did a cicatrix remain. Wardrop's assertion that the operation could be repeated as often as necessary was confirmed by other doctors, according to Sir William Lawrence, who, although himself a skeptic, listed in his *Treatise on the . . . Eye* four positive reports to one negative, quoting a typical response from one who "employs it in every period of acute and subacute iritis . . . when bleeding and other measures failed to relieve. It must be repeated as often as inflammation and pain return: three, four, or more times."[15]

Since there was usually considerable pain in the head (not the eyes) with this condition, and the cornea in some cases might burst spontaneously, resulting in the loss of the eye, Wardrop believed that when there was much pain, the cornea dim and clouded, and vision impaired: "In all such cases the good effects of the operation were instantaneous. . . . When the symptoms have not been relieved by other remedies, the evacuation of the aqueous humor is a practice from which the most beneficial effects may be anticipated. . . . No applications were afterwards necessary but fomentations [hot dressings] around the eye," and for irritation afterward, "vinous tincture of opium."[16] Although this procedure has fallen into disuse, as it can give no long-term relief at all, modern medicine bears out some of Wardrop's assertions: since the cornea has few pain nerve endings, the puncture would not, as he said, be especially trying; moreover, the cornea would, because of its structure, tend to close itself immediately, and the bacterio-static quality of human tears would militate against infection "unless the needle were particularly filthy."[17]

Of particular interest to us, however, is the connection Wardrop seemed to have succeeded in establishing between this set of symptoms and rheumatism. The term "rheumatism" itself had fallen into disuse professionally by the second decade of this century and *ophthalmia rheumatica* before then,[18] but a hundred years earlier Wardrop had differentiated rheumatic eye inflammation from the other types (gouty, gonorrheal, syphilitic, and scrofulous) both because of the portion of the eye it attacked and because of its tendency to alternate with arthritic pain. He posited that the inflamed fibrous membranes of the eye's sclerotic coat were similar to "the kind which are commonly the seat of rheumatism in other parts of the body": when these other parts were inflamed, so would be the eye, sympathetically. Most importantly, the eye disease seemed to alternate with or strike soon after a rheumatic attack, especially after exposure to bad weather or sudden change of temperature, and most typically in the spring—just the season when Emerson's first attack began. Other symptoms, apart from the pain in the head and swelling of the eye, were a temperature that rose in the late afternoon and evening, impaired appetite, increased pulse, and "evacuations always changed in quality."[19] We do not know if Emerson had all these other symptoms, but they are, of course, also symptoms of tuberculosis; eye afflictions, as we shall see, have a long history of association with tuberculosis.

We know from a pamphlet written by Reynolds that he agreed with the prevailing doctrine, advanced by Wardrop, of sympathetic ophthalmic illness, and that he saw the eye and its membranes as a "microcosm" of the body's general state. He wrote in a pamphlet for the wretched and underfed divinity students at Andover who complained about the eyestrain caused by studying Hebrew and Greek in the texts Moses Stuart had personally printed for his students that the eye contained specimens of all the body's membranes: "This similarity of structure and function can alone explain the great variety of diseases with which the eye is affected. There is no organ whose vigour depends more upon the general health of the body than the eye—none, whose diseases arise more evidently from the derangement of the general health—and none which displays more numerous sympathies with every part of the body."[20] Reynolds certainly knew Wardrop's work and may have watched "Mr. Wardrop's procedure" accomplished by the man himself. Expert that Reynolds was at cataract removal, it seems reasonable to infer that, given Emerson's rheumatic symptoms of the same period, this is in fact the operation which his doctor twice performed to give him relief.

If we seek from today's viewpoint to learn the probable etiology of Emerson's ailment, we will find a considerable, but not impenetrable, array of possibilities, for nonsuppurative swelling of the eye, with or without inflammation, can have many causes. The connection seen earlier between the eye and the general state of health is still an axiom, and an uninjured organ may react to disease in an afflicted one in a fashion still described as "sympathetic." Stress, although not clinically measurable, may play a major role, for in stressful situations the adrenal glands produce additional amounts of the steroid hormones, among whose many effects is lowered resistance to infection.[21] Frederick Theodore, an expert on eye disease and allergy, points out that emotional stress may "augment allergic symptoms," that tuberculosis allergy exists, and that "not infrequently the obvious cause precipitating a particular attack" of uveitis may be allergy, for "the eyes and lungs . . . [are] among the most prominent 'shock organs' in the body."[22]

The potential clinical causes of uveitis (defined as the inflammation of the uvea, or posterior part of the iris and choroid coat of the eye) are the complications following rheumatic fever, bacillary dysentery, *herpes zoster,* and tuberculosis. All but one of these, however, can be ruled out. Rheumatic fever can produce both uveitis and arthritis, but the arthritis which follows rheumatic fever is acute and multiple but self-limited: when the patient survives there is no chronic joint pain.[23] Moreover, we have no evidence that the only serious illness we hear of (at age thirteen, mentioned above) was rheumatic fever. As to the second possibility, there is no reference to any dysentery suffered by Emerson at this time. The third alternative, *herpes zoster,* is unlikely because the iritis it produces includes the formation of vesicles which are finally absorbed and leave "focal areas of atrophy with depigmented scars"; it usually produces permanent blindness and is accompanied by long, excruciating pain: none of these effects were present.[24]

The only diagnosis we are left with, one which fits all the known facts and introduces no others, is of uveitis caused by tuberculosis. This is not at all a farfetched diagnosis in view of both Emerson's family history and his subsequent illness. A detailed discussion of this protean disease which could attack throughout the body will be reserved for later pages when Emerson's lung ailment is discussed. Here it is sufficient to say that tuberculosis played a "once dominant role in the etiology of uveitis," and in the days when tuberculosis was still common, it and syphilis were among the first causes looked for when cases of uveitis of uncertain origin appeared in a clinic. A study, for example, made in such a clinic in 1941 and reported by Theodore showed that when all instances of sufferers of uveitis were tested for tuberculosis in 1941, the remarkable proportion of 79 percent either had or had had the disease.[25] (Syphilis, another cause of uveitis, can be ruled out, both because it is virtually certain that Emerson had had no sexual experience at this time, and also because he showed no evidence of this progressive disease.)

The first report of rheumatism, Emerson's second disability, dates from January 1826, shortly after the second operation of his eyes. Back now in the Boston area and able to read for several hours a day and to teach, he returned to the Divinity School in February, after almost a year. Now, however—the timing of his attacks is relevant—the pain in his hip hindered walking. By 30 March he was too lame to leave his room and had to send his brother Charles, bearing a somewhat pathetic note for the librarian requesting renewed borrowing privileges without a personal appearance, as "I am confined by a lameness to my chamber" (*L,* 1:67).

Only two weeks earlier he had written in his journal: "I think that few men ever suffered ⟨in degree, not in . . . amount⟩ more genuine misery than I have suffered" (*J M N*, 3:13). The problem dragged on chronically, yet it also disappeared: we know that two years later Emerson walked twenty miles and possibly much more in a brief period for summer exercise, and eight years later he climbed Mount Washington in only fifteen minutes more than the low normal time.[26]

Arthritis, however, is highly responsive to stress,[27] and we know from other sources that Harvard Divinity School was for Emerson a problematic training ground; what is beginning to accumulate is evidence that his experience there was even more acutely stressful than we have known, and that this expressed itself in somatic symptoms. Emerson's arthritis, however, may also have been tubercular, for tuberculosis of the bones and joints was very common, and the hip was the second most frequent site. A predisposing factor would be a family history of tuberculosis, the age range at onset was primarily through the third decade, and remission with a tendency to relapse was not infrequent: true spontaneous cure was rare. The basic treatment in Emerson's day and afterward until the advent of drugs and safe surgical conditions was rest, good nutrition, and a worry-free environment. Emerson's case would seem to fit the particulars for an early stage of arrested tubercular arthritis, although without a closer description of Emerson's later condition than we have it is best not to assert with certainty a more precise diagnosis than "arthritis."[28]

Despite these problems, Emerson saw no choice but to go on, and in the fall of 1826 was "approbated to preach," a sort of licensing which was less formal than ordination, not requiring examinations, but granted apparently on the grounds of his inability to study because of loss of sight; he later said, "If they had examined me, they probably would not have let me preach at all."[29] He gave his first sermon on 15 October 1826, and the by now familiar pattern emerged again, but more seriously: his lungs now succumbed, and less than six weeks later he embarked for Florida on a sea voyage which, it was hoped, would save his life.

Holmes's (and Rusk's) failure to discuss the nature of his illness has already been mentioned; the silence is the more striking in a biographer whose primary vocation was medicine, especially since Holmes himself had told his students in 1867 that "Every other resident adult you [medical students] meet in these streets is or will be more or less tuberculous. This is not an extravagant estimate, as very nearly one third of the *deaths* of adults in Boston last year [1866] were from phthisis."[30] The evidence suggests that Emerson was one of that 50 percent, and that at the time he left Boston he was undoubtedly suffering from an exacerbated form of the same tuberculosis which in an earlier phase had produced his uveitis and possibly his arthritis. Now under the stress of his intensified vocational crisis it broke out in a more grave expression. We do not know precisely his condition when he embarked in November, but in January 1827 for the first time he described his symptoms: "A certain stricture on the right side of the chest, which always makes itself felt when the air is cold or damp, and the attempt to preach or the like exertion of the lungs is followed by an aching" (*L*, 1:184). His weight had fallen, probably alarmingly, so that in February, three months after he had embarked, he weighed only 141½ pounds, a low figure for a man close to six feet, and he had in fact been gaining. (If after four months he was 10 pounds below the 152 he was to reach in April, a reasonable estimate of his initial weight loss might be 15 to 20 pounds or even more.) In May he wrote, "I am still saddled with the villain stricture, and perhaps he will ride me to death." Oddly but significantly he had written that he had "no symptom any physician extant can recognize or understand" (*L*, 1:192, 198, 184).

This, however, cannot have been the case, for Emerson has given the classic symptoms of pleurisy. Technically an inflammation of the serous membrane enveloping the lungs, pleurisy is not a disease but the name of the chronic chest pain which is made worse by bad weather and exertion of the voice, and which appears more often on the right side. Then as now it was understood to be a sign of mild, chronic, or "indolent" tuberculosis, being caused by lesions which remain on the surface of the lung after an outbreak, but which usually remain localized.[31] Samuel Morton in 1834 began his book, *Illustrations of Pulmonary Consumption,* with a long description of pleurisy precisely because it was known to be a feature of many cases of consumption, describing exactly the one-sided pain, aggravated by every motion of the body, but especially by coughing, speaking, and efforts at full respiration. He knew too that morbid changes in the pleura "do not necessarily involve the life of the patient . . . they are often followed by restoration to health."[32] One should note, however, that we hear of Emerson's pleuritic symptoms only in March; in the late fall when the decision had been made to travel south there may well have been more decisive symptoms of which pleurisy was only the tag end.

The question arises, however, if Emerson did have an exacerbated episode in late 1826 of a chronic mild case of tuberculosis, why he should have said he had "no symptom . . . any physician extant can recognize or

understand" as he did in January 1827, when he wrote William that "I am
not sick; I am not well; but luke-sick" (*L,* 1:184). For we ought not to
underestimate the capacity of contemporary medicine to diagnose consumption.[33] Not only was pleurisy known as one of its signs, but it was
the most familiar of all causes of death, killing more persons in Emerson's age group than all other causes combined, and responsible for from
20 percent to 33 percent of all deaths in the period. (Some estimates ran
higher, some lower.)[34] In the 1860s Holmes, as we have seen, estimated
that it caused one-third of all deaths, and that one-half of all Bostonians
had been touched by it; William Osler at the end of the century quoted the
German proverb, *Jedermann hat am Ende ein bischen Tuberculose*—
"Everyone goes to the grave with a touch of tuberculosis."[35] The formal
lament which opens the chapter on consumption in a contemporary medical text has the air of a set piece: "It is a melancholy truth, verified in
almost every family, that pulmonary consumption constitutes a large
proportion of our bills of mortality, and forms one of the most crowded
avenues to the tomb."[36] Moreover, the disease ran in Emerson's family:
his oldest brother had died of it and his father had had it; while we can only
question it as a possible cause of death for Emerson's two infant sisters, it
is certain that two of his three younger brothers died of consumption
before they were thirty. In addition, medical opinion since Hippocrates
had been that consumption was hereditary (only a few suspected it was
contagious) and ran especially in the families of persons who were fair-
skinned, blue-eyed, and narrow-chested—all characteristics of Emerson
himself.

With such symptomology, family history, and body type, why
would Emerson's doctors not have diagnosed his condition? Common
sense and recognition of the ambiguities then surrounding consumption
may clarify the issue. The disease was much feared, familiarity not
breeding contempt, for there was in fact great ignorance as to its etiology,
duration, and prognosis. Acknowledged to be "protean" in its forms,[37]
tuberculosis could asymptomatically invade many parts of the body and
go undetected; sometimes only autopsy revealed the presence of tubercles. (That the lesions of scrofula, for example, were tubercular was not
known until late in the nineteenth century,[38] and as tubercles per se—
collections of cells which assume a globular or milletlike (miliary) shape
and vary in color from semitransparent to gray—never show up in the
eye, the nature of uveitis's connection with tuberculosis was not clear
until later in the century, when the germ theory had come in.) Part of the
fear sprang from the widely held belief that consumption was almost

invariably fatal,[39] an idea Francis Ramadge set out in 1834 to combat in publishing *Consumption Curable,* but his suggested cure, gradually to expand the lungs by having the patient breathe through tubes of special construction, was no more certain of results than the rigid milk diet advocated by James Thacher and others, or the bloodletting which was still the treatment of choice for diseases of all sorts.[40] Nor was the illness clearly correlated with economic factors, for while a doctor like Morton might adduce evidence that mass starvation increased tuberculosis and write that "affluence is . . . some protection against phthisis," he, like others, simultaneously asserted that it affected persons of every class, without significant distinction.[41]

Diagnosis might be difficult until the disease was well advanced, and even then it might escape detection. The symptoms were many and ambiguous. Coughing, spitting, "hectic" fever that rose in the late afternoons and evenings, pallor, the flush of fever, and loss of appetite and weight were often but not always symptomatic, as was haemoptysis, the coughing of blood. Only such hemorrhaging was considered a sure sign, but even that might not occur; if it did, it might come early and not recur.[42] Ramadge, who maintained a clinic in London for consumptives largely at his own expense and boasted of having performed 3,000 autopsies, thought he could infallibly percuss a tubercular chest and distinguish it by sound alone from a bronchitic one, but his careful description of the process shows how difficult a differential diagnosis might be.[43] Moreover, pulmonary consumption might be painless, the lungs being relatively insensitive, while the tuberculosis might metastasize elsewhere, as into the legs, where a patient might complain of intense pain while feeling nothing in his chest.[44] Statistics were incomplete and often unreliable, causing further confusion.

On one point, however, doctors agreed: "We would encourage cheerfulness of spirits and occupation of the mind," in Edward Smith's words.[45] Tranquility was the great thing, but the opposite also obtained. As W. W. Hall put it, "We then have arrived at a great fact that depressing mental influences are a 'cause' of consumption."[46] He was not unique in thinking that "stress" not only intensified tuberculosis but could cause it. Thus, arguing that the "depressing passions" incite tuberculosis, a German doctor, Avenbrugger, described his dissection of the tubercular bodies of many young conscripts who, shipped to a foreign country, became "hopeless of returning to their beloved country, sad, silent, listless, solitary, musing, and finally quite regardless of all the cares and duties of life. . . . The body gradually wastes away under the pressure of ungratified desires." They died, he concluded, "of the disease called nostalgia"—of which consumption was, in effect, a symptom.[47]

Even with so many variables clouding the picture, it is difficult to understand why Emerson should have reported to his brother that no doctor could understand his symptoms. One expert on the history of medicine believes that it is extremely likely that, given his symptoms, Emerson's doctors would both have diagnosed tuberculosis and informed him of that diagnosis.[48] Certainly, the taboos we associate with tuberculosis—an attitude named *phthisiophobia* by Arnold Klebs in 1909 in working to dispel it—did not spring up until a much later period. But clearly the treatment of choice for tuberculosis was prescribed: the passive exercise and change to a warmer climate afforded by a sea voyage, which would also remove the patient from the specific causes of his anxiety. Emerson evidently wanted to avoid naming his illness. Tuberculosis patients are notoriously euphoric, even unrealistic about the progress of their illness, *spes pthisicorum* being the technical term for their attitude.[49] Probably Emerson knew he had consumption but chose to use what he elsewhere called "the optative mood"—to assume the best, ignore evil possibilities, and control the potential progression from anxiety to depression and despair. We can hardly overestimate the importance of such a lesson as it affected his later modes of thought. Waldo's relation to William may also, however, have affected what he told him, for he may have avoided naming the disease in order to minimize his brother's concern. William's life had already undergone a severe upheaval following the religious crisis that had made him abandon the ministry in 1825, and the sibling who had once been to Waldo "the Mogul" and "your Grace" was now beginning again in poverty, studying law in New York, while eking out his living by tutoring though still longing for an intellectual and literary life.

Seeing that struggle, moreover, may also have influenced Waldo in another way, by suggesting that one could not resolve a religious crisis by abandoning the church for another, uncongenial profession. It might be better to "wrestle with the angel yet a while longer" until he at least knew on what grounds he stood. Such a struggle does seem to have existed and been related to Waldo's breakdown of health, as the precise synchrony of his attacks of illness with the assumption of new professional status so clearly hints. The issues and evidence are too large and complex to be adequately treated here; they are in fact central to a larger study of Emerson's early life and writings which I am now preparing. It may nevertheless be appropriate to sketch briefly some of the dynamics involved. As a mature man, Emerson startlingly described the era when he and his brothers came to adulthood by saying, "The young men were born with knives in their brain." The knife was consciousness itself, the awareness of a "crack in nature" between "intellect and affection," an alienation constituting "a sword such as was never drawn before. It divides and detaches bone and marrow, soul and body, yea, almost the man from himself. . . . The age of . . . criticism has set in" (*W*, 11:311, 307–9). That wracking of body and soul which, as we have seen, was far from metaphorical for Emerson, was complex in origin with sources in religious, vocational, and personal conflicts. One such source was a profound struggle with skepticism that accompanied his prolonged study of Hume—to which he does not refer, there or elsewhere after the fact, but which had a significant effect on his thought.[50] Another source of stress, though as much a symptom as a cause, perhaps, was the high but contradictory nature of his professional self-image and ambition—an ambition first mediated by his aunt but incorporated wholeheartedly by himself, so that for many years he imagined somewhat unrealistically that it would be possible to play a glorious part in the religious life of his country by being simultaneously an insider and an outsider to its establishment, at once a pillar of the church and its purifying critic, a Richard Price, so to speak, and equally an Abdiel.

A third, deeper and less conscious obstacle, however, was his problematic relation to a dead minsterial father who had left him too early for the seven-year-old boy—or his youthful successor—ever to feel entirely comfortable either in relation to that parent's memory or to his profession. A sketch Waldo made in his journal at seventeen might almost be an emblem of his state of mind: titled "A magician of might from the Dead-Sea shore," it depicts a bearded seer, wrapped in something like a shroud, who stares ahead with sightless eyes while bearing a placard whose tiny script appears to be oriental but is meaningless; a youth approaches, supplicatingly, hand outstretched, but the magician does not see him (*JMN*, 1:230 n). To search thus hopelessly in the dead past, embodied occasionally in older men who possess antique, possibly biblical lore but will not share it, was a frequent theme for Waldo during the years 1820–25, and study of his journals reveals how obsessive might be the repetition of the theme of death and its analogues, history and the supernatural, which led across the threshold of death: there might lie that wisdom and identity the youth so consciously sought. He read widely and seriously in history throughout this period, and thought it the chief study of mankind, but his fictive writings, set generally in the historical past, focus on and often seem to be slowly sifting through the meaning of death, sometimes glamorizing it (a tendency one hears in the gothicism of the phrasing, "the moonless night" and "mine ancestors") but also identifying with it, immobilized by the need to reconstruct and get back in some sense to that crucially missing parent, one for whom, significantly, Waldo had not grieved at the time of his loss and of whom, even in his maturity, he had no positive memories.[51]

In later years Emerson understood that only by turning rigorously away from death would he find his sources of energy, but the tone of liberation and exhilaration that rings, for example, through the opening pages of *Nature*—which begins, in fact, with an anathema on our "grop-[ing] among the dry bones of the past"—still lay almost a decade away in the spring of 1827. Nietzsche's insight that "sickness is the answer each time when we are inclined to doubt our right to *our* task, when we begin to make it easier for ourselves in some way," would probably have found assent in Emerson (of whom Nietzsche was an admirer)—assent and an illustration.[52] The brilliance of the aphorism lies in the words, *"our right to our task."* In Saint Augustine, however, the twenty-three-year-old Emerson had to come to terms with death not as fantasy, but as reality, a highly possible end of things for himself before they had begun. His journals and letters suggest the process by which his vision changed. "Sometimes I sail in a boat, sometimes I sit in a chair," he wrote William about his days by the sea; sometimes, clad in clerical black, he drove a green orange down the sand with a stick, watching as it rolled randomly along the shore (*L,* 1:189). Death under these circumstances had no charm; wisdom, if it existed, could not be got by asking others; only he could be his own prophet. Gradually, he changed direction and shifted tropes; the supplicant youth faded away. He began to take up his "task" consciously to choose and renounce. To his aunt he expressed some of this process; in his journal he wrote suddenly that he could now "forego the ambition to shine in the frivolous assemblies of men"—could get beyond the need for acceptance, popularity, for the hope of meeting the expectations of powerful men who would anoint him as one of themselves (*JMN,* 3:78). With that new capacity to define and assume a single, difficult, but compassable role he began also to resolve other conflicts. When he returned to Boston he undertook to preach with some regularity, despite lingering disease; in six months he had met his future wife, and in less than a year he was advising William how to manage the stress which he now knew aggravated and in some sense had caused his own condition:

Have you forgotten that all the Emersons overdo themselves? Don't you die of the leprosy of your race—ill weaved ambition. Pah how it smells, I'll none of it. . . . I can't persuade that wilful brother Edward of mine to use the same sovereign nostrum. If I have written but five lines and find a silly uneasiness in my chest or in my narvous system to use the genuine anile word (and the old women are almost always right . . .) I escape from the writing desk as from a snake and go straight to quarter myself on the first person I can think of in Divinity Hall who can afford to entertain me, i.e. on the person whose time is worth the least. Especially do I court laughing persons; and after a merry or only a gossipping hour where the talk has been mere soap bubbles I have lost all sense of the mouse in my chest, am at ease, and can take my pen or book. I always take as much exercise as my hip can bear, and always at intervals and not in a mass. [*L*, 1:233]

Significantly, Emerson rejects here not all ambition, but that which is "ill weaved"—that which is contradictory and unrealistic, as his own had been. The "old women" who were "almost always right" and pronounced "nervous" with a country accent probably referred to their Aunt Mary, who doubled as Dr. Moody, family physician, when she was not jousting as intellectual opponent of Waldo and his "Garman" philosophers, as she called them, and whom she despised. But she was not *always* right, and he had found that he must move away from her opinions and dreams just as he had from other peoples'. Self-definition (self-reliance, as he was to call it) was the first step towards health. The "mouse in my chest" would vanish and he would speak freely only when he had attached himself in fact, as well as verbally, to the living. Emerson was not quite finished with his moonless night even in 1828, and health problems, including those of a sick, then dying wife, remained. But he had got the upper hand, and the illnesses he had struggled with would not again completely incapacitate him or threaten his life. His later consciousness of occasional debility should obviously be read not as hypochondria but as a response to the intermittent recurrences of an arrested disease which he managed with determination and insight; without such strength and strategy it would probably have killed him as it had killed so many around him. Death henceforth was not romantic, but increasingly sterile, synonymous with evil: "All evil is so much death," he wrote in 1837 and finally, "Life only avails, not the having lived" (*CW*, 2:124, 1:69). His experience gave his words a passion that made of them (though they might also become problematic) an American credo, plangent and urgent, helping paradoxically to bring him the audience and influence he had once sought for and renounced.[53]

"Christ Crucified"

Christology, Identity, and Emerson's Sermon No. 5

WESLEY T. MOTT

In a journal entry in November 1826, Ralph Waldo Emerson wrote: "I would write something worthily on the most affecting of topics[,] upon the personal character & influence & upon the death of Jesus Christ" (*JMN*, 3:55). This idea, hardly surprising coming from an earnest Harvard divinity student who had just delivered his first sermon on 15 October, took shape in two subsequent journal entries and culminated in Sermon No. 5, "Christ Crucified," first preached on 24 June 1827. This sermon is in one sense a milestone marking the beginning of Emerson's "progress" from orthodoxy to transcendentalism, from Christ-reliance to self-reliance; in part it is a conventional conservative-Unitarian homily stressing the beauty and perfection of Jesus' personality while berating in stock Calvinistic terms the human propensity to sin. Although Emerson, perhaps embarrassed by the alternately maudlin and militant tone of the piece, shelved Sermon No. 5 after using it for the twelfth time on 27 July 1828 (*YES,* p. 263), it remains an intriguing expression of his thought and personality during the period from his being licensed to preach (10 October 1826) until several months before his ordination by the Second Church in Boston (11 March 1829).

The months following Emerson's first sermon were a period of profound insecurity, both emotionally and intellectually. His sincere efforts to define his theological beliefs were complicated by deep-seated uncertainty over his vocational choice, an ambivalence tied implicitly to his sense of identity. If, as we now know, the early journals, notebooks, and sermons are the roots of the mature Emerson, Sermon No. 5 represents a formal resolution of his most urgent fears and aspirations during this critical period. The figure of Jesus became pivotal as Emerson sought not only to come to terms with the tenets of Christianity but, more important, to establish his personal sense of mission. The Jesus of Sermon No. 5 is the boldest formulation of the values and virtues Emerson

was working out for himself prior to his ordination. More than a temporary resolution of Emerson's groping toward self-definition at the start of
his ministry, the depiction of Jesus in Sermon No. 5 points toward concepts of heroism that Emerson would proclaim for years to come.

Journal entries of early 1826 show a serious, idealistic young Emerson eager to dedicate himself to some high purpose, but alternately skeptical and hopeful of success. With faith that the meaning of life would be
gradually revealed, he wrote: "I wish it were possible for man to imitate
. . . the way of his maker. It would be an ascent far above the pitch of
ordinary[,] of recorded heroism to dedicate & confine the members of the
body & the members of the mind to the exclusive pursuit of good. 'Tis the
perfection of moral & intellectual nature when nothing is done in vain"
(*JMN*, 3:10). Despite this ideal, his skeptical nature prevented him from
finding adequate heroes in the annals of history. Bonaparte, Byron,
Charles XII—all had shabby sides, convincing young Emerson that
"Much of the good of History is no doubt indirect & general" (*JMN*,
3:6). He comes a bit closer to defining his true hero when he observes that
the "real sovereigns of Britain & France" were not kings but writers and
scientists (*JMN*, 3:13).

History was a mixed record of tyranny (the emergence of false
heroes), of obtuseness in the mass of men (a recurrent motif throughout
Emerson's writings), and of sporadic progress among persons of vision,
permitting the race to grope forward: "Mere conquerors will be first
disregarded as mere units of a crowd and afterwards execrated[,] damned
as destroyers of human happiness. It may be said that these opinions will
always be confined to philosophers for they always have been; & can
never impregnate the inert & sluggish mind of a community which is
always slow to recieve [*sic*] an opinion or dismiss a prejudice. But the
very fact that many men have predicted the reformation is the best warrant
of its fulfilment" (*JMN*, 3:17). Emerson was developing a melioristic
view of history. History comes alive, he believed, when it is morally
instructive: "In the error & the rectitude, in the agreeable & distressing
events, in the education & degeneracy of so many nations of minds there
runs thro' all the same human principle in which our hearts are constrained to find a consanguinity & so to make the registers of history a rule
of life" (*JMN*, 3:21). He believed that "our perception of moral truth is
instinctive," but that "we need a learned experience" to fulfill our "virtue"; it is for this reason that we crave worthy historical models—to

nourish the "growing Godhead within" us (*JMN*, 3:21).[1] History provides, if not examples of perfect greatness, a *universal principle* of "true greatness" which is "always bottomed on goodness," "on sublime motive" (*JMN*, 3:31).

Significant in this light, Emerson wrote with unflinching honesty that for all its beneficial impact on human progress Christianity enjoys no unique status; truth as found throughout history is universal and knows no sects (*JMN*, 3:15). It is perhaps revealing that Emerson's tribute here to the "Unanimity" of truth is sandwiched between two of his most famous journal entries of despair: "I think that few men ever suffered more genuine misery than I have suffered" (16 March, *JMN*, 3:13); and "My years are passing away. Infirmities are already stealing on me that may be the deadly enemies that are to dissolve me to dirt and little is yet done to establish my consideration among my contemporaries & less to get a memory when I am gone" (27 March, *JMN*, 3:15). Emerson's sense of history was, in theory, one of progressive unfolding of purpose. But that Christianity enjoyed no special privileges in this scheme withheld absolute consolation from a young man who was making a commitment to the ministry and who aspired himself to be a "great man."[2]

We have long been aware of Emerson's "problem of vocation" after he resigned from the Second Church pulpit in 1832.[3] But he found himself in 1826–28 in a far more vulnerable crisis as he sought to untangle the threads of philosophy, Christian doctrine, vocational choice, and personal identity which were in his own mind indistinguishable. Temperamental and philosophical receptiveness to the idea of original sin and the need for moral growth combined with family tradition to make the ministry a natural career selection for young Waldo. Moreover, the ministry offered an escape from the schoolteaching which from 1822 Emerson had found demeaning; and it offered an avenue to exercise the "eloquence" he had so long associated with "greatness" (*Life*, chaps. 7 and 8). However restrictive Emerson's ministry appears from the perspective of his later career, it afforded him time and scope to define values that would endure long after he resigned from the Second Church. But he remained unconvinced, given his universalist views of history and truth and his own anxieties about success, that the Christian ministry provided ample range for his talents; and he was unsure whether the figure of Jesus could satisfy his hunger for a hero to worship and to emulate. His ambivalence is expressed in a letter to his Aunt Mary Moody Emerson on 6 April 1826, however self-consciously composed for effect it may have been

(Emerson apparently took it directly from his journal [*JMN*, 3:19–20]). After a moving picture of the "innumerable procession" of mankind, he writes:

At the last an obscure man in an obscure crowd bro't forward a new Scripture of promise & instruction. But the rich & the great leaned to their ancient holdings & the wise distrusted this teacher for they had been often misled before. But the banner inscribed with his Cross has been erected and it has been to some a cloud & to some a pillar of fire.

We too have taken our places in the immeasurable train & must choose our standard & our guide. Is there no venerable tradition whose genuineness & authority we can establish, or must we too hurry onward inglorious in ignorance & misery we know not whence, we know not whither. [*L*, 1:167–68]

The figure of Jesus seems at first to be making a dramatic entry that will change the sad course of human history. Despite Jesus' "promise," his legacy has been inconclusive. Emerson finds himself part of the procession of human history; the images of crowds, of "the immeasurable train," suggest death by smothering throughout Emerson's writings. For Emerson there is the unpalatable choice of following an imperfect tradition or risking the same quiet desperation that has marked all history. The dilemma is that Jesus has left a legacy the validity of which must continually be "established." Emerson makes no attempt here to define the meaning of Christianity for him, leaving open the possibility that his own heroic efforts may be doomed. The passage, with its qualifications and confusing antitheses, frustratingly leaves the dilemma, let alone its articulation, unresolved.

Elsewhere in his journals and letters of the late 1820s, young Emerson more sharply posed to himself and his relatives the philosophical and personal problems that would define his growth during the period of his ministry, problems that would always color his thought. These tensions included internal debates over such theological issues as the nature of divinity and the nature of one's response to intimations of that divinity, and more broadly existential questions over the nature and meaning of experience.

In his journal for 28 May 1826, Emerson is already expressing the confidence in his powers of intuition that marks the mature Emerson of the great essays: "I *feel* immortal. And the evidence of immortality comes better from consciousness than from reason" (*JMN*, 3:25). Yet he is conscious that complete vision is not possible; indeed, "the limits thus set by mind to its daring" offer "an evidence from my instincts of God's existence" (*JMN*, 3:26). While Emerson cannot rest easily with the limits of mind, he can accept, in the manner of Jonathan Edwards, the beautiful necessity of God's will: "I willingly hear an oft unwelcome doctrine, harsh & unwelcome in the ear of poverty & complaint that God has administered a real not apparent equality in the fortunes of men" (*JMN*, 3:13). This perspective enables Emerson to posit a vantage point from which to allay his obsession with the mutability of human life that haunts the early journals (see, for example, *JMN*, 3:50–51).

Emerson's stance of philosophical acceptance did not require a static shelter from the world. In trying further to define a posture that would embrace specific misfortunes within a scheme of cosmic meaning, Emerson proclaimed that human nature was designed to respond to adversity with growth of understanding: happiness "consists in reliefs not in enjoyments[,] and unhappiness is an uneasiness[,] a useful uneasiness in the body or mind prompting to the attainment of some good agreeable to its nature. That is to say All unhappiness tends to happiness" (*JMN*, 3:29). Stasis is neither desirable nor possible, since our experience is ever changing; but the *principle of accepting* flux is an absolute value for Emerson. Emerson's redefinition of happiness resembles the seeds of his concept of "compensation," which begins to appear by that name in the journals in the 1820s. In this context it is clear that Emerson never intended this important concept to be simply a measure of moral reward and punishment, a scale of fixed opposites; rather, "compensation" is a fluid barometer of the state of one's soul. "Compensation" is not simply "conscience," punishing bad acts and rewarding the good. It is a spiritual equilibrium that fosters human improvement, an improvement that needs continual renewal. It moves beyond mere moral approbation to that wisdom in which the mind contemplates its own progress in comprehending and accepting change and adversity.

While Emerson was gradually coming to grips with his sense of self, his relationship to other people posed a problem. His youthful Puritan sense of original sin combined with a constitutional squeamishness about human contact to evoke images of mobs and herds ("screaming" with "unsavoury breath"—*JMN*, 3:52) in depicting the mass of humankind. Young Emerson painfully acknowledged his place in the train of history; yet the "mass" represented a threat to the integrity and achievement of the hero/self. This contradiction echoes throughout the years of Waldo's ministry.

In a somewhat softer assessment of the human condition, Emerson was concerned, in reflecting on the ministry, that "men . . . rest satisfied with the weekly or casual expoundings . . . made by ministers & do not feel themselves under any obligation to think for themselves." While this might argue an inherent limitation of the ministry, Emerson maintained democratically that "moral nature is one & not diverse" (*JMN*, 3:34). He continued to believe in the potential for spiritual growth in all people. And in the martial terms that signified both conventional Christian phraseology and his own youthful yearnings for active heroism, he desired all to be alert for "private tokens from the world of spirits to a militant mind" (*JMN*, 3:35).

For all his reservations about the power of the ministry, Emerson believed religion provided a personal touchstone to measure the attainment of wisdom: "Religion aims to make a man at peace with himself. . . . it is impossible to determine the state of the soul without something outside, some fixed idea as that of God" (*JMN*, 3:106). Religion provides consolation in the face of flux. "Health, action, happiness. How they ebb from me!" Emerson could lament. Yet he went on to imply the solution, asking, "What is Stoicism? what is Christianity? They are for nothing . . . if they cannot set the soul on equilibrium when it leans to the earth under the pressure of calamity" (*JMN*, 3:45). This pairing of references to Stoicism and Christianity, which was to recur significantly in the Divinity School Address some twelve years later, was frequent in Emerson's writings in the 1820s as he tried to come to grips intellectually and emotionally with the institution of Christianity and its benefits. Long before he commenced preaching, Emerson was attacking historical Christianity, the "testimony of crowds and of ages." "But moral evidence," he declared, "the evidence of final causes when it can be procured is unerring & eternal." Still, the value of Christianity could not be overestimated; it explains "the existence of evil, for if man is immortal, this world is his place of discipline & the value of pain is then disclosed." Indeed, he goes on to argue, in terms that foreshadow his celebration of the *essence* of religion in the 1830s, that the monstrous distortions of historical Christianity do not negate the "nature of Xty" (*JMN*, 3:47–49).[4] That Stoicism and Christianity were mingling in his thoughts is suggested in a letter to Aunt Mary on 23 September 1826 that is virtually a blueprint of the Divinity School Address. Identifying with the insistence of "modern philosophy" that "feelings" are superior to the "Bare reason, cold as cucumber," he accepts Christianity as "the expounder of God's moral law" but denies its historical value; he suggests that a minister must speak directly to men, yet he will not rest even in his own newfound convictions: "To grow wise is to grow doubtful" (*L*, 1:174–75).

In the midst of his self-doubt Emerson had been concerned principally with the meaning of history, the nature of belief, and the shortcomings of institutional Christianity. But in Cambridge in November 1826 he
was wishing, we have seen, to write "upon the personal character &
influence & upon the death of Jesus Christ" (*JMN*, 3:55). While a sudden
concern with the person of Jesus is unexpected, it is significant that the
"character" and "influence," even the death, of Jesus lend themselves as
much to character study as to doctrinal formulations. Indeed, as Emerson
pondered this theme on his trip to the South on which he embarked on 25
November, it was the person of Jesus that continued to have appeal, this
at a time when a sense of personal unworthiness was increasingly at war
with Emerson's determination to survive and succeed. The southern
journey, which intensified both Emerson's fear of failure and his sense of
mission, was a turning point enabling him to confront and articulate his
dilemma.

At sea en route to Charleston, released from the familiarity of Boston and Cambridge, Emerson felt a momentary surge of confidence finding as so many nineteenth-century romantics did "a sovereignty in the
mind" that reasserted the centrality of a man amid the turmoil and vastness of nature (*JMN*, 3:57). He remained convinced that, within the
constraints of human frailty, all "partake" of a "universal beam" that
renders man free to travel "the broad or the narrow way"; but for a man
who could never claim a single moment of Christian conversion, and for
whom even transcendental "conversion" would later be an ongoing process, the "development of the mind" remained the key to human spiritual
potential (*JMN*, 3:58).

Into this open-ended view of the spiritual life, Emerson introduced a
universalist interpretation of the importance of Jesus. The "real difference between the sentiments" of dogmatists, he argued, is minimal;
"Hence it happens well that to whatever party names, education or inclination has attached us we sympathize all in the same affecting views of
the life & passion of our Lord" (*JMN*, 3:59). In declining a neat dogmatic solution to nagging intellectual and personal questions Emerson
was perhaps showing courage; but he was also indulging in a sentimen-
talist evasion of important theological issues, which Lawrence Buell has
shown was characteristic of Unitarian ministers of the period.[5] In
Charleston on 4 January 1827 Emerson continued his meditation on "the
great institution of Jesus Christ, the just religion which embodied all that
was known of the human heart & anticipated in its comprehensive revela-

tions all that has since been known." The universality of moral truth did not obscure from Emerson the "prejudice & falsehood" which had marred the history of the search for truth, but he looked hopefully to the time when "the champions of the Cross" will "come at last to the dear & lofty employment of pointing out the secret but affecting passages in the history of the Soul" (*JMN,* 3:61–62).

Emerson, however, was far from solving the problem of his own role in removing the old prejudices and pointing out those lofty "passages in the history of the Soul." To his brother William's suggestion that he apply for a pulpit in New York, he replied on 6 January with obvious homesickness, "For myself, I had rather be a doorkeeper at home than bishop to aliens" (*L,* 1:185). He clearly needed time before committing himself to great effort far from home and without having found his true voice. On 29 January 1827, he wrote William from Saint Augustine, berating himself for frittering away time and worrying that he might never realize his potential: "Here then in Turkey I enact turkey too. I stroll on the sea beach, & drive a green orange over the sand with a stick. Sometimes I sail in a boat, sometimes I sit in a chair. I read & write a little, moulding sermons & sentences for an hour which may never arrive. For tho' there may be much preaching in the world to come yet as it will hardly be after the written fashion of this pragmatic world, if I go to the grave without finding vent for my gift, the universe I fear will afford it no scope beside" (*L,* 1:189). On 2 February 1827 he was lamenting that he was "cold & solitary," unfit to be a "young pilot" to others (*JMN,* 3:72). Since arriving in Saint Augustine, Emerson had been worried anew about mutability, alternately accepting the insecurity of the human condition and doubting the very existence of God for lack of evidence (*JMN,* 3:68–69).

Yet in a matter of days he was recalling and restating his Stoic/ Christian consolation: "I become wise perforce by the progress of life. I strive to be happy but in vain. But every hour and every event fortunate or unfortunate contributes to my wisdom" (*JMN,* 3:74). While the trip South initially intensified Emerson's insecurity, he was soon expressing a new self-confidence. "It is a sound doctrine," he declared near the end of his stay in Saint Augustine, "that faith is virtue. If God sent revelations daily none could plead the merit of faith." As if this were begging the question of belief, he went on: "To what was said above of the death of Christ it should be added, Those words & those sufferings are now a part of human history & how deep a dye they have imparted to all the after fortunes of the race" (*JMN,* 3:76). While the nature of that "dye" is unspecified, that Emerson clearly felt the sublimity of Christ's heroism is an index of his new enthusiasm and sense of the power latent in his chosen profession.

In this more confident mood, Emerson enjoyed his conversations with the stimulating atheist Achille Murat on the return journey. Far from threatening what seems to have been Emerson's ill-defined, if not shaky, faith, Murat challenged Emerson to redefine his convictions and his goals. Though Emerson liked and admired Murat, he wrote of the tenets of Christianity, "My faith in these points is strong & I trust, as I live, indestructible" (*JMN*, 3:77). He felt, moreover, a new sense of purpose by seeing the incompatibility of "greatness in the world & greatness of soul." And he expressed a new trust in his own resourcefulness: "The night is fine; the stars shed down their severe influences upon me and I feel a joy in my solitude that the merriment of vulgar society can never communicate" (*JMN*, 3:78). He continued to worry that his "days" "have no honour among men" nor "grandeur" before God (*JMN*, 3:78–79). But he was learning to find strength (or refuge) from his weaknesses by simply inverting society's values. If he lacked strength and purpose, that was no matter, for the soul was superior to the world and would make its greatness known in time.

Homeward bound, he continued to be fascinated by Jesus ("God the sun, Christ the light") and to associate perception and insight with the private soul: "Nothing can become known to the human mind but thro' the medium of itself—& this the use of revelation" (*JMN*, 3:79). Surprisingly, his imagery now became militant. Speculating on a world in which all had realized their moral potential, he proclaimed, "The young & the old[,] the ardent & the firm would move forward truly & honorably in a Holy War, in the Chivalry of Virtue." The terminology is conventional in Christianity, and certainly Emerson's brand of militancy is based on spiritual, not spatial conquests. But the imagery is important as a sign both of Emerson's confidence in winning his internal debate and of his determination ultimately to translate a passive heroism into some form that would uplift others.[6] Obviously inspired by his own sea voyage, he declared, "When the Sea was stormy the disciples awoke Christ. Let us do so.—" (*JMN*, 3:82). As he returned home Emerson was readying himself to awaken not only the Christ whose sublimity he found so fascinating, but also the heroic springs of his own personality.

Part of Emerson's new assertiveness derived, ironically, from a resolve *not* to commit himself to a new course of action for the present and from a firm retrenching into Boston provincialism.[7] On 7 April 1827 he rejected once and for all William's suggestion that he seek a position in

New York: "I am a bigoted Yankee," he wrote with blunt pride (*L,* 1:195). Again on 3 May, while he admits that being "so bigoted a Yankee" may have blinded him to the beauty of Charleston, he expresses a liking for Baltimore—because it looks like Boston (*L,* 1:196). In mid-May, he is writing his brother Charles in an encouraging tone that stands in sharp contrast to the self-critical letter to William in late January. He advises Charles: "Give yourself to study with boundless ambition. Despising as much as you please the primary & vulgar landmarks of success in the consciousness y^t you aim to raise your rank not among your compeers alone but in that great scale of moral beings which embraces the invisible & the visible" (*L,* 1:200). Emerson, working his way back north, was clearly expressing here his own newfound confidence based on his conviction that there are different measures of success, that one finds greatness in being and in performing according to one's nature; worldly success will follow, if it is to follow, in due order.

Pivotal in Emerson's evolution from the self-flagellation of the letter to William to the hope of the letter to Charles is a letter to Aunt Mary from Saint Augustine in late March 1827. Here Emerson comes to grips with the self-pity that attended his vocational/personal crisis, identifying with the stance of Jesus in the Lord's Prayer in terms that were to reverberate in Sermon No. 5:

It is certainly very easy to conceive of cases wh require more than the exaltation of the martyr's virtue who triumphs at the stake. I mean . . . and who nourishes in silence far from fame the secret virtue the gift of which was accompanied with a consciousness of its worth [*sic*]—than it is for such a youth meekly to surrender his hopes in the outset of his career to forego all these fairy visions & say with uncompromising self devotion Thy will be done. Many a man has died with firmness who yet had never broke his spirit or rather sublimed his spirit to such resignation. Resolution was on his face but regret sat on his heart. Yet we can conceive of one so united to God in his affections that he surveys from the vantage ground of his own virtues the two worlds with equal eye & knowing the true value of the love & praise of men challenges rather the suffrages of immortal souls. And what we can conceive of virtue, it may be we can exhibit. [*L,* 1:195]

As this passage makes clear, Emerson is not denying his anxiety that the world will never know his gift; indeed, the contrast he draws between outward "Resolution" and inward "regret" suggests what had until now been his own situation. Yet he envisions a creative solution: What Emerson is here recommending is neither the glory of martyrdom nor the simple verbal acquiescence of "resignation," but the discovery of that inner resource, that security and maturity of personality, whereby earthly

fame and eternal principle are seen in perspective. This, implicitly, is to
experience personally the "vantage ground" of Jesus himself. Emerson's
stance here reaches back to the Pauline notion that one can *know* only
what one *is*; it derives from Emerson's puritan heritage that insisted that
true sanctification proceeds from justification; and it was nourished by the
liberal Christian ethic of his own time that insisted that deeds and appearances must be judged by the motives that prompted them. On a personal
level it signified for Emerson a glimpse of self-acceptance, a faith in
himself that would "exhibit" its fruit to the world. Instead of worrying
about becoming a "great man," he would *be* one by comprehending the
very struggles that had before seemed to stand in the way of success. In
overcoming anxiety and self-consciousness, in conceiving of vision and
the manifesting of virtue as one, Emerson sensed a new security of
personality.

While much has been written about the importance of Emerson's
European trip following his resignation of the Second Church pulpit, the
southern journey of 1826–27 was crucial as a moratorium allowing the
prospective minister to assess his theological and personal doubts and to
commit himself to a profession that would profoundly affect the stamp of
his future thought. Sermon No. 5 incorporates the major motifs we have
found in the early journals and letters and reveals the constructive impact
of Emerson's ministerial training, which enabled him to identify with the
heroic "character" of Jesus and, in preaching His virtues, to assume the
mantle of eloquence crucial to his own sense of greatness.

Sermon No. 5, which covers the better part of sixteen manuscript
pages, takes as its text part of 1 Corinthians 1:23: "We preach Christ
crucified."[8] Conventionally, the sermon promises to "open" the Scriptures to show how we may rightly appropriate Christ. Emerson's opening,
which derives from a journal entry written at Concord on 19 June 1827,
just five days before the sermon was first delivered, is stern: "It is better,
said Solomon, to go to the house of mourning than to the house of
feasting. There is something more safe & salutary to our virtue in the
influences of sorrow, than in the enticing splendor of scenes of joy. Man
does not stand firm in a high & giddy prosperity. The tender eye of the
mind is dazzled by excessive sunshine. 'We are purified by pity & terror.'" Ralph L. Rusk, in his biography of Emerson, suggests that the
sermon "was full of the sense of the tragic; yet it too implied compensation" in its Aristotelian posture (*Life,* p. 123). Indeed, Emerson elaborated on the journal material, following the reference to Aristotle in the

sermon with five new sentences, explaining just how "By these passions our attention is arrested, our faculties are startled from their sleep into strenuous exertion."[9] Perhaps rationalizing his own earlier enervating introspection by projecting it onto his congregation, he argues that one need not fear the results of contemplating "affliction," "For the animal spirits are not to be long repressed."

The young preacher then takes a direct shot at liberal religion, declaring on the second page that "The religious service of this day seldom has too morose an influence on the rest of the week. That danger departed with a former age." He finds fault with the "great abundance of smooth & pleasant speculation on the agreeable topics" of the day and goes on to question, without really establishing his grounds, "the congratulations that are cheerfully exchanged from every quarter on the distinguished advancement of the age." The gladness of the modern philanthropist and Christian is "just & blameless" (a toughened revision of "just & beautiful" in *JMN*, 3:92); but Emerson discovers sufficient chink in the armor of the popular mind to suggest that, as the wealthy "heir" ought to recall his "benefactor," so "it is a natural & reasonable gratitude on our part which sometimes carries us back in devout recollection to the founder of our spiritual privileges."[10] (Here concludes the material borrowed from *JMN*, 3:91–92.) However gratuitous the pretext for this sermon, it enables Emerson to establish a stance of moral superiority and in purple dramatic tones to invite his congregation away from familiar "pleasant places," "to the field of blood, to a ghastly & atrocious spectacle, to the hill of Calvary & the passion of Christ."

Now, in the middle of the third manuscript page, Emerson announces the moral value of this dramatic reconstruction: "It is good to refresh our virtues by the example of perfect innocence." He focuses attention on Jesus, borrowing, with minor revisions and much amplification, that journal entry from November 1826 (*JMN*, 3:55) in which he desired to "write something worthily on the most affecting of topics": he turns in the sermon

to that most affecting page of human history which pourtrayed in living lines the personal character & the death of Jesus Christ. a being whose character has taken such strong hold of the mind as to divide the opinions of men as to his nature & office more than did ever any question. one so great as to leave foundation for the opinion that he was a portion of the Deity & in the opinions least reverent that he was first of men—a being who would be called renowned did not fame & what men call glory sink before the majesty of his character into things offensive & ridiculous; one whose effect on the fortunes of human society, taking out of

account what may be called supernatural influence, has been far the most powerful impulse that ↑of those yᵗ ever wore the human form↓ ever acted thereon & yet
whose influence on the world is now I had almost said but *beginning* to be felt.

The passage is worth quoting at length because it reveals the
theological significance of Emerson's Jesus, the literary nature of the
sermon, and the kinds of values he found in Jesus worth appropriating to
his own life. Twice he skirts, without explicitly denying, the divinity of
Jesus. The focus is on the "character" of Jesus, a character whose
"majesty" captured the attention of mankind without the kind of overt
achievements and conquests we normally associate with heroism; most
important for Emerson, we shall see, is that while Jesus appeared a failure
by the world's standards, he was *"beginning"* to have "influence on the
world."

Emerson's purpose clearly is to refresh his congregation's sense of
one who, while perhaps not a savior in the conventional sense, is the great
model of moral growth. Emerson's attempt to reach this end is couched in
strikingly literary terms. Where in the journal he longed to "write" on the
"most affecting of topics," he now turns "to that most affecting page of
human history which pourtrayed in living lines the personal character &
the death of Jesus Christ." The layering of imagery of storytelling enables Emerson to play up the "sublimity" of Jesus' life and to work on his
hearers' emotions without committing himself to technicalities of theology; indeed, he sets aside the "supernatural influence" of Jesus, emphasizing instead his "human form." The dramatic unfolding of Jesus'
life and crucifixion marks this sermon as an early example of what Lawrence Buell sees as a "genre" developed in Unitarian preaching: "biblical
fiction."[11]

Not only can Sermon No. 5 be placed in this genre; the "story" it
seeks to tell is not all that original. William Ellery Channing, for example, had anticipated both theme and approach some six years earlier in
"The Evidences of Revealed Religion" (1821). Channing had provided
the obligatory biographical sketch of Jesus' "humble birth and education" as background to describing his grand "character."[12] More concerned than Emerson to establish rational proofs of Christianity, Channing did not depict the melodrama of the Crucifixion as Emerson does;
but he set an example of validating Christianity by appealing not to
miracles but to the benefits of moral development and "character."

While Sermon No. 5 partakes of a "genre" and expresses ideas that
were current in Unitarian circles, it remains an important statement in

Emerson's growth. However common Emerson's techniques and sentiments, his depiction of Jesus represents a turning point in the identity
crisis of his mid-twenties.

We have seen that Emerson was impressed by the "influence"
exerted by Jesus. On the fifth page he goes on to say that most of us pay
heed to "signs of outward splendor" and are influenced "by the pomp of
wealth & power." "But we judge in this matter according to the flesh," he
declares; indeed, Christianity "seems to have been designed to correct
this ancient error." While hardly a novel religious idea, the notion that
this truth is taught not by success but by "affliction" (p. 6) enables
Emerson to assert a professionally and socially approved code that would
legitimize his constitutional introspection, his fear of failure, and his lack
of real power. In this sense, his declaration that "The emblem of our faith
is not a crown but a cross" both certifies his acceptance of general Unitarian doctrine and announces that henceforward he will not be judged by
the world's standards.

To a considerable extent, Emerson's ministry, far from being a
stifling sidetrack from his real literary ambitions, sheltered him from
overwhelming personal crises. Ostensibly, Emerson was *committing*
himself to an acceptable adult role in assuming the ministry.[13] But the
dialectics of Unitarianism also enabled him to redefine the nature of
action and heroism in ways that suited his temperament and convictions.
He asks rhetorically, for example, if Jesus was "born in the lap of grandeur, the child of the Caesars," or pampered "to an effeminate manhood";
and in terms reminiscent of his early journal criticism of military heroes,
he asks in swelling phrases if Jesus was "like the renowned conquerors"
who achieve fame through the misery of others. The obvious implication
is that the world's is not the only measure of greatness.

The familiar details of Jesus' "humble" origins are rehearsed on the
seventh page. This assessment of the power of Jesus' character, while it is
a conventional Unitarian character sketch, is an epitome of Emerson's
evolving personal and professional self-image: "All that was simple &
unpretending in his circumstances was made to show in stronger relief the
majesty of his life: all that was distressing & terrible in his lot to disclose
more manifestly the purity & sublimity of his virtue. It was designed to
set the greatness of the world at nought. It was designed to give us a
perfect pattern of obedience to God at the same time that a confirmation
was added by a holy life as well as wonderful works to the authenticity of
his mission, & the truth of his tidings."

Though he stops short of attributing divine qualities to Jesus, Emerson finds him a staunch model of that sentimentalized revision of Protestant justification, "sublimity." Jesus achieves the lofty stance Emerson had suggested to Aunt Mary in the letter from Saint Augustine (*L,* 1:195). Jesus wins greatness without becoming contaminated by the world (an admirable trait to a young man with a highly refined sense of moral discrimination). And the holy "confirmation" of Jesus' "mission, & the truth of his tidings" had special appeal to one who ministered the faith of Jesus yet longed for validation of his own high calling and the eloquence of his own "tidings," which he had morbidly feared would never find vent or audience.

In the short paragraph at the bottom of the eighth page, Emerson invites us again to the scene of the Crucifixion, the detailed description of which takes up from page nine through the middle of page fifteen. This description, while interesting as a melodramatic *tour de force* unusual in Emerson, is as we have seen conventional "biblical fiction." What is more significant is the further elaboration of Jesus' character, so revealing of Emerson's self-image, and its application to the congregation. Jesus exhibits the kind of transcendence of the shabby material world that Emerson was later to attribute to the poet, naturalist, or scholar. By contrast Herod and the crowd present at the Crucifixion display a stupidity and viciousness in keeping with Emerson's habitual depiction of martial "heroes" and the "mass" of mankind: "They were unable to comprehend in their pitiful ferocity that there is a greatness of soul to which evil fortune & good are accidents . . . a magnanimity so high & serene that mockery & scorn cannot touch its composure. . . . It sleeps to the things of this world in a vision of divine contemplations, an elevation of the soul too sublime to waste itself in idle vaunts & bravado. It is clothed in humility. It walks with God" (p. 9).

We have seen in earlier journal entries Emerson's tentative positing of a stoical equilibrium that provides an impregnable defense against the world's adversities. While it can be argued that Christian revelation transcends the stoic stance, Jesus clearly exhibits the stoical fortitude we find Emerson admiring in the journals. Reverting to the imagery of drawing and storytelling (whether to back off from theology or to emphasize the affecting power of Jesus' life), Emerson continues: "They were skilful hands that sketched in our Scriptures the tragic events of that memorable day. They have told with sad fidelity the story of his sufferings[,] the insane vindictiveness with which his countrymen thirsted for his blood." But while Emerson's vision of transcendence presupposes a hostile mass of men grotesquely waiting for the destruction of the oppressed hero, Emerson is meliorist enough to acknowledge the "consolation" that at the time of man's "deep depravity" (p. 10) Christ "was not wholly abandoned by the sympathies & admiration of men." The mass of mankind may be depraved, but Emerson knew that the congregation at hand must have some hope to hold to, else Christ's life and Emerson's eloquence were for naught.

Accompanying Jesus' noble compassion (he tells his sympathizers to "weep for yourselves & your children") is an ability to perceive the future. Indeed, that Emerson is identifying closely with Jesus here will be obvious to students of Emerson familiar with the importance of eye imagery in the great essays. Jesus' "eye went forward to the future," and "his merciful spirit contemplated" Roman domination, civil turmoil, hunger.[14]

As a seer, Jesus comprehends and transcends the human predicament even as he is victimized by it. In sharp contrast, the "cruel enemies" of Jesus are "ignorant of the future & blinded by passion even to the present" (p. 11). Immediately following this juxtaposition of the man of vision and the uncouth mob comes the journal entry written in Charleston on 6 January 1827 (*JMN* 3:62–64) and comprising pages 11 through 13. The sermon manuscript reveals that Emerson carefully polished the expression of the journal entry and inserted two substantial passages to emphasize the mission of Jesus and the lesson to be drawn from his life and death. The result is an extended passage of antitheses which point up the contrasts between man and Christ, materialism and vision, body and soul, mob and man of vision. "I am anxious," Emerson had begun the journal entry, "to sketch out the form of a sermon I have long had in my head upon the ⟨affecting character⟩ events of the Crucifixion" (*JMN*, 3:63).[15] Despite the cancellation, the sermon makes clear that the "events of the Crucifixion" are graphically presented to throw the "affecting character" of Jesus into sharper relief. Emerson presents the "majesty" of Jesus' agony and describes the sufferer's thoughts of "the painful picture of all the past." In four sentences added to the journal entry he emphasizes that "Man had not found out his immortality, had not found out the God who made him." The mission of Jesus was to restore man to God and to "the purposes to which we exist." Now, "To add to his works of wonder the last testimony he brings his life to bear witness that his doctrine is true." The next sentence, from the original journal entry, states that "now he offers himself a silent victim & feels that he is accomplishing a mighty destiny"; the foregoing new sentences make it clear that to bear witness, to be "a silent victim," is not to be inactive. In a new sentence, Emerson continues that as Jesus "walks amid that raging multitude" his eye looks beyond the "spectacle around him," seeing (in a series of sentences from the journal) "into the future" to perversions of his doctrine "to an unhallowed use of power & pride" (p. 12), until "his calm eye . . . rests on the faithful who in this latter day shall consecrate themselves with pious self devotion" to his cause. Though Jesus is depicted as a passive perceiver, he is a precursor of Emerson's more "active" heroes of the 1830s in that his vision cuts across history. In a long added passage Emerson stresses the ongoing legacy of Jesus' crucifixion ("the death which he is finishing") and emphasizes the imploring invitation of Jesus to "overcome the body in seeking the welfare of the soul." But the implication is that, despite the Christian revelation, history will continue to show the human condition "borne down to the earth" by a "tremendous load of moral depravity." The peace of Christ, always at hand, must forever be won by the select person who responds to Jesus' offer "in imitation of him, to lift that weary head towards God & Heaven" (p. 13).

The moment of moral commitment transcends history, uniting man with Christ, though that commitment must occur within time. Emerson sustains his pattern of antithesis, sharply breaking up even this reverie: "But it was not the hour for meditation; it was the hour of blood. The cry of Crucify him! Crucify him! burst from the savage lips of that enormous multitude & the hills of Judaea rang with the ominous echoes. Then the cross was planted in the earth; & He,—the man who came from God, was hung thereon." The effect of "biblical fiction" in the sermon is to dramatize Christ as an *active* hero despite his outward passivity. The outward action points to death, defeat; the internal spiritual action takes on an heroic sweep that encompasses both history and heaven. Emerson's audience is moved to take sides by emotionally identifying with the victim who is also conqueror, and by making the moral commitment to *imitate* the hero. The pages derived from the Charleston journal entry conclude with a final contrast between the "scoffing" and the "dismal shouting" of the mob, and Jesus' appeal to God to forgive his persecutors.

The "story" of the Crucifixion continues in terms interesting less for originality than for the delight and gusto Emerson takes in completing the sermon. Jesus "is at peace his sufferings are ended, his warfare is accomplished" (p. 14). Emerson declares in apparent imitation of Jesus that our tears should be for Pilate and the priests who now fear Jesus' body may be stolen by disciples to prove his promise of resurrection, but his

tone is unmistakably one of aggressive exaltation: "Alas poor pigmy
actors in this scene of madness & crime." The narrative proper ends not
surprisingly with the Ascension in the middle of page 15. What is surprising, in view of Emerson's earlier tacit denial of Jesus' "supernatural
influence," is that his ecstatic vision of transcendence (or conquest) of the
cruel world betrays him into a literal assessment of the Resurrection. Of
Jesus' persecutors, Emerson declares, God "will baffle you in your folly,
& raise him from the dead. He has burst the bonds of death. He has put on
the garments of glory for a putrid shroud. Ministering angels rolled away
the stone from the door of the sepulchre: the soldiers that watched became
as dead men. He has appeared unto men. He has ascended to his Father in
Heaven."

   In the remaining page and a half Emerson winds down the intensity
of the sermon by explaining the uses of the story. Still taken by the glory
of the Resurrection, he suggests rather morbidly that our deceased friends
continue to observe our behavior and thus act even in death as moral
guides. This view derives, he claims, from the scriptural promise of
Jesus: "'Lo! I am with you alway, even unto the end of the world'" (p.
16). We begin to wonder to what extent Emerson is preaching a religion of
miracles. His final emphasis, however, is on Jesus' moral legacy. "You
can enter into a sublime sympathy with him," he proclaims (in a line that
originally concluded the Crucifixion passage of the Charleston journal
entry [*JMN*, 3:64]) for Jesus provided us with "an example that we
should follow in his steps." Emerson concludes the sermon by declaring
how we achieve "sublime sympathy" with Jesus: "Whensoever you
breathe a pure affection to heaven when you forget yourself to spend your
strength in promoting the happiness of others in every blessed moment
that you resist & overcome the temptations of the world in the pure hope
of becoming more like to our Master, more acceptable in the eye of
God,—in that moment be assured, his heart goes with you, his gentle
spirit commends you, he sees that you acknowledge him on earth & he
shall acknowledge you before his Father in Heaven." The impression is
an odd mixture of genteel sentimentality and evangelical fervor. Emerson is clearly uneasy espousing traditional Christian doctrine. But the
intensity of his feeling reveals a powerful identification with Jesus that
surpasses the bounds of doctrine. It may be true of Emerson as of his
Unitarian contemporaries that, as Buell charges, melodrama was a way
of evading the details of doctrine. What is obvious in reading Sermon No.
5 is Emerson's enthusiasm in embracing the heroic Jesus who overcame
the adversities of sin, mutability, and the spite of men, achieving an inner

peace and vision, and setting an example, which Emerson craved both personally and philosophically. Moreover, proclaiming Jesus' message—or, in this case telling his story—constituted a socially acceptable career that provided an outlet for the eloquence and power Emerson had earlier despaired of achieving. Emerson had assumed a variety of personae—stern Jeremiah, melodramatic storyteller, hopeful evangelist.[16] In so doing, he assumed masks of moral superiority and vision that permitted him, in preaching to men and women who could not but endorse his views, to exorcise the demons of coarse, bloodthirsty mobs who had seemed to threaten his own ideals and aspirations, and to establish a sense of purposeful identity that would endure, with modifications, long after his formal ministry had ended.

Why Jesus could not long serve Emerson as a "hero" is perhaps best exemplified by Emerson himself in "Uses of Great Men" (1850). "Great men," he argued in his middle years, are "a collyrium to clear our eyes from egotism and enable us to see other people and their works" (*W*, 4:25). As such, great men rescue us from the stifling confines of our own claustrophobic personalities; they spur us into new action and discovery by making us aware of the otherness of man and nature. The "danger," according to Emerson, is that influence may become subjugation. For the healthy person, "Every hero becomes a bore at last. Perhaps Voltaire was not bad-hearted, yet he said of the good Jesus, even, 'I pray you, let me never hear that man's name again.'" This reaction Emerson sees as "human nature's indispensable defence" (*W*, 4:27), each man having the *potential*, typified by the hero, of "ascending out of his limits into a catholic existence": "We have never come at the true and best benefit of any genius so long as we believe him an original force. In the moment when he ceases to help us as a cause, he begins to help us more as an effect. Then he appears as an exponent of a vaster mind and will. The opaque self becomes transparent with the light of the First Cause" (*W*, 4:34–35).

After a year of preaching the crucified Jesus in Sermon No. 5, Emerson came to feel that *this* "great man" was thickening into an opaque statue produced by dogmatism. Not that Jesus ceased to interest Emerson in later sermons. But these were different versions of Jesus, designed to meet new emotional and intellectual needs, with fewer references to the specific suffering of the Crucifixion.[17]

The tentativeness of Emerson's satisfaction with the Jesus of Sermon No. 5 is already suggested in a letter to his brother William on the very day he first delivered the sermon. Emerson writes that he has supplied the pulpit at First Church, Chauncy Place, but that already vocational doubts are reasserting themselves: "Meditate now & then total abdication of the profession on the score of ill health. . . . Very sorry— for how to get my bread? Shall I commence author? of prose or of verse. Alack of both the unwilling muse!" (*L*, 1:201).

Aesthetic honesty for Emerson is inseparable from his craving for personal and vocational "power." The timing is perhaps coincidental, but on 15 July 1828, twelve days before Emerson used Sermon No. 5 for the *last* time, the theme of aesthetic power reappears, this time in a letter to his brother Charles, whose "valedictory oration" Waldo criticizes on the grounds that for all his gifts, Charles is "a fine show at which we look, instead of an agent that moves us." In what again is clearly as much self-criticism as criticism of Charles, he anticipates his careful definition of the uses and limitations of great men: "Let him [Charles] remember that the true orator must not wrap himself in himself, but must wholly abandon himself to the sentiment he utters, & to the multitude he addresses;—must become their property, to the end that *they may become his.* . . . Let him for a moment forget himself, & then, assuredly, he will not be forgotten.—" (*L*, 1:238–40). For Emerson, vision, sincerity, and eloquence had become one. Judged by his own standards, Sermon No. 5, however it may have expressed earlier needs, represented now a theological hardening which in turn was restricting him from freely giving of himself as preacher, a situation that in four years would cause him to resign his pastorate altogether to seek new relationships to nature and new modes of expressing those relationships.

In 1826 a painfully introspective young Emerson was dedicating himself to follow his hero, Jesus; increasingly he came to discover *traits* in Jesus that he wished to emulate. By 1836 in *Nature*, as Joel Porte has brilliantly shown, he was actually *identifying* with the visionary *voice* of Christ, (Porte's observation that the first paragraph of *Nature*, with its echo of Christ's warning to the lawyers [Luke 11], "is laced with more anger than we are normally willing to hear" reveals how important Jesus was to the evolution of Emerson's sense of identity: the defensiveness/ aggressiveness suggested by his depiction of militant religious heroism in the early journals had become by 1836 forthright and confident, if angry, prophecy).[18] In this sense *Nature* represents the ultimate stage of Channing's call for man to achieve "likeness to God." Emerson was usually careful to define, as had Channing, Jesus' "inferiority" to God. But the transition from Unitarianism to transcendentalism is perhaps nowhere better illustrated than in Emerson's movement from speaking *about* Jesus to speaking *as* Jesus. *Nature* thus marks an exercising of aesthetic power he began to feel was stifled by writing sermons. This evolution, however, was more gradual than is usually supposed. It would be melodramatic to claim that Emerson, in discovering the liberation of Romantic expression, was rejecting the essential discoveries he had made while a divinity student. If Emerson's new profession and concept of the hero in 1827–28 could not provide final solutions to his anxieties, they provided at least a momentary stay enabling him to build self-confidence and a sense of power even as he denied the "supernatural" properties of Jesus and found the ministry increasingly tedious.

Emerson's satisfaction with the sentiments expressed in Sermon No. 5 is implied, nevertheless, in his journal five days after first preaching the sermon. He expresses that consolation, that compensation that one grows from adversity: "The man who bates no jot of courage when oppressed by fate[,] who missing of his design lays hold with ready hand on the unexpected event & turns it to his own account & in the cruelest suffering has that generosity of perception that he is sensible of a secret joy in the addition this event makes to his knowledge—that man is truly independent . . . of time & chance" (*JMN*, 3:92–93). He continued to maintain, with Stoic fortitude, that "these doubts of ours" are "hints God has interwoven in our condition to remind us of the temper that becomes us; that diffidence & candor suit us better than arrogance & dogmatism" (*JMN*, 3:103).

Philosophical integrity continued to clash, to a painful degree, with Emerson's expectation that a minister exists to "combat prejudices" (*JMN*, 3:108). The old defensiveness concerning what constitutes power resurfaces in the journal on 10 March 1828. Ministers, he explains, are expected by the common folk to appeal for "*Contemplation*"; "But it is not so," Emerson declares. "*We* call them to a life of action" (*JMN*, 3:110). That Emerson was still not equating such a life with a formal occupation is suggested in his letter to William on 3 April 1828, in which he expresses satisfaction at "escaping all engagements at the New Church in Boston." He goes on: "I am embarrassed at present whenever any application is made to me that may lead to permanent engagements. For I fancy myself dependent for my degree of health upon my lounging capricious unfettered mode of life & I keep myself & I slowly multiply my sermons for a day I hope of firmer health & solid power" (*L*, 1:229–30). We find traits of the quiet, inward-looking Jesus of Sermon No. 5 and glimpses of that peculiar transcendental inversion of the value of action in Emerson's assertion that "There are two men in the world: the man of passion, & the man of principle" (*JMN*, 3:129). Indeed, "the silence of a good man" often bespeaks "character" (*JMN*, 3:132). Emerson's new sense that he could learn from adversity and need not force final conclusions on complex reality did not preclude his recourse to terse antithesis and aphorism to justify his passivity.

The "formation of Character," and not outward action, constituted moral development for Emerson. What would seem antisocial under other circumstances he converted into an unimpeachable code. In moments of enthusiasm, he found this vision embodied in his "Idea of the Christian Minister: a man who is separated from men in all the rough courses where defilement can hardly be escaped; & who mixes with men only for purposes that make himself & them better; aloof from the storm of passion, from political hatred, from the jealousy & intrigue of gain, from the contracting influences of low company & little arts" (*JMN*, 3:152). This disembodied figure could be accused of a monklike cloistered virtue only if we forget his antecedents in Emerson's descriptions of Christian heroism in the journals and in Sermon No. 5. The virtues of this "Christian Minister" can be found in substantially the same form in the "poet" and "scholar" of the 1830s and beyond. That the "Christian Minister" is not bound by denominational orthodoxy is already suggested in a journal entry in late November 1828: "I take a pleasure greater than I can express in finding among men out of the influence or [*sic*] Xty the light of Xn sentiment" (*JMN*, 3:144).

Yet the sterner vision expressed in "Christ crucified" is not the antithesis of Emerson's new hero of the 1830s and 1840s. The concept in Sermon No. 5 of the hero and his relationship to society and history continues to inform the great essays. In "Self-Reliance," for example, "we are . . . guides, redeemers, and benefactors, obeying the Almighty effort, and advancing on Chaos and the Dark" (*CW*, 2:28). But the hero still stands against the opposition of a vampiric society: "Society everywhere is in conspiracy against the manhood of every one of its members" (*CW*, 2:29). "Whoso would be a man, must be a nonconformist" for which "the world whips you with its displeasure" (*CW*, 2:32). Images of mobs like those in Sermon No. 5 depict "society": "the sour faces of the multitude," "the discontent of the multitude," "the unintelligent brute force that lies at the bottom of society" (*CW*, 2:33). To be "misunderstood" becomes not just a right but an obligation if one is to be like Jesus "and every pure and wise spirit that ever took flesh" (*CW*, 2:34). While in the moment of vision the soul "shoves Jesus and Judas equally aside" (*CW*, 2:40), Emerson seems to assume the voice of Jesus sending out the twelve apostles (Matt. 10:35–37) when he urges: "Live no longer to the expectation of these deceived and deceiving people with whom we converse. Say to them, 'O father, O mother, O wife, O brother, O friend, I have lived with you after appearances hitherto. Henceforward I am the truth's'" (*CW*, 2:41–42).

Emerson's growing self-confidence and evolving concept of heroism would make him define Jesus in new ways until he would seem but one more "representative man" for the whole person to use selectively.[19] But even by 1838 there are still echoes of the Jesus of Sermon No. 5 in the Divinity School Address; now Jesus is praised as "a true man" (*CW*, 1:81). Moreover, the "formalist" minister, less "real" than the snowstorm because he gives nothing of himself (*CW*, 1:85) is but a version of the orator Emerson had criticized in Charles—and in himself—in 1828. The obstacle here to fulfillment of the minister's office is, as Emerson had believed for over a decade, reliance on historical Christianity. It is the task of preaching, he goes on, to rediscover "the resources of astonishment and power"; otherwise, "The pulpit . . . loses all its inspiration, and gropes after it knows not what. And for want of this culture, the soul of the community is sick and faithless. It wants nothing so much as *a stern, high, stoical, Christian discipline*, to make it know itself and the divinity that speaks through it" (*CW*, 1:87–88; emphasis mine). Though Emerson here completes his early tendency to distill the essence of Christianity from Christ, the Stoic/Christian stance continues to mean self-knowledge, transcendence, impregnable security. Despite the revolutionary reputation of the address, there is also a touch of pathos in Emerson's decree, "Discharge to men the priestly office, and, present or absent, you shall be followed with their love as by an angel" (*CW*, 1:90). As a minister Emerson had craved mission, eloquence, acceptance. The role of minister had provided him with a mask that helped him achieve a "vantage ground" by which to uplift others even as he overcame his own fear of them. His new quest for a broader "congregation" makes poignant his disembodied version of the "priestly office" as a means to win "love," especially in view of his ongoing distrust of "society."[20]

Though he had left his own pulpit, Emerson continued to find hope in the heroic image of Jesus he had conceived in 1826–28, an image of courage and steadfastness, of militant alertness and lofty commitment to truth despite the vagaries of nature and the derision of mankind. Believing vision to be moral action, he found the essence of Christianity a significant touchstone. Though he had rejected the value of the historical Jesus, Emerson continued to find great importance in the "uses" of his first hero—and still representative "great man."

In devoting himself to Jesus, Emerson in a curiously personal way had reenacted the classic Christian experience of finding oneself by losing oneself (Matt. 10:39). Ostensibly, Emerson's intense devotion is a form of subordination of self to a more powerful and perfect hero. The vehemence with which Emerson preaches "Christ crucified" is also a form of defense, if not aggression. But the final meaning of Jesus in Sermon No. 5 is not simply the "Christ crucified" suggested by the short title and by the lurid descriptions and harsh judgments of the sermon. The persecuted Jesus, to be sure, found sympathy from a young minister who needed to project his fears of failure onto a hostile world that could not understand his true gifts. However, Jesus is, in the end, an affirmative image not of passive suffering but of successful heroism. The whole Christian vision, which implies that resurrection follows crucifixion, is expressed in the full context of 1 Corinthians 1:23, which provides the text of Sermon No. 5: "But we preach Christ crucified, unto the Jews a stumblingblock, and unto the Greeks foolishness." Paul had continued, "the foolishness of God is wiser than men; and the weakness of God is stronger than men. . . . and God hath chosen the weak things of the world to confound the things which are mighty. . . . But of him are ye in Christ Jesus, who of God is made unto us wisdom, and righteousness, and sanctification, and redemption." Emerson's Jesus may have been stripped of "supernatural" power. But transformed as he was into the stuff of Unitarian and, later, transcendental myth, Jesus remained in the most important personal way for Emerson the essence of wisdom, righteousness, sanctification, and redemption.

Emerson's Foreground

JEROME LOVING

"God offers to every mind its choice
between Truth and Repose. Take which
you please; you can never have both."
—"The Head"

"The greatest delight which the fields
and woods minister is the suggestion of
an occult relation between man and the
vegetable."—*Nature*

On 10 October 1826, Ralph Waldo Emerson was "approbated" to preach by the Middlesex Association. On 11 September 1832, he resigned as pastor of the Second Church of Boston. And on 9 September 1836, he published his first and in some ways most famous book, *Nature*. These three events punctuate a decade of development in which Emerson ultimately rejected the theological legacy based upon generations of Arminian reform of New England Protestantism and wrote what may be considered an epilogue to the movement. For surely what he inherited from his father, the Reverend William Emerson of the First Church of Boston, was the final chapter—one that opened with the installation of the Reverend Henry Ware, Sr., as Hollis Professor of Divinity at Harvard College in 1805. With that victory, the Arminians or liberals of the church declared the theological frontier of New England conquered; the reform movement which decade after decade in the eighteenth century had witnessed the rejection of innate depravity, original sin, the divinity of Christ—in short, the Calvinistic bedrock upon which the first colonies had been founded—was now concluded. Unitarianism, as the term came into general use by 1819 with William Ellery Channing's famous Baltimore sermon, retained only two of the original puritan concepts: the validity of Scripture as a manifestation of God's will and the conviction that the religious community had an obligation and a right to exercise its influence over society.

When Emerson resigned from the Second Church, he selected as his ostensible reason the applicability of the sacrament of the Lord's Supper, which he believed clothed Christ with "an authority which he never claimed and which distracts the mind of the [Unitarian] worshipper" from God to Jesus (*W,* 11:17). The challenge was not without historical precedent, for the Arminian movement had really begun with an earlier controversy over the same ceremony. Probably more than any other New England Congregational minister, it was Solomon Stoddard who blurred the puritan distinction between the Saints and the Sinners of the church by allowing all of his parishioners, regenerate and unregenerate alike, to receive the sacrament of the Lord's Supper. First-century American Puritanism had thrived on adversity—papism, Anglicism, the wilderness of New England, but most of all the fear of unregenerate souls in its midst. Indeed, the uncertainty of the New World enhanced the Calvinistic principle of innate depravity, for it served as a symbol of the hidden evil in the world. But as the settlers gained a foothold in New England, turning the hostile land into a source of prosperity, their apprehension declined with their fear of the wilderness. This corresponding decline of spiritual determination led to a decline in religious "conversions" by the second generation of Puritans, and by 1662 church leaders instituted the "Half-way Covenant," which allowed the children of the "unconverted" to seek membership in the church. Stoddard merely enlarged this first crack in puritan idealism by using the ceremony as a means to salvation rather than as evidence of justification in the eyes of God and therefore hastened the inevitable disappearance of the concept of innate depravity in the New World. For if everyone could receive the sacrament, how were church leaders to retain a vivid sense of God's election among their congregations?[1]

Of course, there were many attempts by church conservatives to reverse Stoddard's precedent and its liberating effect upon American Calvinism, the most dramatic made by the minister's grandson, the great theologian Jonathan Edwards. He advocated a return to more pristine Calvinistic principles, but after the Great Awakening (1740–45) and its emotional excesses, ministers who had been encouraged by Stoddard's experiment and thus opposed to the concept of regenerate membership in the church began to grow bolder in their views. As Conrad Wright informs us, "The effect of the revival was not so much to spread Arminianism as to prepare the way for its rapid growth. Down to the

Awakening a sense of community in New England still existed. For all of
Stoddard's differences with the Mathers, he still came to Boston every
year at Harvard Commencement time. . . . But after 1745, New England
was so divided that there was a sense of community among the liberals
and a sense of community among the evangelists [Calvinists], but any
wider sense of common purpose was wearing thin."[2]

Emerson's reluctance and ultimate refusal to administer the Lord's
Supper in 1832, then, was the first step in rejecting what the previous
generation of liberals had firmly stopped short of challenging: the validity
of Scripture as proof of God's will. Although they had between the close
of the Awakening and the election of Ware at Harvard adopted the Arian
view that Christ is not divine but an archangel or intermediary between
God and man, they balked at the idea of ceasing to address Christ as God
with the Lord's Supper. In doing so, they acted upon the justified fear that
with the ceremony the Unitarian creed would be open to the Socinian
interpretation of Christ as simply a great man—a view in fact advocated
in 1838 when Emerson complained of the Unitarian preoccupation "with
the noxious exaggeration about the *person* of Jesus" (*CW*, 1:82). And
once Christ was removed from the ambiguous status as an intermediary,
the Unitarians would have been hard pressed to defend the New Testa-
ment as necessary for spiritual progress. Indeed, with the Arian view of
Christ, Unitarianism already came perilously close to English Deism and
a dependence on the empirical principles of Locke. Doubtless, it was
because such Harvard leaders as Ware and Andrews Norton realized the
possible outcome of Arminian reform that they incorporated into the
college curriculum between 1805 and 1819 the writings of the Scottish
commonsense philosophers. Thomas Reid, Dugald Stewart, and
Thomas Brown offered relief from the cold empiricism of Locke by
denying that man's apprehension of God could be gainsaid by logical
analysis; they also maintained that man had an innate moral sense of right
and wrong.[3]

Yet as Perry Miller argues in an essay that is still useful in locating
the source of Emerson's "antinomianism," the New England tradition
"gave with one hand what it took away with the other; it taught that God is
present to their intuitions and in the beauty and terror of nature, but it
disciplined them into subjecting their intuitions to the wisdom of society
and their impressions of nature to the standards of decorum."[4] The Arminians had carried into the nineteenth century many of the social checks
and balances that the original Puritans had used to contain individual
religious fervor. It is not surprising, therefore, that Emerson's epilogue

to the history of his father's religion opens with the complaint that Unitarianism built "sepulchres of the fathers" and also asks for "a religion by revelation to us, and not the history of theirs." For the theological world he assailed in *Nature* was almost as spiritually fixed as that of the first-generation American Puritans.

The clearest origins of the young preacher's misgivings are exemplified by the following journal passage in 1827. Reflecting dubiously on his new calling (from which poor health had temporarily relieved him), Emerson wrote from Saint Augustine, Florida: "Satisfy me beyond the possibility of a doubt of the certainty of all that is told me concerning the other world and I will fulfill the conditions on which my salvation is suspended. The believer tells me he has historical & internal evidence that make the presumption so strong that it is almost a certainty that rests on the highest probabilities. Yes, but change that imperfect to perfect evidence & I too will be a Christian. Now it must be admitted that I am not certain that any of these things are true. The nature of God may be different from what he is represented" (*JMN*, 3:68–69). Although these doubts were real, there were also private ones at the beginning of his preaching career—committed to his journal where he allowed his ideas wide range and free play. Publicly, he was still pledged to the Unitarianism of the day—albeit not as firmly as he had once been. In his undergraduate essay "On Genius" (1820) he had belittled the tendency of modern scholars to overemphasize "their own unassisted exertions" and to underestimate the wisdom "of the wonderful men of old."[5] And in 1827 nature as the source of spiritual elevation was still "an unsubstantial pageant." Yet Emerson's doubts were growing, and being a Unitarian was his way only for the time being. "I will embrace it this time by way of experiment," he decided, "& if it is wrong certainly God can in some manner signify his will in the future" (*JMN*, 3:69). And so he continued to accept his father's theological legacy and went on preaching.

Notwithstanding Emerson's vacillation in 1827, the hundred or so sermons he preached prior to his first wife's death in 1831 suggest that he was clearly trying to fulfill his responsibilities as a Unitarian minister. From "Pray Without Ceasing" (15 October 1826) to "Miracles" (23 January 1831), Emerson—though he occasionally gives hints of his later rebellion—supports traditional Christian concepts. They are duty, conscience, charity, piety, public and private prayer, the pettiness of life compared to the kingdom of God, the need for ceremony (i.e., the Lord's Supper), belief in miracles other than the ordinary works of nature, civic responsibility, God-reliance, underdevelopment of the soul, and so on. His public dedication to the institutional way of knowing God is well demonstrated in "A Feast of Remembrance" (27 September 1829). Although he would conclude his ministerial career with a denunciation of the Lord's Supper, here he sees it as "a means of quickening your moral perceptions and amending your character in its personal and social regards." In "Trust Yourself" (3 December 1830), his theme is not self-reliance but God-reliance. Indeed, it is God-reliance achieved through the religious community: for he announced that "It is the effect of religion [i.e., the institution] to produce a higher respect." Now far from the concept that "society scatters your force," he preaches that one's spiritual growth depends on the quality of his native religion: "cultivate in every soil the grapes of that soil." Finally, in "Miracles," Christ's supernatural accomplishments are regarded as sometimes necessary to startle those who are blind to the presence of God's miracle of nature itself (*YES*, pp. 58, 105, 107, 121).

Emerson's sermons suggest that he was a "Channing Unitarian" between 1826 and 1831. Like the elder William Ellery Channing, the young minister was imaginative in supporting the Arminian concepts that did away with the Calvinistic degradation of human nature, while yet remaining more or less impervious to the subsequent currents of religious thought that blew west from the Romantic movements in England and Germany. Emerson shared Channing's dedication to the idea that Christian churches have an investment in contemporary civilization and must therefore exercise a leadership in the social order. But also like Channing, Emerson stretched the Unitarian reforms to their limits in many of his sermons. In "The Christian Minister" (15 March 1829), his first sermon as ordained junior pastor of the Second Church, he implied the importance of individual spiritual growth by declaring his own preference of preaching to public prayer (because the minister "merely utters the petition which all feel"), and he announced that preaching equal to the demands and hopes of the times "must be manly and flexible and free beyond all the example of the times before us" (*YES*, pp. 25, 27).

Of course, it was the "Gospel and its universal applications" that Emerson intended to advance with such freedom in 1829. Yet in the fashion of Channing's sermon on man's "Likeness to God," Emerson's analogies between man's spiritual life and nature frequently took him into areas of theological ambiguity. Channing, for example, had declared that God "dwells within us" but concluded his sermon with a caveat against "extravagance" in appreciating the concept. "Let none infer from this language," he warned, "that I place religion in an unnatural effort, in straining after excitements which do not belong in the present state, or in any thing separate from the clear and simple duties of life."[6] Generally, Emerson was also content (though he questioned the practice in his journal) "simply to hunt out to exhibit the analogies between moral and material nature in such a manner as to have a bearing upon practice" (*JMN*, 3:130). Ultimately, of course, the means of the analogies became far more enticing than their ends, leading him to the conclusion in 1836 that Unitarianism in its refusal to allow the miracles of nature to supersede those recorded in scripture was groping "among the dry bones of the past."

Perhaps the earliest and most dramatic example of Emerson's shifting focus is found in the sermon entitled "Summer" (14 June 1829). Here he is still preaching in support of "the truth of Religion"—in this case, following the Unitarian practice of adapting Christianity to the eighteenth-century theory of nature as the world machine. (Later, in a sermon on "Providence," he would quote Paley's theology "with pleasure.") In calling "all nature . . . a book on which one lesson is written . . . the omnipresence of God," he cites Scripture as "always appealing" to nature "as the emblems of our mortal estate. It was the history of man in the beginning, and it is the history of man now" (*YES*, pp. 40, 44). Yet in the context of the sermon, which dwells much more on the analogy with nature than on Scripture as a source of the analogy, the biblical references appear obligatory and forced.

In his recent study of Emerson, Joel Porte compares "Summer" to the Divinity School Address, noting that it was last preached almost exactly a year before the Harvard address of 15 July 1838, and therefore seeing it as a kind of translation.[7] There is of course (as Porte demonstrates) a similarity between the opening metaphors—"In this grateful season" and "In this refulgent summer." But since Porte sees the language of the sermon as archaic and flaccid in the shadow of the 1838 address, it may be more accurate to view "Summer" as the earliest precursor to *Nature*. For whereas the Divinity School Address is transcendental doctrine at its Emersonian apex in terms of prose-poetry in the lectures and essays, "Summer" and *Nature* are clearly seminal in doctrine and preoccupied, sometimes laboriously, with the analogy between man's condition and the harmony of nature.

Like the theme of *Nature*, the theme of "Summer" takes the form of a rhetorical question. After cataloging the ways in which nature ministers to man, Emerson asks: "To what end this unmeasured magnificence?"

(*YES*, p. 43). Surely, it has a greater purpose than simple commodity, though "man shuts his eyes to this sovereign goodness, thinks little of the evidence that comes from nature, and looks upon the great system of the world only in parcels as its order happens to affect his petty interest" (*YES*, p. 40). In *Nature* he would remark: "A man is fed, not that he may be fed, but that he may work." And as in the book of 1836, the complaint about man's nearsightedness takes him from the level of commodity to that of beauty in nature. God's benevolence, Emerson says in "Summer," is more profoundly visualized "when it is considered that *the same results might have been brought about without this beauty. . . .* all this food might have been prepared as well without this glorious show." Nature gives us pleasure (the first level of "Beauty" in *Nature*), but "there is more in nature than beauty; there is more to be seen than the outward eye perceives." Nature exists to tell us something about our spiritual destiny—"there is the language of its everlasting analogies" (*YES*, pp. 43–44). Although here Emerson hints at concepts in the next section of *Nature* on "Language," such a detailed analysis of the way nature speaks to man was not to come till he had left the ministry and studied science, biography, and literature in conjunction with his lyceum lectures between 1833 and 1836. Now he is satisfied to imply that nature is somehow the language of the soul. But in doing so, he establishes his definition of nature as the "Not-Me." "There is nothing in external nature," he contends, "but is an emblem, a hieroglyphic of something in us" (*YES*, p. 44). In *Nature* of course he will be more exacting and declare: "Every man's condition is a solution in hieroglyphic."

Like Channing's "Likeness to God," Emerson's "Summer" dwells dangerously close to the later transcendental analogies. Yet it was perhaps because of the Channing sermon—or the Channing influence in general—that Emerson could venture freely into such areas of potential infidelity without offending Unitarian sensibilities. For in "Summer" nature is not what Emanuel Swedenborg called "the dial plate of the invisible" but merely an aid to appreciating the validity of Christian revelation. Here harmony with nature is a means, not an end. The same kind of caution is exercised in Channing's sermon. God may dwell within us, but "God's infinity places him beyond the resemblance and approach of man." In "Summer" man is not "part or particle with God," but merely in orbit around him: "whilst thus directly we depend on this process [of nature], on the punctuality of the sun, on the timely action of saps and seed vessels, and rivers and rains, *are we as punctual to our orbit?*" (*YES*, p. 45).

Sheldon W. Liebman is probably correct when he argues that Emerson's transformation from Unitarian to transcendentalist was gradual and not marked by any particular event, such as Ellen Tucker's death on 8 February 1831.[8] It is certain, however, that Emerson's use of nature became an end in itself rather than a theological tool in his sermons a year after her death. In this sense, the change is *associated* with an external event. For Emerson, 1831 was a watershed year, indeed the year in which he finally decided to act upon the theological doubts that had been piling up in his journals. Ellen's death in the beginning of that year was probably the most traumatic experience of his life. Only the loss of his first son eleven years later can be compared to it for the level of intensity and grief. By 1842, however, his grief was soon assuaged and finally muffled in "Experience" and "Threnody." But in 1831 he was not so well prepared for tragedy. His letters to his brothers William and Charles suggest that his life had lost much of its value without Ellen. This young woman not yet twenty, her person representing everything that was truly good in life, had vanished. Death, it seemed, became attractive as the only means of escaping his misery. Daily he visited his wife's grave, regardless of the weather. On 29 March he recorded in his journal: "I visited Ellen's tomb & opened the coffin." Whether he actually did so is a matter for conjecture—though he did, in fact, open Waldo's coffin in 1857 (*JMN*, 4:7; 14:154). The act suggests the macabre fiction of Edgar Poe. Interestingly, Poe's first "biographer" (and maligner) opened his own wife's coffin in 1842, forty days after her funeral. Rufus Griswold admitted that he entered the burial vault with the aid of a sexton. While alone with the coffin in a fit of melancholy, he pried off the lid and sat "beside the ruin of all that was dearest in the world" till a companion persuaded him to retire. If in fact Emerson is recording an act instead of a dream (and he usually identifies dreams as such in his journals), he would have viewed Ellen's remains at about the same period after death as Griswold. What Griswold saw, he described as "the terrible changes made by Death and Time." He "kissed for the last time her cold black forehead [and] cut off locks of her beautiful hair, damp with the death dews, and sunk down in senseless agony."[9] Since the practice of filling the arterial system with embalming fluid did not begin until the Civil War, the sight must have been a gruesome one. And if Emerson did indeed look upon Ellen in this state, he probably saw little more than the ravages of decomposition—the decay of the emblem that had brought him so much happiness.

The sight must have confirmed what Emerson had declared in

"Consolation for the Mourner," preached twelve days after Ellen's demise. "All that part of man which we call the *character*, survives and ascends. Not a shade, not a thought of it cleaves to the cold clay we have put in the ground" (*YES*, p. 141). Decay, or change in nature, brought death—Ellen's death—but it also brought life. The particular may change—indeed must change—but the universal sense of life remains. What remained and grew, Emerson realized, was *character*, its growth symbolized by the alteration of nature. In 1835, the same year he married Lydia Jackson, Emerson was still assessing the impact of Ellen's death on his thinking. He told his Aunt Mary, the "severest truth would forbid me to say that ever I had made a sacrifice. . . . I loved Ellen, & love her with an affection that would ask nothing but its indulgence to make me blessed. Yet when she was taken from me, the air was still sweet, the sun was not taken down from my firmament, & however sore was that particular loss, I still felt that it was particular, that the Universe remained to us both" (*JMN*, 5:19–20). The confession prefigures "Experience," in which he described life as "a train of moods like a string of beads, and as we pass through them they prove to be so many-colored lenses which paint the world their own hue." Life, he said, is change, and the hope for permanence in the particular is life's greatest illusion.

In "Grief," a sermon preached 27 February 1831, Emerson returned to the orthodox Christian idea that religion makes circumstances indifferent. But that year he must have concluded that religion exalted the particular instead of the universal. For almost exactly a year to the day of Ellen's death—as if emerging from his year of mourning and learning—he reversed himself. In "Find Your Calling" (5 February 1832) Emerson complained, "We hear a great deal of the empire of circumstances over the mind, but not enough of the empire of the mind [or character] over circumstances, that the mind is incapable of exerting this power." To the contrary, he queried his congregation, is there "not reason to think that every man is born with a particular character or having a peculiar determination to some one pursuit or one sort of usefulness[?]" This pursuit may be hidden from him for years because of unfavorable associations or bad advice, "but he will never be at ease, he will never act with efficiency, until he finds it" (*YES*, pp. 164–65, 167). "Find Your Calling" represents most directly his thoughts of 1831—his determination to call forth his own character as it was mirrored in the flux of nature. He took the same theme in "The Genuine Man" (21 October 1832), following the acceptance of his resignation from the office of pastor. The genuine man, he said, "acts always in character because he always acts *from* his character. . . . He therefore speaks what he thinks. He acts his thought" (*YES*, pp. 184–85).

Whereas "Find Your Calling" and "The Genuine Man" are fundamental to Emerson's resignation, "The Lord's Supper" (9 September 1832) is not. The ceremony was but a symptom of a larger malady. To "exalt particular forms, to adhere to one form a moment after it is outgrown," he told his congregation two days before his resignation was tendered, "is unreasonable, and it is alien to the spirit of Christ" (*W*, 11:20). But actually, to exalt the particular in any aspect of life—he had learned during his year of mourning for Ellen—was alien to life itself and hence the development of character. Not only did Unitarianism violate the spirit of its Arminian past by continuing to worship Christ as God, but it also restricted the believer's appreciation of the growth of his character by defining it in terms of tradition instead of insight. Like the corpse of Ellen, the chuch—as he would declare in *Nature*—represented only "the dry bones of the past."

Ellen's death and her husband's reflection on it during 1831 were the catalyst and not the cause of Emerson's resignation. He had already been exposed to various romantic writings, including Coleridge's *Aids to Reflection* and Goethe's memoirs. And he had read Sampson Reed's *Observations on the Growth of the Mind*, finding in it "the aspect of a revelation" (*JMN*, 3:45). His change in vocation was clearly the result of five or more years of inner struggle. Yet it is more than a coincidence that the change is aligned closely with Ellen's demise. It demonstrated to Emerson the importance of the change in nature, which represented the growth of the soul. Looking back in 1837 on his ordeal with the clergy and his decision to leave it he said: "God offers to every mind its choice between Truth and Repose. Take which you please; you can never have both. Between these as a pendulum man oscillates ever. He in whom the love of repose predominates will accept the first creed, the first philosophy, the first political party, he meets,—most likely his father's. He gets rest, commodity, and reputation. But he shuts the door to truth."[10] It was a choice between Repose and Truth. The one exalted the particular symbol (as Emerson would accuse Swedenborg of doing in *Nature*), whereas the other represented a life in touch with the flux of nature. The problem with Christianity was that it fastened its vision on one man who, as Emerson would declare in the Divinity School Address, was merely the first to see that "God incarnates himself in [every] man." The particular example was valuable only insofar as it represented the universal experience.

Christ, as seen through Emerson's version of the Socinian view, was the *first* representative man because he had called forth his character to shape the circumstances of his life.

Five days after Ellen's death Emerson asked himself, "Shall I ever again be able to connect the face of outward nature, the mists of the morn, the star of eve, the flowers, & all poetry, with the heart & life of an enchanting friend?" "No," he concluded, "There is one birth & one baptism & one first love and the affections cannot keep their youth any more than men" (*JMN,* 3:227). Ellen, as he had known her, was no more, and this lesson—learned during his year of mourning—helped him to confront the errors of Christianity. It was no longer mirrored in the flux of nature but mired in the particular of Christ's legacy. As it were, the church had never fully emerged from its period of mourning.

These considerations, we have seen, led him in 1832 to emphasize the growth of individual character in "Find Your Calling" and "The Genuine Man." The idea would later be developed in his most famous essays, especially "The Poet" ("Doubt not, O poet, but persist. Say 'It is in me and shall out.'"). He would need a theory of the soul, however, based upon the visible image in nature before he could enshrine the concept in Neoplatonic terms. For this, he turned to the study of natural history. It has been suggested recently that Emerson's 1833–34 lectures on science "reveal his reading and thinking about science before he had fused his ideas thus derived with the Neoplatonic and 'transcendental' ideas of Plotinus, Swedenborg, Wordsworth, Coleridge, Carlyle, and seventeenth-century English Platonists."[11] But that interest in science and its spiritual relationship began while he was still a minister grappling with the superstitions of the past. His first "lecture" on natural history, therefore, is found in the sermon on "Astronomy" (27 May 1832), in which he suggested that the stars awakened in man religious sentiments that had been distorted by present-day Christianity. "Religion in the later ages, suffering from the caprices and errors of men," he declared, "wanders often far from her object into strange paths; and the attempt is resisted as a sort of violence which strives to reunite Religion with the love of nature." Yet astronomy has always been at hand as the visible image of every truly exalted sentiment: "the song of the morning stars was really the first hymn of praise and will be the last; the face of nature, the breath of the hills, the light of the skies, are to a simple heart the real occasions of devout feeling more than the vestries and sermon hearings; and are those natural checks that are ever exciting an insensible influence to hold us back from fanaticism and keep us with insight of the true God" (*YES*, p. 171).

"Astronomy" also marks the beginning of Emerson's emancipation from anthropomorphic religion: "Even God himself, the infant religion of all nations has clothed in human form. . . . Astronomy corrects all these boastful dreams." And he added (though there is evidence to suggest did not include when the sermon was first delivered to the Second Church): "When the student of nature, quitting the simplicity and perfectness of natural laws, came into the churches and colleges to learn the character of God they [*sic*] there found such gross and unworthy views of him as not agreed but contrasted with their own conclusions respecting the cause of Nature, and as with one voice they rejected these creeds" (*YES*, p. 175). The theme reminds us of Whitman's "When I Heard the Learn'd Astronomer," but it also clearly anticipates Emerson's use of astronomy in *Nature* and the Divinity School Address.[12] In 1832 however Emerson felt obliged to retreat (as he had done in "Summer" and other sermons) from his theory of nature and declare that his observations were "not denial but purification" of the authority of Christ: "Does it take away any authority from his lips? It abridges what belongs to persons, to places and to times but it does not touch moral truth" (*YES*, p. 177). Yet the time was soon approaching when he would unburden himself of Christian doctrine. For astronomy, he thought, "proves theism but disproves dogmatic theology. . . . It operates steadily to establish the moral laws[,] to disconcert & evaporate temporary systems." Therefore, in order to be a "good minister" it was necessary to leave the ministry. "The profession is antiquated," he wrote in his journal for June. "In an altered age, we worship in the dead forms of our forefathers. Were not a Socratic paganism better than an effete super-annuated Christianity?" (*JMN*, 4:26–27). He was almost ready now to act upon the suspicions of 1827: that the nature of God is different "from what he is represented."

The same month Emerson sent a letter to the church committee requesting a change in the communion ceremony. The request was refused, and by the middle of July he decided to resign his pastorate. The formal resignation was presented on 11 September and accepted by the Second Church on 21 October. Emerson's health had been poor during the fall of 1832, and on Christmas day he sailed for Europe in search of a stronger constitution as well as a way to work out his spiritual quandary. Ten months later—on 9 October 1833—he returned to Boston, having regained not only his health but a renewed and more vigorous interest in natural history.

Emerson's experiences in Europe have been recounted in numerous biographies and critical studies. He met John Stuart Mill, Wordsworth, Coleridge, and Carlyle, among others. It has also been noted previously that his visits to the Jardin des Plantes in Paris left him with a feeling only somewhat short of revelation. On 13 July 1833, he wrote in his journal: "The fancy-coloured vests of these elegant beings [in the ornithological chambers] make me as pensive as the hues & forms of a cabinet of shells, formerly. It is a beautiful collection & makes a visiter calm & genial as a bridegroom. The limits of the possible are enlarged, & the real is stranger than the imaginary. . . . Walk down the alleys of the flower garden & you come to the enclosures of the animals where almost all that Adam named or Noah preserved are represented" (*JMN*, 4:198–200). Only with a visit to this Paris sanctuary today perhaps can one fully appreciate the serenity that Emerson must have enjoyed during his tours of the Garden. Originally a botanical garden opened in 1793, it had by Emerson's visit also become the first public zoo in France. Wandering through the sixteen-acre menagerie and attending lectures on science, Emerson seemed to leap forward with a new vision (*Life*, p. 187). The experience confirmed what he had come to accept as his new religion: "Nature is a language & every new fact that we learn is a new word; but rightly seen, taken altogether it is not merely a language, but a scripture which contains the whole truth."[13]

Emerson made his debut as a lecturer on 4 November 1833, when he was asked to speak on the "Uses of Natural History" at the Masonic temple in Boston. The American lyceum movement, begun in 1826, encouraged individuals to speak on various subjects without being "experts" in the fields. Emerson's lecture was assigned to him and sponsored by the Natural History Society of Boston. Yet his theme was similar to that of "Summer" and "Astronomy"—what would become the center-piece of his first book, "To what end is nature?" However, it provides a clearer picture of his future development as an essayist, for it presents his first public discussion of nature, unfettered by the ministerial obligation to align his observations with Christian doctrine.

In inquiring about "the advantages which may be expected to accrue from the greater cultivation of Natural Science," he recalled his experiences in the Jardin des Plantes and the feelings it excited in him. He saw in that collection of life's curiosities "Nature's proof impressions." In his recent assessment of the lecture, Gay Wilson Allen remarks that it clarifies Emerson's famous "transparent eye-ball" passage in *Nature*. Although the passage has been attributed to personal experience, it was more likely an imaginative illustration of the "occult relation" Emerson found between man and the rest of nature. "We feel," he said, "that there is an occult relation between the very worm, the crawling scorpions, and man. I am moved by strange sympathies. I say I will listen to this invitation. I will be a naturalist."[14]

Like the fabled Greek giant Antaeus, whose strength in combat with Hercules was renewed every time he touched the earth, "Man is the broken giant, and in all his weakness he is invigorated by touching his mother earth, that is, by habits of conversation with nature" (*EL*, 1:11). In *Nature* Emerson would write, "The reason why the world lacks unity, and lies broken and in heaps, is, because man is disunited with himself." The idea of unity or correspondence between the material and spiritual worlds had found its first public expression in "Summer" and "Astronomy," but in these sermons the Neoplatonic overtones were vague and absorbed ultimately into Christian doctrine. Although Emerson would not read the Neoplatonists directly till 1837 (and then through the controversial translations of Thomas Taylor), he had been familiar with the doctrine since his college days through Ralph Cudworth's *True Intellectual System of the Universe*.[15] Furthermore, between 1831 and 1834 his journals indicate at least a casual reading of Plotinus and Porphyry. In "Uses of Natural History," however, Emerson was free to develop the Neoplatonic theme of character by dwelling upon the evolutionary process of nature and how it prepared the globe for the advent of man. Astronomy may have suggested the exaltation of true religious sentiment, but geology presented even a stronger case for the use of nature in awakening the "slumbering giant" in man. Coal, for example, was once covered by layers of granite, slate, and chalk. But like so many "coats of the onion," they have been peeled away and vast beds of fuel were brought within the reach of man's puny hands. The discoveries of the geologists suggest that all the workings of nature are made to contribute to man's "pleasure and prosperity at this hour." Finally, this awareness of nature's benevolence produces a "salutary effect" upon man which is directly related to the evolution of his character; indeed, it generates "the highest *state* of character" (*EL*, 1:15–21). For he sees that the whole of nature, or rather its evolution in the particular, is a metaphor for the growth of the human mind or spirit.

The theme is repeated and clarified in his next lecture, "On the Relation of Man to the Globe." Speaking in December, he declared that man is "no upstart in the creation, but has been prophesied in nature for a thousand thousand ages before he appeared" (*EL*, 1:29). And not only has the globe been prepared for man, but necessity has adapted man to the globe. For example, "the history of navigation affords the most striking instances, but by no means the only ones, of the accurate adjustment of the powers to the wants of man. The same balance is kept everywhere. A man is always in danger, and never" (*EL,* 1:38). Certainly, we have here anticipations of Emerson's theory of compensation, but the focus now is really on self-reliance through the realization of character and its constant evolution. Man's adaptation to the globe encourages his love for it—the love of nature for its "accord between man and the external world. Self-reliance, then, is the perception of how truly all his senses, "and beyond the senses, the soul, are tuned to the order of things." For the first time Emerson articulated his distinction between God-reliance and self-reliance. No longer simply in orbit around God, man the naturalist finds in nature a delight that transcends commodity and encourages faith in himself. "I am thrilled with delight," he concluded, "by the choral harmony of the whole. Design! It is all design. It is all beauty. It is all astonishment" (*EL,* 1:44, 49).

In his journal for 22 March 1834, Emerson had determined the subject "that needs most to be presented is the principle of Self reliance, what it is, what it is not, what it requires, how it teaches us to regard our friends" (*JMN,* 4:269). In "Water," delivered to the Boston Mechanics' Institution at the Athaeneum Library on 17 January, he had given his most technical lecture on natural science. Un-Emersonian in its literal rendering of the facts about water and its service to man, it probably conformed more to the spirit of the lyceum movement by emphasizing the practical rather than the moral aspects of scientific inquiry to the working class. His only Neoplatonic "digression" was the observation that there is a parallel between the circulation of water on the globe and the circulation of blood in the body (*EL,* 1:63). But Emerson returned to his Neoplatonic theme in "The Naturalist," addressed to the Boston Natural History Society on 7 May. In his three earlier lectures, he had held back the full force of the implications of natural history for man, much in the same way he had played down in his sermons between 1826 and 1831 the significance of nature as a means of informing (and superseding) Scripture. Now he was ready for a summary of his ideas on natural history which would take for granted Commodity and go directly to the heart of his concern—the "occult relation" between man and nature. "I shall treat this question not for the Natural Philosopher," he began, "but for the Man, and offer you some thoughts upon the intellectual influences of Natural Science" (*EL,* 1:70).

The intellectual influences of nature are not as clearly outlined as they would be in the book of 1836, but as in *Nature* the ultimate result of man's love of nature is self-reliance. First of all, this love persuades man that "Composition is more important than the elegance of individual forms. . . . The most elegant shell in your cabinet [he offered in anticipation of the poem "Each and All"] does not produce such an effect on the eye as the contrast and combination of a group of ordinary shells lying together wet upon the beach." Also, "The tree is not, the botanist finds, a single structure but a vast assemblage of individuals." Second, the realization that the whole is made of individual parts discourages imitation (thus confirming what he had discovered in 1831, that it is baneful to look for permanence in the particular). The study of natural science leads man back to the "Truth" that nature is permanent only in its whole; that indeed, its permanence thrives upon the transitory nature of the particular. "Imitation," he declared, "is [the] servile copying of what is capricious as if it were permanent forms of Nature" (*EL*, 1:73–75).

Much of the doctrine in "The Naturalist" had already been suggested in the first two lectures; here it comes together to suggest a more coherent outline for *Nature*. "The Naturalist" also departs from the others in its attack on society, or the refinements of civilization which keep man from a clear vision of nature. As he had assailed Christianity for imposing barriers between man and God in "Astronomy," he now accused the cities of putting man in danger of forgetting his relation to the planet and the system. "The clock and compass do us harm by hindering us from astronomy," he offered. "We have made civil months until the natural signs, the solstices and the equinoxes, most men do not know. Find me a savage who does not know them." Society took man down the same "strange paths" as he thought Christianity had in "Astronomy." And it resulted in a loss of character that could be repaired only through a rediscovery of nature. "I cannot but think," he said, "that a ramble in the country with the set purpose of observation to most persons whose duties confine them much to the city will be a useful lesson. . . . go out into the woods, break your hours, carry your biscuit in your pocket, and you shall see a day as an astronomical phenomenon" (*EL*, 1:76–77).

It has been said of Walt Whitman that he is one of the very few in the history of world literature who wrote the same book over and again, expanding it but always returning to the same essential theme. Sir Francis Bacon is another who kept beginning again, writing twelve different drafts of the *Novum Organum* in as many years. In a general sense, Emerson also rewrote, beginning with the sermon on "Summer," his book about nature throughout his productive years. His ideas reach their pinnacle in terms of classification in *Nature*, then are applied with greater eloquence and force to individuals in academe, the clergy, and literature. They become somewhat diluted but also more humanized in the biographical sketches of *Representative Men* (1850); yet the idea of biography is implied throughout the successive "versions" of *Nature*. And indeed, as Joel Porte remarks, it was the same with Whitman, whose intuitive grasp of *representation* suggests "uncannily that [the poet] had read not only *Representative Men* but also been given the opportunity to leaf through Emerson's journals."[16] Doubtless, the similarity explains Emerson's "uncanny" ability to see, when no one else could, that Whitman's celebration of self was the work of genius. But back in the winter of 1835, Emerson had still to articulate what he had already known: that natural history by itself had little value—"it is like a single sex. But marry it to human history, & it is poetry" (*JMN*, 4:311). Two more lecture series would be required to complete the rehearsal for *Nature*, one on biography and another on literature.

Between 29 January and 5 March 1835, Emerson delivered six lectures on "Biography" to the Society for the Diffusion of Useful Knowledge at the Masonic temple. As the editors of the first volume of the *Early Lectures* note, the pervasive influence of Plutarch's *Lives* and *Morals* is more apparent than it is on *Representative Men*, "when other influences such as Carlyle's had taken full effect" (*EL*, 1:94). Yet the lectures go far beyond the influence of his early reading in the sense that this series joined for the first time Emerson's observations on natural science to human history as it was best represented (or idealized). Unfortunately, Emerson's intention in the series at the outset can be determined only generally—from the biographical sketches that followed the introductory address; for the manuscript to the opening lecture is lost. His theme anticipates the one of "Uses of Great Men" that introduced *Representative Men*: that history is really a composite of individual biographies of great men which, when strung together, suggests the ideal qualities of the whole or central man. This is more or less confirmed by two journal entries from 1834 to 1835.

"The reason why the Luther, the Newton, the Bonaparte," Emerson wrote in his journal for 19 January 1834, "was made the subject of panegyric, is, that in the writer's opinion, *in some one respect* this par-

ticular man represented the idea of Man" (*JMN*, 4:256; emphasis mine).
In other words, biographies of particular men taken together suggest the
ideal of the whole man, but an individual not really possible on earth.
Instead, he is a paragon to be achieved eventually through change or
amelioration in nature. Therefore (Emerson continued, in his journal for
13 January 1835) biography, or the lives of great men, is "history taken
together [and] is as severely moral in its teaching as the straitest religious
sect." And by studying it, "We recognize with delight a strict likeness
between their noblest passions & our own. . . . We participate in their act
by our thorough understanding of it. . . . that the faintest sentiments
which we have shunned to indulge from fear of singularity are . . . eternal
in man" (*JMN*, 5:11–12).

Emerson chose for his representative men in 1835 Michelangelo,
Martin Luther, John Milton, George Fox, and Edmund Burke. And they
exemplified, respectively, the worshipper of beauty, the epitome of self-
reliance, the gifts of the poet, the exaltation of religious sentiment, and
the philosopher as statesman. Of Michelangelo, Emerson said he was
"so true to the laws of the human mind that his character and works . . .
seem rather a part of Nature than arbitrary productions of the human will"
(*EL*, 1:99). Yet the essay is really about beauty and the artist's perception
of it. It is the great whole which the understanding cannot embrace. Of
course, reason—or its potential—resides in all men, but most men are
able to use it only to *appreciate* beauty. This is called taste. But
Michelangelo was an artist who possessed the ability to reconstruct the
conversations with nature that lesser men can only grasp through taste.
Martin Luther was also a poet in this sense: "He wrote no poems, but he
walked in a charmed world. Everything to his eye assumed a symbolical
aspect." And "No man in history ever assumed a more commanding
attitude or expressed a more perfect self-reliance." In opposing the sale of
indulgences and other corruptive practices of the Roman Catholic
church, he operated on the sensible world by "taking his stand in the
Invisible World" (*EL*, 1:132, 136, 143).

John Milton, Emerson said in an essay that can still be considered
more or less sound today, was a poet in the literal sense because he had the
power of language to clothe the invisible world with words. His language
was what Emerson called "the secondary power" of reason. To the
antique heroism of Virgil, "Milton added the genius of the Christian
sanctity" (*EL*, 1:156). To the pagan philosopher's celebration of individ-
uality, Milton added religious sentiment:

> Henceforth I learn, that to obey is best,
> And love with fear the only God, to walk
> As in his presence, ever to observe
> His providence, and on him sole depend.
> [*Paradise Lost* 12. 561–64]

"Was there not a fitness in the undertaking of such a person," Emerson asked, "to write a poem on the subject of Adam, the first man?" In other words, Milton achieved what the Virgil of Dante's *Commedia* could not, that of escorting Man through the Wall of Flames back into the Garden of Eden. Milton's poem was "of the *heroic* life of man" (*EL*, 1:160, 162; emphasis mine).

In discussing George Fox, founder of the Quakers as a protest against Presbyterianism in England, Emerson touched again upon his theme of the need for constant evolution in religious worship. "All attempts to confine and transmit the religious feeling of one man or sect to another age, by means of formulas the most accurate, or rites the most punctual, have hitherto proved abortive," he said. "You might as easily preserve light or electricity in barrels. It must be lived" if true exaltation of religious sentiment is to be achieved (*EL*, 1:167–68). Like Emerson, Fox had opposed the use of the Lord's Supper as well as other church ceremonies. He did so, Emerson said, in the spirit of reform, for "The creed, the rites of one age can never fit the next. . . . Nature never fails. Instantly, the divine Light rekindles in some one or other obscure heart who denounces the deadness of the church and cries aloud for new and more appropriate practices." Fox and his followers laid stress "upon the doctrine of the infinitude of Man as seen in the conviction that his soul is a temple in which the Divine Being resides" (*EL*, 1:174, 180–81).

In introducing the final lecture in the series, the editors of the *Early Lectures* remark that the role that Edmund Burke filled as statesman "had less personal appeal for Emerson than did those of poet, philosopher, and religious leader" (*EL*, 1:183). Yet Emerson's interest in Burke was aligned with his enthusiasm for the others in the series. Indeed, it might be compared to our own yearning for the statesman instead of the politician in American politics. Burke was not merely a statesman but "the *philosophical politician,* not a man who, quoting Latin and German, Aristotle and Hume, acted with total disregard to general principles,— but one who, drawing from the same fountain with these theorists, brought principles to bear upon the public business of England" (*EL*, 1:189). As the philosopher in action, Burke anticipates Emerson's model for the American Scholar. But as we shall see, he also contributes to the central man theory that lies at the heart of *Nature*.

Of course, the most *central* man for Emerson was the poet, and hence the biographical sketch of Milton was appropriately the center-piece of the series. Emerson's favorite poet for years, Milton combined to a lesser extent all the qualities that the others represent. He perceived the whole of beauty in nature. Certainly, he was self-reliant, writing with failing eyesight his greatest works. And he possessed the moral sentiment to celebrate in his poetry man as "Adam in the garden again" (*W*, 8:31). Finally, as Emerson remarked in his sketch, Milton was the philosopher in action and "obtained great respect from his contemporaries as an accomplished scholar, and a formidable controvertist. . . . His prose writings, especially the 'Defence of the English People,' seem to have been read with avidity" (*EL*, 1:146). Emerson also made reference to *Areopagitica* and other pamphlets having to do with public affairs.

In his biography of Emerson, Allen writes of the lectures on English literature: "None of these lectures is of particular importance in Emerson's biography except his Introduction, in which he explained his theory of literature. . . . it was a dress rehearsal for *Nature*."[17] It is true that the series was hastily prepared and often careless in its use of factual material. Indeed, Emerson's assessment of Chaucer, for example, as a talented imitator sounds ridiculous today. It is also true that many of the observations in the introductory lecture were lifted almost unchanged into *Nature*. But this lecture, delivered 5 November 1835, while certainly the closest thing to *Nature*, is perhaps more important as a benchmark in the development of Emerson's theory of language. We have seen in the sermons and earlier lectures many of the ideas that went into *Nature*, but that development had stopped short of anticipating "Language," one of the most important sections in *Nature*. In "English Literature: Introductory," Emerson finally laid the foundation for this section which most directly presented his theory of poetry. And with this accomplished, he had served his apprenticeship as the prophet of the American literary renaissance. In this sense, Allen is correct in calling the introductory lecture a dress rehearsal for *Nature*; for once the "Language" section had been worked out, the sections on "Discipline," "Idealism," "Spirit," and "Prospects" followed almost automatically.

We must keep in mind that Emerson's greatness lies in his use of language, not in any philosophy he originated. Meaning for him was possible only through language—in its ability to clothe the spiritual world with words. "Of the various ways in which man endeavors to utter the great invisible nature which gives him life," he said in the opening lecture to "English Literature," "the most perfect vehicle of his meaning is Language" (*EL*, 1:219). What followed will be familiar to every student of *Nature*: "Every word which is used to express a moral or intellectual fact, if traced to its root, is found to be borrowed from some corporeal or animal fact. *Right* originally means *straight; wrong* means *twisted*. Spirit primarily means *wind*. Transgression, the *crossing a line*. Supercillious, the *raising of the eyebrow*." And further on: "It is not words only that are emblematic; it is things which are emblematic. Every fact in outward nature answers to some state of the mind and that state of the mind can only be described by presenting that natural fact as a picture" (*EL*, 1:220). Good writing, then, is a perpetual allegory representing man's connection with the Unseen. Only the poet, of course, is capable of this level of discourse—which teaches us the emblematic character of the flux of the material world: "He converts the solid globe, the land, the sea, the sun, the animals into symbols of thought. . . . it is his office to show this beautiful relation, to utter the oracles of the mind in appropriate images from nature. And this is Literature" (*EL*, 1:224–25).

Like the series on biography, "English Literature" focuses upon representative men but now solely those gifted in the highest form of expression—the "august geniuses . . . who had just views on their vocation as Teachers." They did not sing the tune of their times but obeyed the spirit within them, preferring "its whisper to the applause of their contemporaries" (*EL*, 1:231–32). Their fables were true allegories of Man.

Though Emerson failed to appreciate Chaucer's gift for satire, he did say of the bard that he "never writes with timidity. He speaks like one who knows the law, and has a right to be heard" (*EL*, 1:274). And like Milton, Chaucer was a moralist and a reformer, lashing out at the clergy (though Emerson failed to cite "The Pardoner's Tale" as an example of his satire on the religious community). Emerson considered Spenser for his next lecture but chose Shakespeare instead, probably because he thought the poet's example better fitted his theory of language. "The power of the Poet," he said, "depends on the fact that the material world is a symbol or expression of the human mind and part for part. Every natural fact is a symbol of some spiritual fact." Also in "Shakspear" (which was delivered in two parts), Emerson gave the definition he would apply to his Orphic Poet in *Nature:* "He converts the solid globe, the land, the sea, the air, the sun, the animals into symbols of thought. . . . And this act or vision of the mind is called Imagination. It is the use which

the Reason makes of the material world, for purposes of expression"
(*EL*, 1:289). Again as in the introductory lecture—and indeed as far back
as Emerson's discovery of the meaning of character in 1831—the fluidity
of nature is paramount.

Bacon's *Novum Organum* was certainly a logical continuation of
this theme, for Emerson clearly appreciated Bacon's argument that experience is the source of all knowledge and induction is its method. The
syllogism, or deductive reasoning, Bacon said, "is no match for the
subtlety of nature." Of the other writers covered in the series (Jonson,
Herrick, Herbert, and Wotton), only the observations on the author of
"Upon Julia's Clothes" add any new facts about Emerson's future as a
writer and a judge of poetry. Although he commended the poet for his
lyrics "upon the objects of common life," he also censured Herrick for
his sexual pieces: "Herrick by the choice often of base and even disgust-
ing themes, has pushed this [poetic] privilege too far, rather I think out of
the very wantonness of poetic power. . . . to make his book sell, by
feeding the grosser palates of his public" (*EL*, 1:346–47). (Ironically, he
would advise Whitman that the sexual poems in "Children of Adam"
would keep *Leaves of Grass* from selling.)[18] Herrick's propensity to feed
"the grosser palates" aside, he joined the others in the series in his ability
to clothe the Invisible World with words. And with the lectures on "English Literature," Emerson completed the triad that became the main
ingredients of *Nature*: natural history, biography, and poetry.

Since the shock with which the Unitarians received Emerson's
"transparent eye-ball" passage, critics have pointed to it as the eclectic
statement in *Nature*, calling it a description of a mystical experience. Yet
I agree with Gay Wilson Allen that it is more likely an imaginative
illustration of man's occult relation with nature. Allen cites the passage
from "Uses of Natural History," but I would like to note that it is
repeated in *Nature*, and further, that it is a more accurate, if less imaginative, description of what the transcendentalist experiences: "The greatest
delight which the fields and woods minister, is the suggestion of an occult
relation between man and the vegetable. I am not alone and unacknowl-
edged. They nod to me, and I to them." The transcendentalist is the
central man, representative of all men in their finest moments. But a
description of these is beyond the language skills of most men, and only
the poet can freeze the music of nature's song. It is only he—the epitome
of the representative man—Emerson would say again in "Prospects,"
who can help us "become sensible of a certain occult recognition and

sympathy in regard to the most unwieldy and eccentric forms of beast, fish, and insect.''

This sensibility the poet brings to us is the subject of "Language" and indeed one of the central themes of *Nature*. He makes the veil of society (a theme in "The Naturalist") somewhat diaphanous; he lifts "our discourse above the ground line of familiar facts" by clothing the spirit with images. "The poet, the orator bred in the woods [Burke, for an example of the latter], whose senses have been nourished by their fair and appeasing changes, year after year, without design and without heed— [does not] lose their lesson altogether, in the roar of the cities or the broil of politics." This master of language, who sees a fact as "the end or last issue of the spirit," also teaches us that "Nature is a discipline." He comprehends the laws of physics, for he sees that "a leaf, a drop, a crystal, a moment in time is related to the whole, and partakes of the perfection of the whole." In a sentence, Emerson remarks in "Discipline," the language of the poet helps the understanding to approach intellectual or spiritual truths—the poet shapes "the Hand of the mind." Which is perhaps as far as most men can soar in their appreciation of nature and how its flux mirrors the growth of their character.

The poet knows that with discipline "all parts of nature conspire," Emerson says in the "Idealism" section. And it matters not to the poet "whether nature enjoy a substantial existence without, or is only in the apocalypse of the mind." For like the genuine man of 1832, he shapes the circumstances of his life and finds meaning. Now in 1836 Emerson reiterates his theme of the self-willed evolution of character: whereas "The sensual man conforms thoughts to things; the poet conforms things to his thoughts. The one esteems nature as rooted and fast; the other, as fluid, and impresses his being thereon." And relying on Shakespeare again, he likens the poet to the magician Prospero of *The Tempest* to illustrate the "transfiguration which all material objects" receive under the power of the poet's language. When Prospero calls for music to soothe his companions:

> A solemn air, and the best comforter
> To an unsettled fancy, cure thy brains
> Now useless, boiled within thy skull.

Through reason and the gift of language, the poet transfers "nature into the mind, and [leaves] matter like an outcast corpse." He detects, Emerson continues in "Spirit," "God in the coarse." Finally, in "Prospects" he advises, "Build, therefore, your own world."

Of course, *Nature* is general doctrine, the so-called bible of transcendentalism. It urges man to undergo a change of character—to act from character. But underlying all is the message that we need an intermediary or archangel, and he is the poet—just as Christ had been, he would say two years later at the Harvard Divinity School, to the first Christians. And by acting from his own character, the poet perceives the fluid world and acts for us all. This is the poet that Emerson endeavored to summon forth in himself, in *Nature*. But the task, as he discovered in his first book, was not an easy one. For to delight in God in nature—as he does in the "transparent eye-ball" passage—is difficult within the community. Even "the poet," he confessed at the end of "Spirit," "finds something ridiculous in his delight, until he is out of the sight of men."

Emerson, therefore, was not yet free from the intimidation of society, not quite out of the "ministry" in *Nature*. No longer able to evoke the authority of Christ for his "higher flight" and yet not fully able to evoke his character either, he turned to the Orphic Poet: "I shall therefore conclude this essay with some traditions of man and nature, which a certain poet sang to me." Some critics have thought this to be a reference to Amos Bronson Alcott, whose draft of "Psyche" Emerson had read and criticized in 1836. But since he found the manuscript "deficient in variety of thought & illustration," it is unlikely that the "Orphic Philosopher" served as a model for the Orphic Poet in "Prospects." Rather, the Orphic Poet is the self or voice Emerson was still trying to bring forth—the voice of his true character that had begun as a murmur back in 1827, when he entertained the doubt that "the nature of God may be different from what he is represented" (*JMN*, 3:69). *Nature*, therefore, served as Emerson's bridge between the realms of the understanding and the reason. It was the catalyst and catharsis that took him from the expository prose of the preacher-lecturer to the freer, more irresponsible speech of the poet.

Emerson on "Making" in Literature

His Problem of Professionalism, 1836–1841

GLEN M. JOHNSON

If the five years preceding *Nature* were crucial to Emerson's developing philosophy of the universe and of man's place in it, the five years after 1836 were equally vital to his sense of himself as an artist and a professional. Emerson had set out in *Nature* to write a "first philosophy"—his ambition for at least a dozen years—but had, after much intellectual difficulty, produced a poem in prose.[1] From that experience, he learned to accept his gifts as a writer: his mission and his method were, he would say in 1838, to use metaphor, not syllogism, to "suggest the majestic Presence to the soul" (*EL*, 3:20). And yet, after *Nature*, Emerson waited almost five years to produce what he conceived as his "book of Genesis," the *Essays* of 1841 (*L*, 2:194). In the interim, he perfected his art before the limited but immediate audiences for his orations and lectures. Perhaps equally important to his future, he worked in public and in private to develop a sense of himself as a professional man of letters.

For Emerson, professionalism necessitated coming to terms with two problems—one social, the other aesthetic. The problem of vocation, Emerson's need to discover a cultural role for himself, has been carefully analyzed by Ralph Rusk, Stephen Whicher, and Henry Nash Smith.[2] The related problem, however, has received relatively little attention: Emerson's need to develop a theory of creation consistent with the demands of writing for a vocation. Emerson believed in afflatus, but in the late 1830s he committed himself to a career that required production by schedule, "inspiration" or none. As he prepared his subscription lectures, and later his first "professional" book, he was seeking not only to produce but to convince himself that he *could* produce without sacrificing the quality he valued most in literature. As a result of this theoretical struggle within himself, he developed by 1841 a concept of "making" in literature, a theory allowing him confidence in both his professionalism and his allegiance to the spirit. The present essay analyzes that theory as it took shape in the journals, lectures, and essays of 1836–41.

For Emerson, literature proceeded from—and in the reader led to—a state of vision. Like other romantic thinkers, Emerson identified this state sometimes with the earliest stages of human history—his imagery here clearly Edenic—and sometimes with the youth of every individual. In either case, a prelapsarian condition presumably once existed and certainly could exist again. In such a state, all men live by intuition, and thus all thought and all expression are spontaneous; all men are artists. Or, from another perspective often assumed by Emerson, all existence is spontaneous and "art," thereby rendered superfluous, ceases to exist: "Why should a man spend years in carving an Apollo, who looked Apollos into the landscape with every glance he threw?" (*EL,* 3:93).

Believing in the potential reestablishment of intuitional existence, and setting himself to service as "teacher of the coming age" (*JMN,* 4:93), Emerson devoted most of his public statements in the 1830s to describing this renewed Eden and the receptive attitude that would bring it about. And so it is true that Emerson's aesthetic—in its pure, optative form—glorifies creativity in such a way as to make art as we conceive it impracticable. Indeed, in moments of influx from the Over-Soul—one name for which is "the wise silence"—any kind of willed activity, language included, obtrudes and hinders. "The ancient sentence said, Let us be silent, for so are the gods" (*CW,* 2:160, 202–3).

During the period of his transcendental genesis, Emerson believed that the revolution which would restore spontaneity to human existence was—given some exhortation from him—imminent. But implicit in his acts of exhortation was a recognition that man's present state was depraved and that flashes of pure inspiration came spasmodically, if at all. "A man is a god in ruins," says the poet-persona of *Nature*, and Emerson accounted for this anomaly with a version of the Fall from grace. About the causes of the Fall Emerson was more vague than his Puritan ancestors had been—usually blaming social complexity and pressures to conform—and he almost always treated the Fall as myth rather than as historical fact. Nevertheless, the myth of a Fall is prominent in his writings of the late 1830s; it is made explicit in the words of the poet at the end of *Nature* and in the "fable" of divided man at the beginning of "The American Scholar." The clearest statement, however, comes at the beginning of "The Protest" (January 1839), the sixth lecture in Emerson's subscription series on "Human Life." Part of the significance of "The Protest" is the fact that Emerson paired it in the series with one of the most transcendental of all his lectures, "Genius." The sequence of "Genius" and "The Protest" reveals in unusually pure form Emerson's

habit of juxtaposing his visions of human possibility and actuality—
heaven and hell, so to speak—and shows him still trying to make inspiration consistent with the professional's "skill of practice."

Considered in isolation, "Genius" seems to justify the charge that
Emerson regarded literary expression as inspired automatic writing.
"Genius is the spontaneous perception and exhibition of truth," Emerson
tells his audience; and he denies any essential distinction between perception and exhibition. Genius is "not a knack, a habit, a skill of practice, a
working by a rule, nor any empirical skill whatever"; it is, rather, an
"energy" whose source almost seems external, a "power which over-
awes," an "enthusiasm not subject to . . . control" (*EL,* 3:70–71).
Genius finally boils down to self-reliance ("To believe your thought,—
that is genius"), but in such a context self-reliance seems largely passive.
Only when one passes on to "The Protest" does it become apparent that
"Genius" describes a visionary state which has existed only for a few
men, and then intermittently. Certainly—and this was Emerson's problem of professionalism—it does not describe the usual conditions under
which literature is, and for the professional must be, produced.

In "The Protest," Emerson shifts from the optative mood into the
indicative; he begins by noting the "extreme paucity" of genius as he has
described it, citing Doctor Johnson's opinion that the world contains "no
men of entirely sane mind." Emerson then proceeds to analyze the discrepancy between potentiality and actuality, revealing a fatalism that is,
intentionally, startling in its juxtaposition with the vision of "Genius":

> The dissonance of which I speak is involuntary and necessary. It is a neces-
> sity flowing from the nature of things. What is the front the world always shows to
> the young spirit? Strange to say, The Fall of Man. The Fall of Man is the first
> word of history and the last fact of experience. In the written annals or in the older
> tradition of every nation this dark legend is told of the depravation of a once pure
> and happy society. And in the experience of every individual somewhat analo-
> gous is recognized.

> The life of the soul in men is ordinarily not continuous and sustained but
> impulsive. But the life of the senses is continuous and usurping.

> The fact is very strange and the cause of it perhaps too deep in our constitu-
> tion and too subtle to be explored. [*EL,* 3:86–87]

The extent of Emerson's concern here is indicated by his calling
upon the myth of the fall—explicitly, without the cover of a persona or a

fable, and with a full awareness of the associations the myth carried for his contemporaries—to explain the "dissonance" which seems, in "the nature of things," to block the life of art by shutting a man off from his genius. Still, Emerson is not ready to admit that the state of vision cannot exist in the present world, and so he begins immediately to outline a strategy for confronting the fall of man, a strategy that provides an important function for art.

"Young men"—Emerson's metaphor for those who refuse to accept the fall—begin as militant perfectionists: "All literature, all art is really below and not above the aspirations of the youth. Nothing that is done satisfies him. He wishes the perfect, the illimitable. He finds in it instantly the bonds of the Finite. . . . And hence, as the poets say, in the first age, the sons of God printed no epics, carved no stone, painted no canvas, built no railroad, for the sculpture, the poetry, the music and architecture were in the man. . . . If we felt that the Universe was ours, that we dwelled in Eternity and advanced into all wisdom we should be less covetous of these sparks and cinders" (*EL*, 3:92–93). This all-or-nothing attitude is essentially identical to that which informs Emerson's own position in "Genius." In "The Protest," however, Emerson expresses reservations about the attitude, even while he defends it. The problem is this: given the Fall of Man, the "youth's" unyielding insistence upon the illimitable sets him in opposition to his fellows; paradoxically, perfectionism becomes self-destructive and can actually block progress toward the desired general revolution: "Now this hostile attitude of young persons . . . makes them very undesireable companions to their friends: querulous, opinionative, impracticable; and, furthermore, it makes them unhappy in their own solitude. If it continue too long, it makes shiftless and morose men" (*EL*, 3:99). Thus Emerson anticipates by over a century Charles Feidelson's objection to his "impracticable" theory of literature.[3]

Faced with an apparent impasse between his millennial vision and his recognition of actual conditions, Emerson sets himself to working out a compromise that neither sacrifices the former nor ignores the latter. As he sees it, the all-or-nothing position of the visionary is "a temporary state," "an unavoidable preliminary to vigorous and effective action." In the new myth of regeneration, the youth's "warlike" perfectionism "is made good by new impulses from within," resulting in a "position of perpetual inquiry." "Then it is presently revealed to him how he should live and work. Quite naturally his own path opens before him; his object appears; his aim becomes simple and, . . . he begins to work according to his faculty. He has done protesting: now he begins to affirm: all art affirms: and with every new stroke with greater serenity and joy." As he begins to work, the "immortal youth" finds himself part of a movement: "Friendly faces look over the wall into his acre; laborers in all divers crafts show him that they also have one purpose with him, and their works forward each other" (*EL,* 3:99–101).

The central concept in this passage is that of vocation; the key words are "action" and "work"; and the one kind of work mentioned specifically is art. In "The Protest," Emerson has begun to shift his emphasis—subtly and tentatively, to be sure—from passive reception to active creation. The individual is still at the center of his philosophy, but Emerson is more conscious than before of man's social duty in a fallen world. Consequently, his ethics of individual purification now shares place with his ethics of vocation; his vision of the individual alone with God is complemented by a vision of individuals working together to achieve the regeneration of all men. None of these elements is new in Emerson's thought, of course; but "The Protest" does record a change in emphasis, the beginnings of a new synthesis which reflects Emerson's greater respect for the intractability of the actual and his awareness of the need to work actively against it. The synthesis has great significance for Emerson's theory of literature, since artistic creation is unavoidably a social act, and the aesthetic artifact is fundamentally a made thing, the result of conscious working. Previously, Emerson has mostly ignored the social dimension of art, except to find it shameful that any man should take his "own rejected thoughts" from another (*EL,* 3:77). And he has generally evaded the question of "making" by asserting, as in "Genius," that expression, like acquisition, is intuitive and facile. These positions, however, have run up against the undeniable "fact of experience" that "the life of the soul in men," Emerson included, is "not continuous and sustained." For Emerson in 1839, the inconsecutiveness of inspiration was especially troublesome, for his chosen profession committed him to continuous and sustained production. And he had learned that his own best art—the most obvious example is the carefully crafted epiphany on the bare common in *Nature*[4]—was the result of labor rather than of inspired overflow. And so by 1840 he could record a lesson, learned from the "hateful experience" of struggling to compose over five dozen lectures in six years: "nothing grand ever grew" without hours and days of laborious making (*JMN,* 7:339).

As he usually did when confronted by a discrepancy between theory and practice, Emerson began, particularly in the "Human Life" lectures of 1838–39, to adapt his aesthetic to his experience as a writer. Indeed, as

Gene Bluestein has noted in his reinterpretation of the "Language" chapter of *Nature*, Emerson's theory always contained one perspective which sees literary composition as a means of evoking inspiration. The artist's task is, as Bluestein glosses Emerson, to use words to call forth the "natural facts" which symbolize spiritual truths. If the words and the natural facts are in a proper symbolic relationship, "then the channels open and the underlying spiritual truths come into focus. . . . As Emerson gives it, the creative process is by definition an indirect one," a way for fallen man to pierce the opaque mist that separates him from the spirit—to fight his way back to truth.[5] From this point of view, Emerson was able, even in his most transcendental period, to see truth as the end of the creative process rather than the beginning, thus disarming the Platonic objection to literature twice-removed from reality. And he was able to regard art, in an important, if limited, sense, as the *making* of truth. Although truth has absolute existence, man in his fallen state can generally approach it only through art, through "calculated use of language."

In Emerson's earlier works this more practical perspective is generally subordinated to the perfectionist's view; under the pressure of experience, however, it gradually comes to equal prominence. The advantages of the new synthesis for the professional author are obvious. First, it gives literary endeavor a specific and respectable social function, a power to show fallen man the way to truth. Second, it aggrandizes the artist's vocation, combining in him the scholar's insight and the hero's active power. Emerson's American Scholar, to whom he paid tribute a year after *Nature*, was "man thinking," where thinking remained largely a passive event. In "The Protest," one sees the emergence of man creating, an emergence that will continue in "Intellect" (1841) and culminate in "The Poet" (1844). Third, Emerson's new synthesis, in its emphasis on action or work, makes room for a conception of art as making. Emerson now begins to admit the role of the understanding in creation, the need for technical proficiency and the synthetic operations of the mind.

The central text here is "The School," a lecture delivered in the "Human Life" series three weeks before "Genius." Emerson begins with a reference to the capriciousness of inspiration: "That Nature which we all share has not been vouchsafed to us in like measures. . . . Here is this great Tragedy, shall I call it, of More and Less." But here also is a way around tragedy: "My great brothers have seen that which I have not seen, which I cannot see; they have created that which I can understand and enjoy and the book is their depository of the treasure." In his explanation of this fact, Emerson makes—for the first time in a formal statement—a clear distinction "between *perception* and *creation*," between "perfect understanding" of truth and "*the faculty of subordinating that rapture to the Will*" (*EL*, 3:44–45; Emerson's emphasis). The faculty works in two ways. It enables the artist "*to conjoin and record*" his infrequent moments of direct, pure inspiration. And, although the precise mechanism is mysterious and the final step beyond conscious control, it can in some way actually provoke inspiration, break through to truth. As Emerson has already noted in "The Head" (1837), and will repeat in "Intellect" (1841), "the oracle comes because we had previously laid siege to the shrine. . . . So now you must labor with your brains, and now you must forbear your activity and see what the Great Soul showeth" (*EL*, 2:252; *CW*, 2:197). Literature, then, both records inspiration for all to see and—through the labor of the brains—helps man break through the actual to the vision.

Two parallel developments confirm a shift in Emerson's thinking about literature around the time of "Human Life." The first is a change in his conception of his own primary genre. Up to the time of the Divinity School Address, Emerson's preferred form was the lecture or oration, at least partly because it provided the feeling, if not the fact, of spontaneity. Even though he apparently read his speeches verbatim from prepared texts, he praised the lecture, as opposed to the written statement, for its greater approximation to ecstasy: "There is a limit to the effect of written eloquence. It may do much, but the miracles of eloquence can only be expected from the man who thinks on his legs; he who thinks may thunder; on him the Holy Ghost may fall & from him pass" (*JMN*, 7:41). Faced with the unsettling reaction to his address, however, Emerson began to consider the "much" that a published statement could do. His journals for this period record a number of arguments in favor of the book. It could be more comprehensive than an oration, or even a lecture series, and thus could make more clear the "one doctrine" behind his diverse previous statements. Its influence could be greater in both space and time, thus fitting it for the tougher task of the "teacher" fighting against the Fall of Man. And a written statement could be more carefully prepared, more highly wrought, than a lecture, with less need to "economize" and "cheapen" (see *JMN*, 7:342, 339, 242).

The second development is Emerson's increasing interest, also reflected in the journals of 1838–40, in literary techniques and in justifications for "making" in art. Such interests are not absent in his earlier writings, of course. In 1835, for example, Emerson wrote, as a gloss of one of Bacon's aphorisms, that a great literary work results from "a multitude of trials & a thousand rejections & the using & perusing of what was already written" (*JMN*, 5:39). About the time of the Divinity School Address, however, there was a marked increase in both the frequency and the specificity of such statements. This criticism of Wordsworth, for example, dates from August 1838:

> In hearing one of Wordsworth's poems read, I feel, as often before, that it has the merit of a just moral perception, but not that of deft poetic execution. . . . The Rylstone Doe might be all improvised. . . . These are such verses as in a just state of culture should be *verse de societé,* such as every gentleman could write, but none would then think of printing, or claiming a Poet's laurel for making. The Pindar, the Shakspear, the Milton, whilst they have the just & open soul, have also the eye to see the dimmest star that glimmers in the Milky Way, the notches of every leaf, the test objects of the microscope, and then the tongue to utter the same things in words and engrave them on all the ears of mankind. The poet demands all gifts & not one or two only. Yet see the frugality of nature. The men of strength & crowded sense run into affectation. The men of Simplicity have no density of meaning. [*JMN,* 7:43–44]

This passage anticipates the new emphasis of "Human Life" by combining a vision of man's fallen state with a version of the poet's vocation. And it differentiates the poet from the "gentleman" not only on the basis of perception but also on the basis of his "deftness" in using words, his ability to "engrave them on all the ears of mankind."

On the day after he recorded his thoughts on Wordsworth, Emerson lightheartedly pictured himself as the "inventor of a new pleasure." If someone should offer a reward for the invention, "I would tell him to write an oration & then *print* it & setting himself diligently to the correction let him strike out a blunder & insert the right word just ere the press falls, & he shall know a new pleasure" (*JMN,* 7:44). Eleven days later, reflecting on the printed Divinity School *Address* and *Literary Ethics,* which had "cost me no small labor," he stated his case more seriously: "There goes a great deal of work into a correct literary paper, though of few pages. . . . It cannot be overseen & exhausted except by analysis as faithful as this synthesis. But negligence in the author is inexcusable. I know & will know no such thing as haste in composition" (*JMN,* 7:53). Practical statements on various aspects of the artist's "great deal of work" appeared regularly in 1838, 1839, and 1840.[6] In June 1839, Emerson returned to the theoretical plane to justify his own working to the "young persons" who figure so prominently in "The Protest": "It may be said in defence of this practice of *Composition* which seems to young persons so mechanical & so *un*inspired that to men working in Time all literary effort must be more or less of this kind, to Byron, to Goethe, to De Stael, not less than to Scott & Southey. Succession, moments, parts are their destiny & not wholes & worlds & eternity" (*JMN,* 7:216). The tone of this statement is sad; it records the loss of the young artist's ecstatic expectations of creativity. But the passage also reflects assurance gained through experience. It clearly marks Emerson's achieved sense of himself as a professional.

"Human Life" marks the culmination of Emerson's internal debate over whether a highly wrought work of literature could comprehend—reflect, or perhaps provoke—inspiration. This question had concerned him, as indeed it must concern any romantic artist or theorist, at least since the period of his transcendental genesis in the early 1830s. But in the years immediately following *Nature*, "making" became an insistent topic in his journals and, directly or indirectly, in his lectures. As usual with Emerson, theoretical debate originated in a practical problem, and experience dictated the direction his thinking took. After *Nature*, Emerson had committed himself to literature as not just his vehicle but his profession. And a professional had of necessity to be a maker.

By 1839, Emerson had worked out for himself a satisfactory theory to justify craft or "skill of practice," without sacrificing afflatus and ecstasy as either source or result of literature. The debate was not finished, of course, since Emerson sought not a synthesis but—as in the pairing of "Genius" and "The Protest"—a balance of perspectives. That the achieved balance was fruitful for him is obvious. Shortly after completing "Human Life," Emerson began his most ambitious artistic project, *Essays,* and ushered in a period of extraordinary professional productivity. When he called *Essays* his book of genesis, he indicated his sense of beginning anew, as a man of letters.

The Method of Nature and Emerson's Period of Crisis

DAVID ROBINSON

After a delay of almost a year because of the necessity of lecturing, Emerson sent his second book, *Essays,* to press on 1 January 1841. Although it was begun in 1839, Emerson found it financially necessary to put it aside in order to write a new series of lectures, "The Present Age," for the winter of 1839–40. Plans for the book, or one like it, go back several years in Emerson's career, even before he had written *Nature*.[1] But when he did complete the volume, he did so by postponing at least one part of it, another essay on "Nature" which he intended as a conclusion.[2] Emerson did finally fulfill that intention, as Richard Lee Francis has noted, with the concluding essay of *Essays: Second Series* (1844), entitled "Nature."[3] But he also achieved at least a partial fulfillment earlier, when in the summer of 1841, he delivered an oration on *The Method of Nature* at Waterville, Maine. The address is comparatively little known despite its crucial place in Emerson's career, and its centrally important subject matter. Carlyle thought it the "best *written*" (*CEC,* p. 312) of Emerson's works to date, but a more prevailing attitude is exemplified in Robert Spiller's remark that the address lacks "power and clarity" despite some excellent passages (*CW,* 1:117).[4] Moreover, if a reader has any initial suspicion of the essay's disjointedness, the feeling is further confirmed if he knows of Emerson's apparent difficulty in finishing the piece, and of the cold reception it received in Maine.[5] Still, Emerson felt the oration was "written in the heat and happiness of what I thought a real inspiration,"[6] and a fair reconsideration of it will certainly augment its stature in the Emerson canon, particularly in the light of recent issues in Emerson criticism. Spiller, despite his reservations, notes that the address "marks the low point in a time of personal crisis which has only recently been identified" (*CW,* 1:117).[7] It is the relation of the address to Emerson's time of crisis that will concern me here, for the address not only helps us identify the time period of that crisis but deals explicitly with the intellectual paradox that prompted it: the impermanent result of the quest for permanence.

Emerson is intent on defining nature's method in the address as one of flux or movement. "Its [nature's] permanence is perpetual inchoation" (*CW*, 1:124), he asserts, and the entire oration is an attempt to establish the fact of this perpetual change and to assess its impact on the mind. The theme is no new one for Emerson, dating back well into the speculations on science and natural theology during his ministry which led to *Nature*.[8] Moreover, the centrality of that theme in Emerson's thinking is gaining increasing recognition, and versions of it have been called, in Leonard Neufeldt's phrase, the "law of permutation,"[9] or by Brian Harding and Daniel Shea a vision of "metamorphosis."[10] While this realization of nature's "flux" was generally regarded by Emerson as a key to a triumphantly positive vision of organic growth, it did have disturbing implications for his faith in the possible culture of the soul. These disturbing qualities of nature's impermanence were manifest most clearly during what Stephen Whicher has labeled the period of crisis in Emerson's works, the late 1830s and early 1840s.[11] Large parts of *Essays* can be seen as a response to that manifestation,[12] and in *The Method of Nature,* Emerson continues his meditations on the soul's never-ending quest for permanence, which is so forcefully symbolized in nature. But the address also raises the crucial question of the source of spiritual vision, placing enormous stress on moments of ecstatic insight at the same time that it subtly questions the human capacity to achieve such experiences. Emerson's journal entries preceding the address suggest that these questions of vision were becoming increasingly crucial to him personally, and the address itself is a precarious balance of hope and doubt. Although it is supported by the foundations of natural theology and visionary mysticism he had constructed during the 1830s, it looks ahead to the curious blend of trust and fatalism that characterizes his later work.

No piece of Emerson's is more clarified by its biographical context than *The Method of Nature,* and no piece has a deeper center in Emerson's thinking. It is an important link in a chain of speculation about the moral uses of nature which began with some of his earlier sermons, and included his early lectures on science, *Nature*, significant parts of both series of essays, and the late *Natural History of Intellect*.[13] While these works cumulatively show Emerson's response to nineteenth-century scientific thought, particularly to doctrines of biological and geological evolution, their initial context is an eighteenth-century one, reflecting

Emerson's early immersion in the Unitarian blend of natural theology and revealed religion which Conrad Wright has called "supernatural rationalism."[14] The commitment which Emerson absorbed from his Unitarian forerunners—Channing was the most influential—was to view nature as a confirmation of biblical truths. Further, as Harry Hayden Clark has shown, natural theologians such as William Paley and Joseph Butler, who argued for the existence and attributes of God from the design of nature, were important parts of Emerson's training at Harvard.[15] This intellectual blend of reason and faith was not difficult for Emerson to accept in one respect. The abstract idea of God's existence, never seriously in doubt for him, seemed indeed to be confirmed by the design of nature, and in early manhood he was somewhat jarred by the experience of having met an intelligent and sincere atheist.[16]

But Emerson demanded not only an existent but a moral God and found both revealed religion and natural science less satisfying on this issue. Eighteenth-century moral philosophy, and his own deep conviction, had convinced him of an innate moral sense in the soul, but his growing rationalism and heterodoxy made biblical support for that sense less satisfying. The question he began to ask in the late 1820s was whether nature could provide that needed support of the moral sense. He had in one sense based his entire theological position on moral grounds, as some early sermons suggest. One sermon, first preached in September 1828 (and last preached as late as 1837), is devoted to the idea that belief in God is innate and argues for the validity of design rather than chance in the universe because of the presence of conscience in man.[17] Earlier that year, he had preached on "the very striking proof [conscience] furnishes, of the existence & government of God," calling it "the master work of the Deity," a law sure enough to be "the gravitation of the moral world."[18] Clearly he saw the moral sense as a foundation for a theology based on nature's design; but conversely, he also began to look to nature as a confirmation of the moral sense. He hoped, as he put it in one journal entry, to find "the ethics of the creation" (*JMN*, 3:186).

He began to find that support through his growing conviction in the evolutionary or dynamic qualities of nature, based in his scientific reading in the early 1830s and confirmed by his visit to the Jardin des Plantes in Paris in 1832. What he saw was a natural world which revealed its design not in static perfection but rather in constant change and flux. He called this new vision a "Theory of Animated Nature" (*EL*, 1:83); its appeal lay in the fact that it mirrored the potential for the growth of the soul.[19] Nature's deepest moral lesson was therefore one of the organic development from seed to fruit, a lesson which Emerson worked out in detail in *Nature*, concluding with the assertion of the "Orphic poet" that "Nature is not fixed but fluid," and the corollary admonition to "Build, therefore, your own world" through the expansion of an inner vision (*CW*, 1:44–45).

Emerson's work immediately following *Nature*, which includes the lectures of the late 1830s and *Essays,* can be seen essentially as a following out of this admonition to moral growth. The "Human Culture" lectures (1837–38) are an important expression of this period, proposing a model of the soul whose essence is that of continual growth, what he termed a "constitutional aspiration" which is "the centrifugal force in moral nature, the principle of expansion resisting the tendency to consolidation and rest" (*EL*, 2:218). But out of this stress on the progress of the soul, based on the ever-renewing sense of an "Ideal" or "Better" still to be pursued (*EL*, 2:217), a curious skepticism began to develop, which counterpoints the strenuously affirmative stance of *Essays*. It is revealed most clearly in "Circles," superficially one of the most positive essays in the book, but which raises the specter of what Emerson labeled "pyrrhonism" (*CW*, 2:188), an attitude which renders all intellectual pursuit valueless, because its goal of truth can never be achieved with finality.[20] As one's perception increases, so does one's sense of the incomprehensible magnitude of what is to be known. Emerson therefore depicts a "flying Perfect, around which the hands of man can never meet" (*CW*, 2:179).

Emerson's response to this dilemma is complex, and very important to our sense of his career. One can readily see the grave implications that a recognition of the elusive nature of truth might have for a man who, after much struggle, has forged a vocation of truth-seeking for himself, in the form of his conception of the "scholar."[21] This is his major concern in *The Method of Nature,* one which is appropriate to the occasion of the literary exercises at the Waterville College commencement, but which also taps a source of very personal concern for Emerson himself. In "Circles," he had argued that this dilemma of the receding Ideal was in fact a source of strength, if viewed from the perspective of continued progress, and his stress in that essay's peroration on "old age" as the only enemy (*W*, 2:188–89) is in fact a plea for a perpetual youthful exertion to extend further into an ever-renewing "Better." But while this argument is the dominant strain in "Circles," it has a counterpoint in less prominent emphasis on the experience of mystical timelessness, which sidesteps the whole problem of spiritual progress and the teleology of the soul's expansion. In the "power of divine moments," Emerson writes, "I no longer reckon lost time." The reason is that "these moments confer a sort of omnipresence and omnipotence which asks nothing of duration, but sees that the energy of the mind is commensurate with the work to be done, without time" (*CW*, 2:188). It is this faith in momentary inspiration that allows Emerson to respond to the danger of pyrrhonism with the stance of "an endless seeker with no Past at my back" (*CW*, 2:188). But there is a certain bravado in the stance which suggests the depths of the problem to which it responds.

The entries in Emerson's Journal E for the first months of 1841 suggest that he was undergoing a mild depression, centered around his literary work. "But lately it is a sort of general winter with me" (*JMN*, 7:419), he wrote on 4 February.[22] The immediate source of this depression was doubtless an emotional letdown upon the completion of *Essays*, furthered by the aggravation of last-time revisions and proof-corrections. As he wrote his brother, William, on 5 February, "It is disgraceful when you thought you had done your chapters, to be obliged to waste days & weeks in parsing & spelling & punctuating, & repairing rotten metaphors, & bringing tropes safe into port, & inspecting suspicious places in your logic, & inventing transitions like solder to weld irreconcileable metals; and other such tinkering arts" (*L*, 2:378). Behind these minor aggravations, however, lay more serious problems of maintaining the delicate balance between inspiration and communication in art, and Emerson's very real fear that necessary inspiration would not be forthcoming. Such inspiration was not only the cornerstone of his art; he felt it to be a requirement of his soul as well, and sought it with desperate urgency throughout his period of crisis. The journal entries which record Emerson's wrestling with these problems provide an immediate context for *The Method of Nature*.

Hints of Emerson's depression can be gathered from several entries which compare "books," "words," or "language" with "nature," and try to resolve the tension between the artificiality of art and the reality of nature's potential inspiration. "Books lead us from extasy" (*JMN*, 7:412), reads one isolated comment, which is followed by another entry, containing notable revisions which are preserved in the Harvard edition of the *Journals:* "We have exhausted ⟨words⟩ ↑nature↓ but we read one of the masters & instantly are made aware of new classes of laws ⟨so⟩ and this world ⟨be⟩ casts itself into types so smiling grand & so equal to the sense that we get a new idea of wealth & grow impatient of our words

& think we will never use them again, like boys who have had a ⟨toy⟩ ↑rocking↓ horse or a boat & then are mounted on a live horse or a sailboat ⟨they never wish for⟩ ↑despise↓ their toys" (*JMN*, 7:412). Emerson's initial substitution of "nature" for "words" is striking, suggesting his sense of the close relation between difficulties of vision and of expression. The "exhaustion" of nature (originally, of words) is relieved by the master who reveals "this world" in a new way, but which renders us "impatient of our words." Vision thus comes at the price of expression, a problem which was not new to Emerson, but which was asserting itself with some force in this period.[23] Only a few days later, he takes up the theme again by remarking, "Happy is the man who hears: unhappy the man who speaks." As he expands on this idea, its relevance to his immediate situation becomes apparent: "The reason is obvious: it is better to be poor & helpless in doing because our heart is preoccupied & astonished with the immensit⟨y⟩ies of God than to be at leisure to adorn & finish our trivial works because communication with the Deity is no longer open to us" (*JMN*, 7:414). For Emerson, the crisis of a lack of artistic inspiration was fundamentally a religious crisis. Committed to the necessity of writing, for both vocational and psychological reasons, he was in search of a way to preserve the purity of inspiration from the need for expression.

Emerson's frustration with words was qualified, however, by his sense of their potential value. The earlier entry in which he suggests the power of a "master" to reopen nature to him suggests the value of words; an entry dated 21 January, the day after his above complaint about the lack of "communication with the Deity," further confirms this sense. The passage arises from a comparison of words with nature: the "sweeping sleet amid the pine woods," he writes, make his sentences look "contemptible." But those sentences are contrasted with "words prompted by an irresistible charity . . . whose path from the heart to the lips I cannot follow." The distinction between these forms of words can be found in their differing sources. One arises from "this lust of imparting, as from ⟨ourselves⟩ *us,* ⟨this⟩ the desire to be loved, the wish to be recognized as individuals," and is therefore "finite" and "of a lower strain." But the other form of words arises from "God rushing into multiform." The artist too often finds himself captive of finite words, and, as Emerson feels himself to be now, unable to formulate those words which are prompted by "an irresistible charity." This explains Emerson's earlier depiction of the artist's (and his own) plight: "It is pitiful to be an artist when by forbearing to be artists we might be vessels filled with the divine overflowings" (*JMN*, 7:415; *CW*, 1:130).[24] Despite this problematic opposition of vision and expression, Emerson still left room for a possible healing of that split, as a journal entry some two months later confirms: "Should not man be sacred to man? What are these thoughts we utter but the reason of our incarnation? To utter these thoughts we took flesh, missionaries of the everlasting Word which will be spoken" (*JMN*, 7:434; see also *CW*, 1:129). The biblical allusion to the "Word" here indicates that such expression is neither finite nor artistic, in the limited sense in which Emerson had described them earlier, but linked to a kind of expression he would term infinite and essentially religious.

What is notable about this solution is that it posits an ongoing process of expression, predicated on a continual opening of new vision or revelation to the mind. The nature of this expression renders previous and existing expression unsatisfactory, and even potentially damaging, if one finds himself in some way tied to those words, as Emerson did in early 1841. The nature of this possible solution can be clarified further if we examine an analogous problem which Emerson also confronted in his journal during these months, the details of which were eventually incorporated directly into *The Method of Nature*.

In the same entry of mid-January that he had spoken of the exhaustion of nature and words, Emerson noted that "Nature is the mercury of our progress" (*JMN*, 7:412), a theme central to his thinking, as we have seen, since the early 1830s. In another entry, apparently of the same period, he also wrote that "the love of nature . . . is . . . but the presentiment of intelligence of it: nature preparing to become a language to us" (*JMN*, 7:412). These thoughts are presumably connected to the chapter of nature that he did not finish, and they suggest the extent to which Emerson still looked to what he saw as the moral perfection of nature for both guidance and stimulation. "Nature," is of course an amorphous term; for Emerson, its immediate meaning was usually the woods around Concord, though he did regularly read in natural history, and engage in more rigorous forms of nature study, from time to time. In April, he was reading the astronomer John Pringle Nichol, whose description of the planetary system and the cosmos both unsettled and fascinated him.[25] He had, by this time, received the invitation to speak at Waterville, and his thoughts seem to be coalescing around the themes he would treat there.[26]

He is moved by Nichol's portrayal of the vastness of the universe, what Emerson terms "this wasteful hospitality with which boon nature turns off new firmaments without end" to create "suns and planets hospitable to souls." The emotional connotations of the terms "waste" and "hospitable" suggest that Emerson reacts to the fact of the sheer immensity of the universe with both fear for the insignificance of humanity, and exultation at mankind's part in this system. Yet he is also reminded, in his alternate reading of Saint Simon and his descriptions of the French court, of the poor purposes to which men put such cosmic hospitality. He thus concludes that "one can hardly help asking if this planet is a fair specimen of the so generous astronomy, and, if so, whether the experiment have not failed" (*JMN*, 7:427; see also *CW*, 1:125–26). His personal dejection seems here to be enlarged to a sense of general human failure, and the relative perfection of nature only exaggerates that failure by contrast. This attitude reveals elements of Emerson's increasing social concern, which had recently been given expression in "Man the Reformer" (25 January 1841; see *CW*, 1:145–60); his period of personal crisis coincided with a period rife with social alienation and a corresponding desire for reform.[27]

In reflecting on this problem, Emerson offers two solutions, each of which marks out a direction which his thought would take as he completed the oration. He first explores the answer which "astronomy itself may furnish" but notes that this answer is "certainly not the highest." It is a version of his theory of metamorphosis, positing that "all grows, all is nascent, infant" (*JMN*, 7:427). This sense of universal change comforts us with the sense that we can find nothing "final"; nature manifests itself as "tendency" everywhere: "the planet, the system, the firmament, the nebula, the total appearance is growing like a field of maize, or a human embryo, or the grub of a moth; is becoming somewhat else; is in the most rapid & active state of metamorphosis" (*JMN*, 7:428). This realization leads Emerson to the coda for this entire phase of his thinking: "Metamorphosis is nature." Such a vision is comforting because it leads to the belief that even the mean actions of humanity can be ultimately transformed by this same law: "every valet that grimaces in the French Court is related bodily to that heaven which Lagrange has been searching & works every moment by the same laws we thought so grand up there" (*JMN*, 7:428). The fact of natural change holds out to Emerson the hope for moral progress.

But since this answer was "not the highest," Emerson continues this long meditation by discussing "the true answer." This answer is not based on a projection of human or natural metamorphosis, and therefore on future improvement, but on an immediate assertion of human power. "I am of the Maker not of the Made. The vastness of the Universe[,] the portentous year of Mizar & Alcor, are not vastness[,] no longevity to me.

In the eternity of truth[,] in the almightiness of love I slight these monsters. Through all the running sea of forms I am truth, I am love and immutable, I transcend form as I do time & space" (*JMN*, 7:428–29).[28] The response here thunders as if from on high, and the "I" who speaks gains increasing affinity with God as the passage continues. The final claim of transcendence of time and space confirms the mystical identification of self and God and it also emphasizes the radical difference of this second answer, which is completely independent of any process of change in time. It represents the very kind of divine inspiration Emerson always hoped for, but only rarely achieved.

If we return to the earlier question of Emerson's problem of artistic expression, the connection to this problem of faith in nature and man seems clear. Both stem from an absence of vision or illuminations and both are easily dismissed when vision is available. But both can also be seen as instances of a complex dialectic of growth or achievement, in which metamorphosis is proposed as a solution to the recurring conviction of the bankruptcy of the present. Emerson's dissatisfaction with his art, with the present state of the language he had molded, is a personal instance of his more general dissatisfaction with the moral state of mankind. Both levels of this problem, personal and universal, continued to weigh on him as he composed *The Method of Nature*.

It is on the note of general, not personal, dissatisfaction that Emerson begins the address, appealing to his audience in the broadest terms to support the social role of the scholar. The nature of that role entails a recognition of social failure, for scholars "stand for the spiritual interest of the world, and it is a common calamity if they neglect their post in a country where the material interest is so predominant as it is in America" (*CW*, 1:120). In "Man the Reformer," delivered the previous January, he had lamented the fact that the prevalent abuses in commerce require "more vigor and resources than can be expected of every young man, to right himself in them" (*CW*, 1:147). Now the social evil seems more widespread: "The rapid wealth which hundreds in the community acquire in trade, or by the incessant expansions of our population and arts, enchants the eyes of all the rest; the luck of one is the hope of thousands, and the proximity of the bribe acts like the neighborhood of a gold mine to impoverish the farm, the school, the church, the house, and the very body and feature of man" (*CW*, 1:120). Emerson is relying on the biblical paradox that wealth impoverishes, and applying it here not to an individual but a nation. But as his argument unfolds, this social indictment is narrowed to emphasize that the real cost of such impoverishment is individual. "There is no man; there hath never been. The Intellect still asks that a man may be born" (*CW*, 1:122). Emerson means, of course, that there is no complete individual, no one who lives up to the potential which the intellect discerns. The call for such a man is reminiscent of the image of the universal man in "The American Scholar"; moreover, it parallels the argument in "Human Culture" that a sense of the Ideal or the Better continually demands reform and progress. What Emerson labels here as "the old want" for human greatness (*CW*, 1:122) thus grounds the oration in a context of thought which he had forged in the late 1830s.

Our sense of the depth of his personal involvement in these issues is heightened by what appears to be a clear autobiographical reference to his first book *Nature*: "The new book says "I will give you the key to nature," and we expect to go like a thunderbolt to the centre. But the thunder is a surface phenomenon, makes a skin-deep cut, and so does the sage" (*CW*, 1:123). The autobiographical nature of this hint reinforces the sense that *The Method of Nature* deals centrally with unfinished business which grew out of *Nature* and remained at issue in *Essays*. By introducing these questions in the first paragraphs, he establishes the direction of his inquiry: "In the absence of man we turn to nature, which stands next." Nature's use, ultimately, is to reveal mind, a process which Emerson expresses in a vivid natural metaphor: "[Nature] existed already in the mind in solution: now, it has been precipitated, and the bright sediment is the world" (*CW*, 1:123). This near identity of nature and mind suggests the function of nature as "a convenient standard, and the meter of our rise and fall." We must "study the mind in nature . . . as we explore the face of the sun in a pool, when our eyes cannot brook his direct splendors" (*CW*, 1:123). Thus he calls upon his audience to explore *"the method of nature"* with the goal of finding "how far it is transferable to the literary life" (*CW*, 1:123). This purpose is a direct answer to the problems with which he had struggled in his journal earlier in the year.

Emerson's description of nature initially suggests the influence of Plotinus, whom he had been reading the previous winter and spring.[29] "Every natural fact is an emanation, and that from which it emanates is an emanation also, and from every emanation is a new emanation" (*CW*, 1:124). But while this vision of emanation immediately raises the question of an ultimate source of nature, Emerson is more intent to analyze the endless process of emanation itself. The source must simply be recognized as "a metaphysical and eternal spring" which is "a mysterious principle of life." Its mystery finally baffles the delving intellect: "Known it will not be, but gladly beloved and enjoyed" (*CW*, 1:124–25).

It is not, therefore, the cause, but the "ever novel effect" (*CW*, 1:124) of nature's emanation which initially interests the mind; but lest we assume that this "effect" can be interpreted as a unified purpose or end of nature, Emerson cautions that nature has "innumerable ends without the least emphasis or preference to any." He elaborates this notion with one of his favorite images, the circle, and introduces the key term "ecstacy" to describe nature's purposes: "Nature can only be conceived as existing to a universal and not to a particular end, to a universe of ends, and not to one,—a mark of *ecstacy*, to be represented by a circular movement, as intention might be signified by a straight line of definite length" (*CW*, 1:125). Emerson's position here marks a significant departure from his earlier interpretations of nature, although it is a departure that has been in preparation for some time. By denying that nature can be thought of as a line, or as a movement from one fixed point to another, he denies a teleological interpretation of nature which places man at the center of its design. The circle, which for Emerson had divine and mystical connotations,[30] suggests a view of nature in which humanity is part of a larger whole, whose ultimate ends may conflict with an individual will.

To make this suggestion explicit, Emerson returns to the empirical fact of human failure, which, as we have seen, had concerned him in journal entries of the previous spring. We may be sure that "no single end" can be attributed to nature, for "if man himself be considered as the end, and it be assumed that no final cause of the world is to make holy or wise or beautiful men, we see that it has not succeeded" (*CW*, 1:125).[31] Emerson's position brings to mind the question which framed his earlier book *Nature*: "to what end is nature?" (*CW*, 1:7). He seemed to have answered that question, temporarily at least, in the chapter "Discipline," when he wrote that "This ethical character so penetrates the bone and marrow of nature, as to seem the end for which it was made" (*CW*, 1:26). Clearly, however, something now seems to be missing from this formula, as Emerson tests it against the ethical character of men as he finds them. To be at all tenable, the assumption of nature's moral quality must be adjusted to account in some way for the state of humanity.

Part of Emerson's answer to this problem is taken directly from his journal entry of the previous April: "To questions of this sort, nature replies, 'I grow, I grow'" (*CW*, 1:126; see *JMN*, 7:427). The continual progress of nature is suggested as the antidote to disillusionment, as it has been in much of the writing of the late 1830s. But if we remember that in his journal Emerson had called this answer "not the highest," we can understand why, in the next paragraph, he offers a second answer, which is far different. In this case, nature directly refuses the kind of moral stewardship over man which Emerson had set forth in *Nature*. "'I have ventured so great a stake as my success, in no single creature'" (*CW*, 1:126), is nature's direct reply, a rebuke of human pretentions, but also a subtle rebuke of Emerson's own early position that human moral action is the culmination of nature's purpose.

It is in this context that Emerson's use of the term "ecstasy" comes into play as a process which replaces the previous conception of human moral progress as nature's end. Nature "does not exist to any one or to any number of particular ends, but to numberless and endless benefit," a benefit that Emerson describes as a "redundancy or excess of life which in conscious beings we call *ecstasy*" (*CW*, 1:126–27). The term has certain mystical connotations, which suggest the kind of direct experience of divinity so important to Emerson in both a personal and artistic sense. The etymology of the word, whose root meaning is to stand outside oneself, augments its mystical associations, and Emerson uses the word in a sense very close to that one by insisting that nature respects "no private will" (*CW*, 1:127). To comprehend the natural process, therefore, one must see it from a perspective that transcends private hopes and interests.

This is not to say, however, that Emerson, a moralist from first to last, abandoned his long-standing commitment to moral philosophy, though it is apparent that he is reformulating its basis. He does make one important distinction that helps to clarify his stance, when he introduces a concept of different levels or "platforms" from which man and nature can be viewed: "Self-accusation, remorse, and the didactic morals of self-denial of strife with sin, are in the view we are constrained by our constitution to take of the fact seen from the platform of action; but seen from the platform of intellection, there is nothing for us but praise and wonder" (*CW*, 1:127). The concept and terminology of different platforms of perception had been a key part of the essay "Circles," where Emerson had combined it with the metaphor of the circle to suggest the growth of the soul as an upward spiral of ever-broadening knowledge and power (*CW*, 2:184–86). But it is less the hope of progress than the comfort of an alternative to the moral struggle that makes this concept appealing to him here.

Emerson's distinction between the platforms of intellect and action as a point for evaluating human worth also contains within it an important temporal distinction that should be noted. This distinction arises from the elevation of the importance of the present moment which the term "ecstasy" implies. In using the term, Emerson is calling for a complete openness to the immediate possibility of a divine presence, and a corresponding awareness of nature, which can be a means to that presence. In so doing he subtly reverses the tendency of his entire address to minimize the place of mankind in the scheme of nature. By changing his stress to momentary fulfillment, he is able to argue that "The fact of facts is the termination of the world in a man"; and even to launch into an ode to "rich and various man" which concludes with the flat assertion that "An individual man is a fruit which it cost the foregoing ages to form and ripen" (*CW*, 1:127–28). This certainly seems at first to be a point-blank contradiction of the whole of the earlier essay, and it tempts us to remember Emerson's strictures on "foolish consistency" (*CW*, 2:33). But the saving fact here is that Emerson is basing his praise of human nature not on the sum total of human moral actions, which he had convincingly dismissed earlier in the essay, but on the possibility of isolated moments of acute perception, whose intensity outweighs their rarity as a measure of human worth. Thus a human "is not strong to do, but to live" and is important "not as an agent, but as a fact" (*CW*, 1:128). The future-oriented quality of action renders it secondary to the kind of heightened perception that is here put forward as the culmination of the present.

Such a state of perception has implications for the creation of art, of course, and as Emerson comes to consider them, he returns to one of the most fundamental, and personal, questions behind the address, the relation of vision and artistic creation. The crux of this issue lies in the fact that he considers the experience of "ecstasy" to be a passive one, based purely on a person's receptivity to divine promptings. "His health and greatness consist in his being the channel through which heaven flows to earth, in short, in the fulness in which an esctatical state takes place in him" (*CW*, 1:130). Such inspiration is, for Emerson, necessary for art, but paradoxically, art can be its enemy, as he immediately adds, drawing on his journal entry of the previous winter: "it is pitiful to be an artist when by forbearing to be artists we must be vessels filled with divine overflowings, enriched by the circulations of omniscience and omnipresence" (*CW*, 1:130; see *JMN*, 7:415, quoted earlier). But now in *The Method of Nature,* he is able to make the basis of this opposition more explicit, by linking artistic expression not only to a narrow egotism, as he had done in his journal, but to a pursuit of limited ends and "action." So the same problem arises with art that arises with the struggle for moral improvement: each endeavor can detract from the consciousness of the present that the ecstatical state demands. Each is, to an extent, performed for an end to be realized in the future.

But just as Emerson has subtly turned his address before, he does so again with a change of perspective and emphasis when he comes to describe the poet in greater detail. While he has argued that art can be the barrier to ecstasy, he also begins to emphasize that it can also serve as the evidence of that ecstasy when seen from the perspective of history. And more importantly, because it stands as such evidence, it can also serve as an example or inspiration for ecstasy. According to Emerson, history has always suggested that the poet spoke from a divine authority, given rather than self–created: "we rather envied his [the poet's] circumstance than his talent. We too could have gladly prophesied standing in that place. We so quote our Scriptures; and the Greeks so quoted Homer, Theognis, Pindar, and the rest. If the theory has receded out of modern criticism, it is because we have not had poets. Whenever they appear, they will redeem their own credit" (CW, 1:130–31). By the poet's "circumstance," Emerson means the fact of his inspiration or ecstasy as recorded in the poem itself. That fact may in itself be enough to serve as an inducement for further inspiration, but Emerson adds to it an implied call for a rebirth of vision in poetry, through his reference to the dearth of modern poetry. This call is the message he would amplify later in "The Poet."

At the center of this connection between art and ecstasy is nature, rightly used. The right use of nature must be stressed, however, because Emerson warns of the potential danger of nature seen with a prospective end in mind. If we come to nature with the motive of use, or "commodity" as he termed it in *Nature*, then "nature is debased" (CW, 1:131). If the motive is pleasure, the danger is even greater, for the power of material objects threatens to possess the mind. Emerson's warning is clear: "Therefore man must be on his guard against this cup of enchantments, and must look at nature with a supernatural eye" (CW, 1:131). To see nature supernaturally, he goes on to explain, is to see "the cause of nature" (CW, 1:131), which is in fact a restatement of the need to pursue the ecstatic state. Emerson establishes the connection between the perception of nature and the pursuit of ecstasy in these terms: "as the power or genius of nature is ecstatic, so must its science or the description of it be. The poet must be a rhapsodist: his inspiration a sort of bright casualty: his will in it only the surrender of will to the Universal Power, which will not be seen face to face, but must be received and sympathetically known"

(*CW*, 1:132). This description of the poet reaffirms the call for a poetry that excludes egotism, and thus makes possible the simultaneous existence of inspiration and expression.

This connection between nature and ecstasy which Emerson establishes as the address comes to a close reminds us that he had earlier defined nature as a "rushing stream" (*CW*, 1:124) which is always "in rapid metamorphosis" (*CW*, 1:126). To an extent, the momentary, even atemporal, quality of ecstasy places it in opposition to nature's growth or progress through time, and seems to stand as an alternative to the similar process of growth or culture of the soul. While this polarity is central to the address, and to Emerson's intellectual concerns at the time, he is able to suggest something of a synthesis between the two by changing the grounds on which he associates dynamism with nature. Nature changes, he suggests, not only because its dynamic essence but because the perceiving mind changes, deepening its grasp of the cause of nature as it grows. Nature will always support, therefore, "the best meaning of the wisest man," which is to say that it will always confirm the vision revealed in the ecstatic state. Emerson emphasizes this idea by returning to the image of the river, adding to Heraclitus's well-known analogy an interpretation of his own: "'You cannot bathe twice in the same river,' said Heraclitus, for it is renewed every moment; and I add, a man never sees the same object twice: with his own enlargement the object acquires new aspects" (*CW*, 1:132). This position affirms momentary insight at the same time that it affirms the progress of the soul over time, by suggesting that progress is, in fact, the accumulation of insight, each moment of which grows from a previous such moment. Nature is, typically for Emerson, a kind of standard of measurement of growth, whose function is to prove the depth of insight by opening to ever deeper symbolic interpretations. These interpretations are ultimately possible because the symbolic aspect of nature is only a manifestation of its source in the spiritual realm.

Thus out of the complicated entanglements of moral growth and mystical perception, of time and the timeless, of nature as end and as means, Emerson is able to fashion a fragile synthesis, whose final result seems consistent with his earlier work, but whose grounds are inexorably shifting. We still find the appeal to human moral capacity, the vision of nature as a moral guide, and the insistence on a loss of self in a larger will, all of which were present in *Nature*. Now, however, Emerson depends even more heavily on an ecstatic experience but realizes that its necessity is no guarantee of its availability. Even when he celebrates this experience, his language betrays what was becoming the central problem of his spiritual and intellectual life: "There is virtue, there is genius, there is success, or there is not. There is the incoming or the receding of God: that is all we can affirm; and we can show neither how nor why" (*CW*, 1:127). In these very questions of "how" and "why" lie the seeds of Emerson's later work, particularly as we find it in "Experience" (1844) and "Fate" (1860).

But the synthesis allows Emerson to conclude the debate with a series of five applications, containing comments on several diverse aspects of human life. To end an address with "applications" or "uses" is a device which Emerson inherited in the New England sermon form, and which he adapted and used extensively in both his secular lectures and his published essays. In this address, the reader is well into the series of applications before he recognizes it as such, for the first of these uses was in fact his treatment of nature, discussed above, in which he cautioned against the use of nature as an end, or for the purposes of commodity or sensual pleasure.[32] This first application serves as a paradigm for the last four—virtue, love, genius and history (*CW*, 1:132–35). In each case, Emerson stresses the necessity of avoiding conscious purpose or intention, which is always linked with ego and the limitations of self, in favor of what he labels "tendency," a kind of progress of soul not restricted to a specific goal. This distinction is made most concrete in the second application, which deals with "virtue" or "conscience," and which leads Emerson to argue the weakness of movements for specific reform. The tendency to disillusionment which he detects in many reformers is the product of their limiting the reform effort to specific causes such as temperance or antislavery, which "are poor bitter things when prosecuted for themselves as an end" (*CW*, 1:132). The reason, as Emerson sees it, is that "the soul can be appeased not by a deed but by a tendency" (*CW*, 1:133). The specific nature of a goal tends to tie the soul to what is finally limited, while the soul can grow and prosper only as it ties its aspirations to the infinite—which is also to say, the unspecified. Emerson's position here takes the form of a clear warning to reformers of limited goals: "I say to you plainly there is no end to which your practical faculty can aim, so sacred or so large, that, if pursued for itself, will not at last become carrion and an offence to the nostril" (*CW*, 1:133). Emerson's imagery here suggests the link between death and a too-limited object for the soul. The soul's life, conversely, is preserved by a tendency toward an infinite good.

The same analysis also applies to love, which should not be "self-possessed or prudent" but, rather, "all abandonment." It can be nurtured only by "a living and expanding soul," which allows the lovers always to aspire further. Similarly, genius, which is only "finer love," cannot be tied to "models and methods and ends in society," as talent is, but instead "draws its means and the style of its architecture from within" (*CW*, 1:134). The association of genius with nature, continual expansion, and ultimately, with divinity is confirmed by Emerson's use of river image again: "yet when Genius arrives, its speech is like a river, it has no straining to describe, more than there is straining in nature to exist" (*CW*, 1:134). But if genius shows the workings of a tendency toward unknown ends on an individual level, history shows the same on a universal level, for history is "the work of ideas, a record of the incomputable energy which his infinite aspirations infuse into man" (*CW*, 1:134). The word infinite must be stressed here, because the finite ends of which man may be conscious do not explain fully the course of history. Emerson's example is New England Puritanism, which cannot be completely explained by political, theological, or economic motives, but whose influence flows out of its culture of self-denial and service to others, rather than any of the more tangible ends which its adherents might have had, such as church reform or political liberty. Again, the important ends are those which are unknown to the agent, arising from a source that transcends individual will or purpose.

This series of applications leads into Emerson's peroration, which opens on the theme of Puritan piety. He asks how that piety, which is now slipping away, can be regained. Much as he shared in the Unitarian aversion to Calvinist dogma, Emerson felt acutely that the modern age had witnessed a lapse from the actual practice of Puritan piety. He rises to almost revivalist terms on this topic, insisting that his hearers can be "children of the light" and "worship the mighty and transcendant Soul" (*CW*, 1:135). But even as he argues that "[o]ur health and reason" depend upon such a worshipful stance, he raises two very pertinent questions which finally seem as revealing as the positive tone of his preacherly exhortation. Perhaps because of the earlier references to Puritanism, and certainly because the problem was beginning to weigh on him, Emerson raises the question of determinism, by asking whether the state of ecstasy that his address calls for can be the product of the human will: "If you say, "the acceptance of the vision is also the act of God:"—I shall not seek to penetrate the mystery, I admit the force of what you say" (*CW*, 1:136). It should be noted that Emerson introduces this doubt in the voice of a skeptical listener, which tends to put some distance between his own stance and the opinion which is suggested by the question. But the device also dramatizes the question, and, perhaps quite purposefully, calls attention to Emerson's confessed inability to respond to it. It is quickly followed by another question, the thrust of which is also to raise doubts about human capacity for the attainment of vision: "If you ask, "How can any rules be given for the attainment of gifts so sublime?"—I shall only remark that the solicitations of this spirit, as long as there is life, are never forborne" (*CW*, 1:136). While he stops short of offering a formula for ecstasy in this response, Emerson does return to a stress on the universal availability of the spirit's promptings, which he goes on to amplify with the assertion that these promptings "court us from every object in nature, from every fact in life, from every thought in the mind" (*CW*, 1:136). Again, this reply is not responsive to the doubts of his imagined skeptical hearer, and Emerson seems in part to be contrasting his own stance of faith with a skepticism born of arid logic. His closing call for attitudes of joy, awe, and wonder confirm this, but the power of Emerson's rhetoric of faith cannot completely obscure the very questions he himself has raised.

Nor could he obscure these questions in his later work, where they come to play an increasingly important role. What we have seen in this close analysis of the background and text of *The Method of Nature* is the process by which Emerson came to place heavier and heavier stress on momentary illumination, as opposed to purposeful self-culture, as the means of affirming the value of the soul. While he is able to preserve the vision of metamorphic nature as a moral guide, he is able to do this primarily on the grounds of successively higher moments of vision, or ecstasy. But as the nagging questions about human ability at the end of this address suggest, the stress on momentary illumination was itself plagued by the question of the source of that illumination. Could any kind of human activity or preparation result in such an experience? This was the question that Emerson's stress on ecstasy inevitably raised. It might be noted that just such a question, framed in more explicitly theological terms, had plagued Emerson's Puritan ancestors in New England.[33] Given the nature of the doubts we have seen him raise, it is not surprising to find that his answer to the question was increasingly negative as his career progressed. Insight comes when *it* will, he stressed increasingly, and not according to the will of the individual. Therefore, such optimism as we find in the later work was necessarily formulated within the limits of such uncertainty. "Experience" depicts a bleakness and alienation which is remedied only by the "surprise" of newness (*W*, 3:67–70); the term "surprise" itself implies that insight is neither willed nor even expected. "Fate" frankly calls for us to "build altars to the Beautiful Necessity" (*W*, 6:48), and in that essay, Emerson leaves no doubt that whatever the beauty of fate, there is no avoiding its necessity. Such a conception does not rule out the "ecstasy" that he calls for in *The Method of Nature*, but it does make it clear that such ecstasy, when it exists, will be given and not made.[34]

The Poet and Experience
Essays: Second Series

RICHARD LEE FRANCIS

Essays: Second Series constitutes unfinished business in the development of the Emersonian canon. Emerson was unable to complete his second essay on "Nature" for inclusion in *Essays*, where he originally looked upon it as a balance for "Art"—or so he said in a letter to William Emerson (*L*, 2:387). In December 1841, he gave the lecture series on "The Times" from which he was to mine much of the material for the new volume of essays, though he also reached as far back in his journals as 1838 for inspiration. Ralph Rusk remarked in his biography of Emerson that his essays were arranged "in hardly more than haphazard order" (*Life*, p. 300). Even if that is not true, the fact of the matter is that Emerson apparently contracted for the second volume shortly after finishing the first, on the quite reasonable assumption that he had a sufficient amount of material left over from which to fashion the second series. But in reality his thinking was moving in other directions, as the lecture series "The Times" makes clear. The titles of those lectures, while reflecting something of the concerns of the earlier series ("Manners," "Character," "Relation of Man to Nature"), were also moving toward his later conception of representative men ("The Conservative," "The Poet," "The Transcendentalist"). In a letter to his brother William on 4 December 1841, he commented: "I think to take Universal Whiggery for my text next week & perhaps call the next lecture 'The Conservative' and perhaps the following 'The Transcendentalist.' One I have written called 'The Poet' and another in prospect called 'The Fashionist' & so we will go on with our portrait gallery" (*L*, 2:469). The latter was never written, but the whole idea, somewhat superficial here, was to blossom later as *Representative Men* (1850).

Why Emerson did not pursue this scheme for his volume; why he selected "The Poet" for the initial essay of *Essays: Second Series*, rather than his second essay on "Nature," is not clear. But undoubtedly it involved a sense of incompletion in his evolving sense of the self. The

focus of the final essays of the first series points toward a singular vocation for man—that of "Poet." As his Waterville College oration, "The
Method of Nature," makes clear, it was toward defining this role, rather
than reexamining nature, that Emerson pursued the unfinished business
of the essayist. For it is the poet who represents the final realization of
Emerson's vocational quest, the fullest embodiment of all the previous
roles of naturalist, moralist, and scholar. To that extent, "The Poet"
(together with its complement, "Experience") rounded out Emerson's
structure, leaving the rest of *Essays: Second Series* as essentially an
exercise in elaboration. "The Poet" is therefore analogous to *Nature* in
its complex statement and stylistic intricacy. Having found the "Method
of Nature" elusive, Emerson discovered instead the method of the self.
With a clear grasp of that, he was able to deal both with the sphere of daily
life and that of the transcendent. Like Karl Barth many years later,
Emerson learned that man "himself is the creature on the boundary
between heaven and earth."[1]

Like most of Emerson's truly significant essays, "The Poet" was
slow in developing. He wrote Margaret Fuller on 10 April 1842, "My
reading lately is to the subject of Poetry" (*L*, 3:47), and on 3 June, "My
chapter on the Poet grows very slowly; it is like the Concord River,—one
may sometimes suspect it moves backward" (*L*, 3:59). The labor left its
mark. When, in February 1844, he responded to an inquiry from his
brother William, Emerson replied: "You asked about my book. 'The
Poet' is only one of its chapters though much the longest" (*L*, 3:242). The
long germination of *Essays: Second Series* is difficult to account for,
though there is evidence in the correspondence that a great amount of
Emerson's time from 1842 to 1844 was taken up in editing the *Dial*, in
lecturing extensively along the northeastern seaboard, and in tending to
family problems and finances. But the years 1840–41 had been almost as
busy, and yet he managed the composition of the first series. Certainly the
first part of 1842 was blighted by the death of his son Waldo in January,
and undoubtedly the more complex answer lies in the elusive realm of
psychological motivation. Did the death of Waldo provide the kind of
expressive impetus which the earlier death of his brother Charles provoked, or was it a constricting impediment?

Less than two weeks after the tragedy of Waldo's death, he was in
Providence, delivering his lectures on "The Times," and there is no
conclusive evidence in either the letters or the journals of extended grief.
Indeed, there is evidence of the Stoic discipline that Emerson both practiced and preached. Within ten days of Waldo's death, Emerson wrote

Caroline Sturgis, "the days of our mourning ought, no doubt, to be accomplished ere this, & innocent & beautiful should not be sourly & gloomily lamented, but with music & fragrant thought & sportive recollections" (*L*, 3:9). The principal problem was, as Emerson recorded it, "I chiefly grieve that I cannot grieve." A few passages in the J journal display the restrained understatement of classic tragedy (*JMN*, 8:163–66), and much of this material reappears in poetic form in the first version of "Threnody" (1846). While experiencing the natural personal grief of a father, Emerson reacted to Waldo's death in ways that suggest it did not affect his sense of himself as deeply as Charles's death did, probably because he had by then already crystallized much of what he had been personally searching for during the years from 1832 to 1844, and with that self-assurance could absorb tragedy more readily.

"The Poet" not only represented the finding of an acceptable sense of vocation, but it also brought into sharp focus the transcendental vision that Emerson had uniquely developed and which he did not like to leave identified as a collective philosophy, as a letter to his wife on 1 March 1842 makes clear: "I am in all my theory, ethics & politics a poet and of no more use in . . . New York than a rainbow or a firefly. Meantime they fasten me in their thought to 'Transcendentalism,' whereof you know I am wholly guiltless, and which is spoken of as a known & fixed element like salt or meal" (*L*, 3:18). In delivering his lectures on "The Times" in New York that March, Emerson shifted the lecture on "The Poet" to primary position immediately after the Introductory Lecture.

Defining the function of the poet was not easy for Emerson, and he made several attempts before arriving at the initial "chapter" in *Essays: Second Series*. On 3 November 1841 he delivered a lecture at the Concord Lyceum on "Nature and the Powers of the Poet" and in December he included a lecture on "The Poet" in his series "The Times," delivered in Boston and elsewhere. There are two significant dimensions to this latter effort: first, very little of it was used in the essay of the same title (five passages, mostly phrases or sentences; only one of paragraph length); secondly, the title is misleading, conforming mainly to the general title format of the series (i.e., "The Conservative," "The Transcendentalist"). The purpose of the lecture is not to define the generic identity of the poet (as in the later essay) but, rather, to consider "the part he plays in these times" (*EL*, 3:348). The early part of the lecture is devoted to exploring the nature of poetry and expression and man's need for them: "besides the need which every man has of doing something, and making his mark somewhere, which is the first result of the eternal impulse at the heart of things, it needs that not only his will, or the direction of his practical faculties should have this justice done it, but that his science or his perception of things in the intellect, should have an expression also" (*EL*, 3:351–52). Emerson then turned to his familiar argument that nature is a "sympathetic cipher or alphabet" in which all things are symbols. From this section come all but one of the passages used in the later essay. Instead of focusing on the implications of the poet as "the universal knower and singer" (*EL*, 3:357), Emerson turned to a discussion of language and meters. Significantly these sections of the lecture were mined for his late essay, "Poetry and Imagination" (1872).

Clearly, then, the work which opens *Essays: Second Series* is the result of Emerson's rethinking of the whole question of who the poet is and what his vocation was to be. A close examination of the essay is not only appropriate but essential.

The essays in *Essays: Second Series* are consistently prefaced by mottoes. "The Poet" is prefaced by two. The process of searching is the subject of the first: the "moody child" pursued a game that involved cosmic vision, rending "the dark with private ray," over the horizon's edge. The child is possessed of "Apollo's privilege"—the Olympian bard's capacity to penetrate everywhere in search of "musical order." The second motto, from Emerson's "Ode to Beauty," is on the same subject but more cryptic: "Olympian bards who sung / Divine ideas below, / Which always find us young, / And always keep us so." The images of the second motto clarify the structure of the space through which the "moody child" peered. It is vertical. And those who enjoy "Apollo's privilege" convey "divine ideas" of a higher realm to a lower one. These have the capacity, in a figurative sense at least, to obliterate time. The poet, from his pivotal position, imparts the ideas inspired by his vision of the transcendent realm to those below in the realm of experience. In its evolution, the essay elaborated this concept of the poet's function.

Like most of Emerson's major essays, "The Poet" has several rather well defined divisions which shed light on the evolution of its statement. After an initial introductory paragraph, Emerson devoted nine paragraphs to a discussion of the nature of the poet and of poetry. The next section begins with the assertion, "The Universe is the externization of the soul" (*W*, 3:14), and for eight paragraphs explores the way in which symbolic language verifies that relation (in this way it resembles the chapter on language in *Nature*). The next thirteen paragraphs explore the means by which the imagination makes possible the passage of the soul to higher forms and the possibility for every man possessed of imagination to be a poet. The final three paragraphs constitute a typical peroration of considerable rhetorical intensity in which Emerson sought to bring together his central ideas and images. Thus in quantitative terms the essay is as much about the imagination as about the poet; but in terms of intensive imagery and epigrammatic style, the section on the nature of poetry and the poet is more commanding in its assertions.

As the first paragraph makes clear, the essay had as its intent the exploration of a "doctrine of forms"—to consider the interrelation of spirit to fact (*W*, 3:3). Most intellectual men in their calling—even most theologians and poets—do not accept this "essential dependence." But for Emerson, "the highest minds of the world have never ceased to explore the double meaning . . . or much more manifold meaning of every sensuous fact" (*W*, 3:4). Only the master artist recognizes the Platonic reality, that "the fountains whence all this river of Time and its creatures floweth are intrinsically ideal and beautiful." Accordingly the essay directs its purpose to "consideration of the nature and functions of the poet, or the man of beauty; to the means and materials he uses, and to the general aspect of the art in the present time." The poet, we learn, is a representative man: "He stands among partial men for the complete man" (*W*, 3:5). Most men are partial because they do not express themselves, are unable to call upon the forces in themselves and their world, or else they are men on whom the "impressions of nature" register too feebly (*W*, 3:6). By contrast: "The poet is the person in whom these powers are in balance, the man without impediment, who sees and handles that which others dream of, traverses the whole scale of experience, and is representative of man, in virtue of being the largest power to receive and to impart."

What follows this succinct definition is Emerson's most elaborate piece of mythmaking and the most explicit expression (within the mythic metaphor) of his imagistic structure. In it he wedded his abstract personification of man to traditional cultural and religious personae and suggested their archetypal dimensions: "For the universe has three children, born at one time, which reappear under different names in every system of thought, whether they be called cause, operation and effect; or, more poetically, Jove, Pluto, Neptune; or, theologically, the Father, the Spirit and the Son; but which we will call here the Knower, the Doer and the Sayer. These stand respectively for the love of truth, for the love of good, and for the love of beauty. These three are equal. Each is that which he is, essentially, so that he cannot be surmounted or analyzed, and each of these three has the power of the others latent in him and his own, patent" (*W*, 3:6–7).

The focal point of the essay is the poet who "stands on the centre" and is the sayer. Since "Beauty is the creator of the universe" and the poet is "emperor in his own right," creativity as expressed by the sayer is the central reality at the core of the Emersonian structure (*W*, 3:7). Beauty, then, becomes the visual manifestation of the eternal reality of which truth and goodness are also components. It presents special problems, however, because beauty principally expresses itself in the finite realm. If it is to have the validity and stature that Emerson claimed for it, then it would have to possess certain indestructible qualities. If art were possessed of archetypal scope, then it could solve this paradox. Thus the somewhat gnostic Emersonian assertion, "For poetry was all written before time was," combined with: "Words and deeds are quite different modes of the divine energy. Words are also actions, and actions are a kind of words" (*W*, 3:8). The poet is one who "announces that which no man foretold." Thus the man of beauty perceives and describes what has always existed but which has previously been inadequately expressed for his time and place. His commerce is with both realms: the eternal or infinite and the transitory or finite. The true poet is accordingly someone who is concerned with more than the superficial dimensions of art. Thus Emerson spoke deprecatingly of lyrists, men of mere talent, who were not true poets because they placed form ahead of argument in importance.

Emerson's doctrine of form, viewed in this context, becomes quite clear despite its paradoxical epigrammatic quality: "It is not metres, but a metre-making argument that makes a poem" (*W*, 3:9). Emerson made a distinction between time and genesis, a distinction in his structure between horizontal and vertical. Thought and form, he declared, are equal in time; but thought is prior to form in genesis. Thus the poet has a new thought, which is new to him but part of all that was written before time was. Since words are actions, the poet has had a new experience as he articulates his new thought. In telling us "how it was with him," the poet creates a new reality within the finite realm of human experience, although the origin of the experience has been in the eternality of thought from which he has received his insight or inspiration (*W*, 3:10). Experience, then, is creative expression in the finite realm which the poet describes in his capacity as sayer (this definition is central to the essay that follows with its more revealing original title, "Lords of Life").

In this fashion Emerson reconciles his insistence on the eternality of art and its fluxional manifestation which is human creativity. To confirm this function he described the effect of the poet's art on one who has recognized its validity. The images confirm the dual spheres of his structure and the centrality of the poet's position between them: "I shall mount above these clouds and opaque airs in which I live,—opaque, though they seem transparent,—and from the heaven of truth I shall see and comprehend my relations. That will reconcile me to life and renovate nature, to see trifles animated by a tendency, and to know what I am doing" (*W*, 3:12). Even his discussion of the poet-manqué that follows affirms the idea, for the vivid images are of an Icarian figure who does not "know the way into the heavens" and who cannot inhabit the "all-piercing, all-feeding and ocular air of heaven."

The natural world for the true poet is a "picture-language" (*W*, 3:13). Emerson quoted Jamblichus, " 'Things more excellent than every image are expressed through images' " and he added: "Things admit of being used as symbols because nature is a symbol, in the whole, and in every part." Thus a series of analogous relationships are established, pointing to one end: "The beautiful rests on the foundations of the necessary." And, quoting a passage from Edmund Spenser, Emerson expressed the concept in terms of his concern with form: " 'For, of the soul, the body form doth take, / For soul is form, and doth the body make' " (*W*, 3:14). Finite form (body) is merely in its truest sense, then, a manifestation of spiritual form (soul). In recognizing this truth, we stand in a "holy place," before the "secret of the world." In terms of the structure, we are at that point "where Being passes into Appearance and Unity into Variety." Macrocosm is microcosm: "The Universe is the externization of the soul." Science is related to religion and metaphysics. All things connect. This interconnectedness is why the Poet's function as namer or language-maker is so important. For, as Emerson echoed his earlier discussion of language in *Nature*, everyone uses symbols and emblems in the everyday discourse of life. But it is the poet's function to make sure that our use of symbolic language does not become dislocated or detached through reductive overuse. The poet "re-attaches things to nature and the Whole,—re-attaching even artificial things and violation of nature, to nature by a deeper insight" (*W*, 3:18). What many men, who have not realized their potential as poets, see as prosaic and pedestrian, the poet sees falling "within the great Order not less than the beehive or the spider's geometrical web" (*W*, 3:19). The poet is possessed of a "centred mind."

Moreover, like the mythical Lyncaeus who could see through the world, the poet, "turns the world to glass, and shows us all things in their right series and procession" (*W*, 3:20). This procession is evolutionary: "within the form of every creature is a force impelling it to ascend into a higher form; and following with his eyes the life, uses the forms which express that life, and so his speech flows with the flowing of nature" (*W*, 3:20–21). Emerson again anticipated the 1849 revision of the motto for *Nature* with its emphasis on the evolutionary spires of form. Man, as the ultimate creature, uses "forms according to the life, and not according to the form" (*W*, 3:21). This seeming paradox is resolved if we consider the singular *form* as the precedent archetypal form and the plural *forms* as the finite particularized things of the physical world. The poet, however, "does not stop at these facts, but employs them as signs." The poet is in touch with the realm of *form*; most men only with the realm of *forms* or facts. It is a question, as Sherman Paul has conclusively demonstrated of the "angle of vision." The poet's central position gives him, like the transparent eye-ball, the capacity to see into both spheres, to comprehend the facts of the natural world and to relate them to the realm of eternal form. Thus in his capacity as language-maker or namer, the poet sometimes names things after their "appearance" and sometimes after their "essence."

Accordingly the function of language is highly metaphoric, though in many cases words once vividly descriptive of essence have degenerated to "secondary use" and no longer evoke their poetic origin (*W*, 3:22). The poet's function is to revivify the primary meaning of words, to restore language as a "fossil poetry" to vitality. This undertaking is not really "art, but a second nature, grown out of the first, as a leaf out of a tree." This process of metamorphosis is described in the allegoric imagery of a "certain poet," whose conception of the poet's process is akin to the discharge of spores by fungus (a not entirely happy image).[2] The literal level soon establishes the seed as the soul of the poet and the spores as its songs, which finally metamorphosized as melodies, "leap and pierce into the deeps of infinite time" (*W*, 3:24). The allegory reminded Emerson of a more appropriate tale to express the passage of the soul to higher forms—that of the sculptor who was so emotionally moved by the dawn one morning that he strove for days to express in stone his tranquillity. He succeeded in producing a statue of Phosphorus, the mythic representation of the morning star, which left those who saw it in awe.

The poet operates in much the same way. "The expression is organic." The process involves the imagination: "This insight, which expresses itself by what is called Imagination, is a very high sort of seeing, which does not come by study, but by the intellect being where and what it sees; by sharing the path or circuit of things through forms, and so making them translucid to others. . . . The condition of true naming, on the poet's part, is his resigning himself to the divine *aura* which breathes through forms, and accompanying that" (*W*, 3:26). The intellect functions in this condition—not as detached reason—but as agent of "its celestial life" (*W*, 3:27). In such a way new vistas are opened and "the mind flows into and through things hardest and highest, and the metamorphosis is possible." By this process the poet finds another world within the outer world; he functions tropologically. By stimulating others through tropological insight, poets for Emerson are "liberating gods" (*W*, 3:30). They unlock and emancipate the minds and lives of those to whom their imaginations reach. Their language is "vehicular and transitive"; their symbols are "fluxional" (*W*, 3:34). It is this fluidity that distinguishes the poet from the mystic (who "nails a symbol to one sense"). But such a poet is hard to find: "Time and nature yield us many gifts, but not yet the timely man, the new religion, the reconciler, whom all things await. Dante's praise is that he dared to write his autobiography in colossal cipher, or into universality. We have yet had no genius in America" (*W*, 3:37).

Emerson had only to wait another decade for someone who would agree with him that "America is a poem in our eyes; its ample geography dazzles the imagination" (*W*, 3:38). His initial enthusiasm for Walt Whitman's *Leaves of Grass* is foreshadowed here. But beyond that we encounter the clearest definition of what it is Emerson has been constructing. The "timely man" is he who is both appropriate to the moment and capable of functioning within the existing society, as the mystic is not. He is distinguished as a reconciler—one capable of bringing together the disparate spheres of experience and spirit, of justifying the unseen to the seen—in that sense creating "the new religion" in the manner of Dante. That is, the poet elevates his own vision of existence into a universal statement of man's quest for the ideal, the paradisical. Art is the means by which he achieves that end. In the act of creating, the poet strives to express himself "symmetrically and abundantly" (*W*, 3:39). In so doing the "ideal shall be real" (*W*, 3:42). The final apostrophe of the essay, addressed to the poet, achieves epical sweep:

Thou shalt have the whole land for thy park and manor, the sea for thy bath and navigation, without tax and without envy; the woods and the rivers thou shalt own, and thou shalt possess that wherein others are only tenants and boarders. Thou true land-lord! sea-lord! air-lord! Wherever snow falls or water flows or birds fly, whereever day and night meet in twilight, wherever the blue heaven is

hung by clouds or sown with stars, wherever are forms with transparent bound-
aries, wherever are outlets into celestial space, wherever is danger, and awe, and
love,—there is Beauty, plenteous as rain, shed for thee, and though thou shouldst
walk the world over, thou shalt not be able to find a condition inopportune or
ignoble. [*W*, 3:42]

To move from this high rhetoric to the motto of "Experience" is to
encounter one of the most difficult verse prefaces that Emerson wrote.
But if we have read the later poetry, particularly "Days" (1851), we
recognize resemblances between the lords of life and the daughters of
time. The more persuasive clue, however, is found in the essay itself,
when—near the end—Emerson invokes the classical Greek myth of the
Eumenides or Furies. Within the assumptions of that myth, they were
indeed lords of life, and in terms of their characteristics, they seem very
close to the description which Emerson made in the poem, being "om-
nipresent without name." It is only the latter part of the motto that truly
perplexes. Who the "little man, least of all," is to whom nature whispers,
"The founder thou! these are thy race," remains enigmatic. In light of the
evolving essay, he is probably the "fragment" of man discussed near the
end of the essay. For where the focus of "The Poet" had been on the
integrating dimension of man's existence, that of "Experience" is on its
fragmentations.

The opening question asserts this condition. "Where do we find
ourselves?" it asks (*W*, 3:45). The image that follows is not unfamiliar
from the evolving images of the preceding essays—"We wake and find
ourselves on a stair; there are stairs below us, which we seem to have
ascended; there are stairs above us, many a one, which go upward and out
of sight." This Dantesque metaphor crystallizes the vertical ascending
motif that Emerson increasingly evoked in the 1840s, as his concept of the
"spires of form" took its dominant place in his imagistic structure. What
is important here is that the figure on the stairs is not spheral man. What he
lacks is perception. The overdose of lethe, which induces a lethargy that
cannot be shaken off, blurs perception even if it does not threaten life:
"Dream delivers us to dream, and there is no end to illusion. Life is a train
of moods like a string of beads, and as we pass through them they prove to
be many-colored lenses which paint the world their own hue, and each
shows only what lies in its focus" (*W*, 3:50). Partly it is a question of
"temperament" for it "shuts us in a prison of glass which we cannot see"
(*W*, 3:52). It is "the veto or limitation-power in the constitution" of man
(*W*, 3:54). It constitutes a platform on which "one lives in a sty of
sensualism, and would soon come to suicide." But, shifting the metaphor

slightly, there is a door that is never closed "through which the creator passes" to revive the creative power of man. "The intellect, seeker of absolute truth, or the heart, lover of absolute good, intervenes for our succor, and at one whisper of these high powers we awake from ineffectual struggles with this nightmare. We hurl it into its own hell, and cannot again contract ourselves to so base a state" (*W*, 3:54–55).

Such a course of action is available to the man of intellect or heart, but much in other men's lives does not respond to these depths or heights. Such lives are merely "sturdy" rather than intellectual or critical. "We live," Emerson observed, "amid surfaces, and the true art of life is to skate well on them" (*W*, 3:59). Part of that art is the avoidance of excess. On the one hand is "the thin and cold realm of pure geometry and lifeless science," on the other mere sensation (*W*, 3:62). "Between these extremes is the equator of life, of thought, of spirit, of poetry,—a narrow belt." This "mid-world" Emerson described as "best," because it is the place where the two elements of human life—power and form—can be kept in proportion (*W*, 3:64). Even so, an individual finds it difficult to calculate life—no matter what vision or sense of its structure he might have. That is why the ancient cultures tended to elevate chance to a divinity. But Emerson affirmed the opposite. Beyond the fragments, the distractions, he saw the "coetaneous growth of the parts" united and harmonized (*W*, 3:70). "Underneath the inharmonious and trivial particulars, is a musical perfection; the Ideal journeying always with us, the heaven without rent or seam" (*W*, 3:71).

An awareness of this fact comes with growing consciousness in man. It is a "sliding scale, which identifies him now with the First Cause, and now with the flesh of his body" (*W*, 3:72). This consciousness is analogous to the vast-flowing vigor of Eastern thought; in Western philosophy we call it "Being" (*W*, 3:73). Unfortunately in Western experience, "Being" is too frequently seen as a wall rather than "interminable oceans" of vast-flowing vigor. This negative response is reinforced by the weight of the principal theological doctrine of Western man—the Fall: "Ever afterwards we suspect our instruments. We have learned that we do not see directly, but mediately, and that we have no means of correcting these colored and distorting lenses which we are, or of computing the amount of their errors" (*W*, 3:75). But the clear-eyed vision of spheral man defines its own world, its own horizon. Human existence, human relations develop through the "great and crescive self, rooted in absolute nature" (*W*, 3:77). What follows is an incredibly compacted series of images which are at the very heart of the Emersonian structure.

There will be the same gulf between every me and thee as between the original and the picture. The universe is the bride of the soul. All private sympathy is partial. Two human beings are like globes, which can touch only in a point, and whilst they remain in contact all other points of each of the spheres are inert; their turn must also come, and the longer a particular union lasts the more energy of appetency the parts not in union acquire.

Life will be imaged, but cannot be divided nor doubled. Any invasion of its unity would be chaos. The soul is not twinborn but the only begotten, and though revealing itself as a child in time, child in appearance, is of a fatal and universal power, admitting no co-life. [*W*, 3:77–78]

In this fashion Emerson endeavored to reaffirm his monistic conception of the soul and at the same time to allow for the increased complexity of the dialectical, dualistic structure that had slowly evolved in his writings and for which "The Poet" and "Experience" offer confirmation. The tension between the two is particularly acute in regard to the concept of evil which he had first defined in the Divinity School Address and later reexamined in his discussion of dualism in "Compensation." The distinction this time is between *thought* and *conscience*. In terms of the former, sin is a "diminution"; in terms of the latter it is "pravity or *bad*" (*W*, 3:79). "The intellect names it shade, absence of light, and no essence. The conscience must feel it as essence, essential evil. This it is not; it has an objective existence, but no subjective." The theological implications of these assertions were less important to Emerson than the methodological ones. If the self does not accept the essential existence of evil, then it does not need to account for it in its subjective scheme. "Thus inevitably does the universe wear our color, and every object fall successively into the subject itself" (*W*, 3:79). As the subject expands, everything falls into place in its scheme of things.

For Emerson the central doctrine might be expressed: "As I am, so I see." For the first time since *Nature*, Emerson seemed to acknowledge the other dimension of the existential equation. So much emphasis in the early essays was on the act of seeing as a means of comprehending the self; here the emphasis is reversed, and what the self is affects what it sees. The spheral man is necessary for spheral vision: "The partial action of each strong mind in one direction is a telescope for the objects on which it is pointed. But every other part of knowledge is to be pushed to the same extravagance, ere the soul attains her due sphericity" (*W*, 3:80).

Nonetheless, there are marked spheres of possibilities for most mortal men, as Emerson's illustration from *The Oresteia* reminds us. Describing the Flaxman drawings of the Aeschylean Eumenides, Emerson observed that Apollo's face revealed "the irreconcilableness of the two spheres" (*W*, 3:82). The description of Apollo is revealing for its analogies to the Emersonian poet: "He is born into other politics, into the eternal and beautiful. The man at his feet asks for his interest in turmoils of the earth, into which his nature cannot enter. And the Eumenides there lying express pictorially this disparity. The god is surcharged with his divine destiny." But it is, of course, Orestes in the myth who represents man placed between inexorable fate and divine mercy. The Emersonian man has for most of the essays been the poet, the spheral man, more godlike than human. What the conclusion to "Experience" does is to adjust this new reality to the elaborate evolving structure of the self and to make the necessary choice which will affect the rest of Emerson's endeavors as poet-sayer, as scholar-essayist: "Illusion, Temperament, Succession, Surface, Surprise, Reality, Subjectiveness,—these are threads on the loom of time, these are the lords of life. I dare not assume to give their order, but I name them as I find them in my way. I know better than to claim any completeness for my picture. I am a fragment, and this is a fragment of me. I can very confidently announce one or another law, which throws itself into relief and form, but I am too young yet by some ages to compile a code" (*W*, 3:82–83).

Thus the early Emersonian expectation to project a meaningful structure for human life by ordering the self and extending that order to all other selves cannot simplistically be achieved. This insight did not discourage Emerson to the point of despair or cynicism. It merely meant a reformulation of the role of the new teacher who has now discovered—in discovering himself—that he is not the new messiah leading the chosen to a new society. It meant an acceptance of limitations: "I know that the world I converse with in the city and in the farms, is not the world I *think*. I observe that difference, and shall observe it. One day I shall know the value and law of this discrepance" (*W*, 3:84). It meant a return to solitude and its values: "in the solitude to which every man is always returning, he has a sanity and revelations which in his passage into new worlds he will carry with him" (*W*, 3:85). The new course of action is outlined in the final lines of the essay, in which the realm of the spirit, through which genius operates, would be transformed and realized in the realm of experience by what Emerson called "practical power." The remainder of *Essays: Second Series* (as well as the subsequent volumes on *Representative Men* and *The Conduct of Life*) take shape from this premise.

In arriving, then, at some realization of the self, in refining the structure that he vowed to build in *Nature*, Emerson could move from the somewhat egocentric, romantic projection of the self as the paradigm of society to a more restrained, more qualified consideration of what the constituents of the good society might be once the self no longer served as an archetypal model. The diminution in both style and statement that is so noticeable in the second series of essays following "Experience," the failure to write another version of *Nature* equal to the first, the particular emphasis of the final two major volumes of 1850 and 1860 (*Representative Men* and *The Conduct of Life*) all testify to a major shift in this endeavor. Not, I think, because Emerson was forced to choose between "Freedom" and "Fate," but because the initial aims and aspirations of his work were realized in the creation of the persona of the poet and the acceptance of the vocation of essayist.

In his journal for 1842, Emerson observed, "My life is optical not practical. I go out to walk for exercise & not to answer a necessity. I speculate on virtue, not burn with love" (*JMN*, 8:170). This optical existence placed him apart from other men. With this realization Emerson was able to turn his attention to the other sphere of experience where most men labored with Orestes' dilemma (though perhaps not in "quiet desperation" as Thoreau was to have it). The youthful ardor which exhorted every man to build his own world had cooled. But the sober, patient persistence to help other men bring order to the chaos of their everyday lives was logically to extend his role as mediator between an ideal world that his own genius had envisioned and the experiential world which he now accepted as one in which only practical power could achieve the ordered society that the harmony of the soul required. It is perhaps a fitting irony that Emerson's great public acceptance after the publication of *Essays: Second Series* should correspond to that period of his life which he devoted to explicating the world of ordinary men, while his literary reputation rests securely on the earlier period when he was engaged in the great poetic visions that were the artistic transformations of his own searching into the elaborate labyrinth that provided this intricate key to the self.

Emerson's Eumenides

Textual Evidence and the Interpretation of "Experience"

DAVID W. HILL

The history of Emerson's essay "Experience" as we can see it in *The Journals and Miscellaneous Notebooks* leads up to a point—probably in the late spring or the summer of 1844—when Emerson decided to leave incomplete and unstated many of the conclusions, ideas, or assertions he had prepared for the essay in his journals. He decided to dramatize the implications of a theme he stated succinctly in a list of materials for the essay, probably from 1844: "Our moods never trans⟨ferab⟩lateable by words. Selfreliance. E 129" (*JMN*, 12:547). The passage to which Emerson refers, from 3 May 1840, says that the best record of an experience does not prepare us for the return of that experience or its appearance in someone else—"The *life* of it is untranslateable by words" (*JMN*, 7:345–46). The structure of the essay—the seven "lords of life," or moods, labeled as if they were ideas—moves through incomplete states of thought and feeling to the image Emerson built from Flaxman's drawing of the *Eumenides* of Aeschylus. The suffering Orestes speaks to Apollo but cannot bring the god into the orbit of his human experience. We speak. Others may hear, may even listen, but they can understand and respond only within the limits of their own lives. Even within one's own life, moods cannot communicate with each other. At the end of the essay Emerson did not resolve his theme of the incoherence of experiences with each other; instead he invented a new mood, a new self that was able to accept and include the disparate voices which had spoken the earlier sections of the essay.

Four kinds of evidence from the *JMN* inform my reading of the essay. The first two are relatively straightforward. One is, of course, Emerson's revisions of wording and emphasis between journal entries and essay passages (because "Experience" did not grow out of a lecture or identifiable group of lectures, the relation between journal entry and essay passage is more immediate than in many cases). The second range of evidence involves Emerson's manipulations of contexts. The meaning of an entry—often the meaning of its words and sentences as well as its general drift—within its context in Emerson's journal was often changed (and sometimes reversed) when he placed the journal entry into a different context in his essay.

The third kind of evidence is more complicated to identify. There are two kinds of outlines for many lectures and essays: traditional, organized outlines, and the looser conflations of journal materials I will call "scans." For "Experience," as is often the case in Emerson's writing, the more conventional outlines come earlier in his composing process than do the scans in which Emerson recorded surveys of his journals for passages he wanted to use and experimental patterns of combination. (These scans appear mainly in the lecture notebooks that are concentrated in volumes six and twelve of the *JMN*.) While the outlines, recorded in the journal Emerson used in the spring and summer of 1843, propose one kind of essay, the scans reflect more closely the very different essay Emerson sent to the printer in the late summer of 1844. The scans of the journals for "Experience" are in places so close to the published essay in their selection and ordering of material that they appear in this case (as in so many others) to be the models Emerson used for composition. In his scans Emerson usually entered a word or phrase and the journal title and page; he probably used them as guides to find the passage he wished to copy or revise and to locate the subsequent journal source he wanted to fuse or juxtapose with the first. The lecture notebook scans for "Experience" record how Emerson constructed a secondary self, a modified, sometimes transformed self out of the pieces of writing he found in his journals. Among other things, the scans for "Experience" in Lecture Notebooks Phi and Index Minor show us how intimately that essay is related to "The Poet" and "Nominalist and Realist," both of which Emerson was composing at the same time as "Experience."

The fourth range of evidence involves what might be called the comparative geology of the journals and the essay which grew out of them. What veins of thought and feeling did Emerson tap when he composed the essay? How does the mixture of tones in the essay compare to that in the journals? How much granite is there? How much limestone, and in what proportions? My appropriation of metaphors from W. H. Auden's "In Praise of Limestone" reflects my sense that to study the relation between journal sources and essay products—to study Emerson's method of composition—we need to pay attention not only to the evidence but to the categories we apply to it. The Emerson who composed "Experience" is a complex imaginative force who requires for interpretation not only the categories critics have explored since the publication of Stephen Whicher's *Freedom and Fate* but also categories that attempt to describe the writing self which recognized, manipulated, and composed the sides of itself Whicher identified with freedom and fate. Whicher's "free" Emerson rushes in his early writing toward exaltation of the private self, insistently pressing on toward meaning and its comprehension in ways that both exhilarate readers and, as David Porter has suggested in relation to the verse, may rob some of his published writing of the sense of experienced life that twentieth-century readers expect to find in resonant imaginative writing.[1] The other side is an Emerson who passively expresses his helplessness, either in a quietistic acceptance of all-encompassing spirit or in acknowledgement of his limited ability to perceive and control his life very fully. But another pair of Emersons emerges when one thinks about what he did as an artist as he rearranged, modified, and commented upon the bits of himself he found in the journals. The man of granite sometimes chose to convert apparent surrenders into obdurate assertions of sovereign selfhood, while the man of limestone could find assertions which seemed to him to be defeats. Particularly in journal passages in which Emerson comments on other passages, these two opposed selves meet, combine, and depart from each other in complex, unpredictable ways, leaving the reader of the journals in a literary version of what sedimentary geologists call radical discontinuities. It is in the lectures and essays that the artful writer invented patterns which could convert these discontinuous identities into a series of usable selves.

The "lords of life" in "Experience" are neither logical steps toward a developed assertion nor a series of merely casually assembled pieces of fine writing. Instead they are steps toward a usable self, contributions toward the artfully constructed voice which closes the essay. At the beginning as at the end, there is a paradox: While spiritual illumination is available to people in exhilarating and reassuring moments of vision, that fact is not of very much help to us most of the time. The seven lords of life are tonal variations on this theme; they are seven ways of looking at a self. None of these variations drowns out the others; rather, they accumulate until the end of the "Subjectiveness" section, when their interplay is interrupted by the voice they have produced, an artful construction which avoids both despair and abstract consolation, both fate and freedom. Each "lord" is a construction which Emerson dissolved into his next construction. Each is "a momentary stay against confusion"—to use a Frostian metaphor which seems to me to explain one source for Frost's admiration for Emerson—a stay which, because it is momentary, would if pursued become a constriction, a corset-stay, a cause itself of confusion. And each one of these stays is itself a dissolution or deconstruction which Emerson had carried out on the phrases, sentences, and discussions he found in his journals.

The history of Emerson's ideas about the essay overturns some apparently commonsense assumptions about it. First, the concentration of journal sources and cross-references to other sources in Journal R, which he used from March to July 1843, indicates that Emerson was working intensively on the essay (tentatively titled "Life") at that time.[2] But the importance and distribution in the essay of entries from Journal U, used from August 1843 to the spring of 1844, and from Journal V, begun two months before the essay went into proofs in August 1844 (see *L*, 3:259), indicate that "Experience" did not take its final form until shortly before it went to the printer. An 1843 outline in Journal R calls the divisions of the essay "the capital lessons of life" instead of "lords," and arranges them in a logical progression which moves from the fact of "Subjectiveness" to a final recognition of the power of "Temperament" (*JMN*, 8:411–12), an order which is almost the reverse of that in the published form. Emerson headed the outline with an assertion that he undercut in his structural design for the published essay: "It is greatest to believe & hope well of the world, because he who does so, quits the world of experience, & makes the world he lives in." Another outline, in Lecture Notebook Phi, reflects one general drift in the essay, but uses a quasi-logical structure to come to a pair of mutually canceling assertions:

Culture ends in headache R 101, 109

———

Experience therefore indispensable.
But all is musty again without Idea [*JMN*, 12:321–22][3]

Only in a scan in Lecture Notebook Index Minor, which contains materials from as late as the summer of 1844, did Emerson abandon quasi-logical structures which renounced the "world of experience" for a realm of ideal value. His ideas about the essay and its subject became more problematical the further he was in time from the death of his son Waldo in January 1842—the event to which many commentators attribute the uncertainty and darkness of tone in the essay.

Second, the time at which various journal sources were written also calls into question oversimplified identifications of Emerson's initial grief at his son's death with the problematic nature of the essay. The

"Illusion" and "Temperament" sections of "Experience," darker in tone
than the rest, are the most highly synthetic, drawing materials from
almost all of the journals Emerson used between 1838 and 1844. The
"Surprise," "Reality," and "Subjectiveness" sections, which contain
the writing in the essay that is closest to what F. O. Matthiessen called
"the optative mood," draw heavily on journal materials written in the
year immediately after Waldo died. While the death of his son, the latest
payment of "the costly price of sons and lovers" by this much-bereaved
man, certainly triggered the release into published prose of darker strains
in Emerson's writing, the history of the essay does not amount to a simple
progression from grief in 1842 to attentuated hope in 1844. The essay taps
in a complex way veins of feeling which stretch back to the journals of the
1820s.

    If one considers only immediate sources for the essay, a rough count
shows that while the "dark" "Illusions" section contains much material
drawn from the journals used in the year after Waldo's death (Journals K,
J [pp. 70–end], N, E [pp. 330–end], Zᴀ, and Books Small [Sequence I]),
as many passages come from the journals he used in the four years before
his son's death (Journals D, E [pp. 1–330], G, H, and J [pp. 1–70]) and
those he used in 1843 and 1844 (Journals R, U, and V). Material from
the first year of Emerson's bereavement is particularly prominent in the
"Surface," "Reality," and "Subjectiveness" sections of the essay. Material from the years just before Waldo's death is most significant at the
beginning of the essay, while the great number of sources from Journal R
and the less numerous but thematically important materials from Journals
U and V are distributed fairly evenly through the essay.[4] Emerson linked
these materials to each other by means of his revisions of wording and
context, establishing the unified tones of voice in which each of the lords
of life speaks and constructing the links between the voices which create
the dramatic interplay which releases "the particular angle" in which
Emerson could see in these apparently discontinuous journal entries a
concern about himself which he had been struggling to identify and
understand since his early manhood. His writing self was, by the spring
or summer of 1844, able to turn the "bit of Labrador spar" so that it would
show "deep and beautiful colors" (*W*, 3:57).

    In the highly synthetic first paragraph of the essay, Emerson con-
structed a single tone out of disparate materials written between 1840 and
1844. The dark-tinted picture of a Lethe-drenched, insubstantial,
ghostlike man who awakes briefly to find himself on a stair with "stairs
below us, which we seem to have ascended" and "stairs above us, many a

one, which go upward and out of sight" (*W*, 3:45), is not so dark in the source, Journal K (p. 106), probably from April 1842. There, as Joel Porte has noted, the stairs "go up to heaven," in a more apparent reference to Jacob's Ladder,[5] and the cluster of entries of which the source is a part (*JMN*, 8:237–38) contains the "new America in the West" entry which Emerson used over twenty printed pages later in the "Reality" section of the essay. He improved the wording of a later sentence—in the journal source, "Sleep lurks all day about the corners of my eyes as night lurks all day about the stem of a pinetree"; in the essay, "Sleep lingers all our lifetime about our eyes, as night hovers all day in the boughs of the fir tree" (*JMN*, 7:508; *W*, 3:45)—but modified it even more by removing it from the context set by verses about the relation between dreams and waking reality. Its essay context, which creates its new tone and import, is set by the sentence which precedes it, in which the "Genius" mixed the cup of Lethe "too strongly" when we entered the world, so that "we cannot shake off the lethargy now at noonday." That sentence, which seems to invoke the spirit as well as a motif of Wordsworth's "Ode: Intimations of Immortality," echoes an 1843 journal sentence in which the affinities are, instead, to *A Midsummer Night's Dream*: "Nature lives by making fools of us all, adds a drop of nectar to every man's cup" (*JMN*, 8:397). A few sentences later Emerson again refracted rather than reflected the significance of what he found in his journals. While the essay sentence is "Ghostlike we glide through nature, and should not know our place again," in the journal we glide through "life & should not know *the* place again" (*JMN*, 8:173; emphasis mine). The change of wording from "life" to "nature" sharpens the thrust of the essay paragraph, but the change from "the place" to a question of whether or not we should know "*our* place" reinforces the affinities to the Intimations Ode by making it ambiguous whether or not a nature we can barely see really is "our" place.[6] Emerson pulled apart the units of language and thought he found in his journals in order to construct a single tone which would accord with that in the pun about our "Genius" and the image of the millers that he drew from an 1843–44 journal (*JMN*, 9:23, 30). The voice of "Illusion," which sees and expresses nature and perception as dark, baffling mysteries, was not an immediate response to the death of Emerson's son in 1842. Instead, it was an artful construction in which Emerson sometimes "darkened" journal entries from that time.

After the images of exhaustion in the first paragraph, Emerson built the even more highly synthetic second paragraph around the experiential fact which, in the organization of the essay as a whole, would be called

"Surprise." Despite our incapacity, things happen—not many, but enough to indicate that the first paragraph does not say all there is to say. Within the context of the "Illusion" section, Emerson does not name this lord; he can, speaking in this voice, only begin to identify it. The word "intercalate," here used in the reference to "Of Isis and Osiris" from Plutarch's *Morals*, encapsulates both the element that will later emerge as "Surprise" and emphasizes, through its contrast with the everyday, what Emerson will say in a different key in the "Succession" section. An 1841 journal entry uses the word, but in a context which highlights the minor key in which "Illusion" is set: "We hoe all day or curry horses or sell stocks or read books & a moment of serenity & sight intercalates the routine[,] one patch of blue sky which presently is lost again amid all these fogs. In the progress of character the Blue will vein & reticulate the whole web of particulars" (*JMN*, 8:6).

A similar relation holds between some of the images in the famous third paragraph of the essay and Emerson's earlier uses of these motifs and images. The failure of grief to be sufficiently powerful, to engage us fully enough, is the burden of the paragraph. Compare it to this statement about an earlier bereavement, this time from the loss of Emerson's first wife:

I loved Ellen, & love her with an affection that would ask nothing but its indulgence to make me blessed. Yet when she was taken from me, the air was still sweet, the sun was not taken down from my firmament, & however sore was that particular loss, I still felt that it was particular, that the Universe remained to us both. . . . Distress never, trifles never threaten my trust. Only this Lethean stream that washes through us, that gives sometimes a haze of unreality, a suggestion that, as C[harles Emerson]. said of Concord society, "we are on the way back to Annihilation" only this threatens my trust. [*JMN*, 5:19–20]

Another discussion of the same complex of themes speaks more directly to the shape of the essay paragraph:

I saw clearly that if my wife, my child, my mother, should be taken from me, I should still remain whole with the same capacity of cheap enjoyment from all things. I should not grieve enough, although I love them. But could I make them feel what I feel—the boundless resources of the soul,—remaining entire when particular threads of relation are snapped,—I should then dismiss forever the little remains of uneasiness I have in regard to them. [*JMN*, 7:132]

The Emerson who wrote these two passages differed from the writer of "Experience" not only in the degree of his confidence in spiritual wholeness but also in his lack of artistic purpose. Much of what he says about faith in these passages appears in "Experience" in the "Reality" and "Subjectiveness" sections.

Another passage in the same paragraph, the veiled allusion to Southey's *The Curse of Kehama*, is the outcome of a series of journal entries which embodies rather fully the process of dissolution and transmutation of journal materials we can glimpse in the entries about bereavement. Here is the passage from "Experience": "The Indian who was laid under a curse, that the wind should not blow on him, nor water flow to him, nor fire burn him, is a type of us all. The dearest events are summer-rain, and we the Para coats that shed every drop" (*W*, 3:49). Compare it to this passage near the end of "The Poet": "And this is the reward; that the impressions of the actual world shall fall like summer rain, copious but not troublesome to thy invulnerable essence" (*W*, 3:42). The immediate sources of these contrasting passages are within five pages in Journal R, where Kehama's curse is the poet's blessing on one page and Emerson's curse on another (*JMN*, 8:405, 407). Both uses of the allusion to Southey grow out of a complex passage in Journal E, probably from 1839:

It is the necessity of my nature to shed all influences. Who can come near to Kehama? Neither the wind, neither the warm ray of love, nor the touch of human hand. It seemed, as I mused in the street, in Boston, on the unpropitious effect of the town on my humor, that there needs a certain deliberation & tenacity in the entertainment of a thought,—a certain longanimity to make that confidence & stability which can meet the demand others make on us. I am too quickeyed and unstable. My thoughts are too short, as they say my sentences are. I step along from stone to stone over the Lethe which gurgles around my path, but the odds are that my companion encounters me just as I leave one stone & before my foot has well reached the other & down I tumble into Lethe water. [*JMN*, 7:326–27]

The self-observing Emerson untangled in 1843 the complexities of this earlier meditation about himself, letting the vein of granite crop out in the use he made of this entry in "The Poet," and simplifying and dramatizing in "Experience" the complaint that the man of limestone made in the journal. One of his several selves—the self that wrote the "Illusion" section of the essay—yearned for attachment to that world which another self would sacrifice in order to secure its "invulnerable essence."

The next section of the essay is built around materials from 1843–44 journal entries in which Emerson presents the limitations of temperament, dramatizes the tone of voice which accepts temperament as a limitation to selfhood, and finally rejects in disgust that voice and its conclusions (see *JMN*, 9:109, 55–56, 120–21). But in order to establish that voice Emerson returned to materials from earlier in the decade and quoted from the impassioned evocation of the transforming power of imagination that he used in "The Poet," which he composed at the same time as "Experience." The passage, drawn from an 1841 journal entry, celebrates an imaginative liberty which makes it "mean . . . to study, when merely an emotion communicates to the intellect this power to sap and upheave nature." In this trance of imaginative ecstasy, "dream delivers us to dream, and whilst the drunkenness lasts, we will sell our bed, our philosophy, our religion, in our opulence" (*JMN*, 8:101; *W*, 3:32–33). While in "The Poet" he was ambivalent about the radically anarchistic implications of his doctrine of absolute imaginative force, in the different context set by his different purpose in "Experience," that force is clearly insufficient to give order and meaning to experience. The fact that "dream delivers us to dream" shows us only that "there is no end to illusion" (*W*, 3:50). In the same paragraph Emerson used a sentence out of its journal context, where it began an entry about the way in which one mood notices only a few anecdotes from the past. The end of the journal entry—"All the passages will in turn be brought out"—sets a context which established a meaning for the first sentence—"We animate what we can, and we see what we animate" (*JMN*, 8:48)—quite different from that in the essay. Emerson's rewording of the next sentence changes the weight of the succeeding passage about the effect of mood on our ability to "relish nature or criticism." The journal sentence would fit into the later "Subjectiveness" section: "Nature & literature prove subjective phenomena" (*JMN*, 7:464). But the tone of the essay sentence is unmistakeably one of the early, less commanding voices: "Nature and books belong to the eyes that see them" (*W*, 3:50).[7]

Similar manipulations of wording and context establish the tones and progressions between tones in Emerson's subsequent variations of his theme—lack of coherence between everyday experiences of living and momentary experiences of visionary Being. One example of the progressions between tones occurs in the "Temperament" and "Succession" sections, where an image from an 1842 passage, "the revolving barrel of the music box," is linked to an apparently very different image from an 1843 journal. The music box image in the "Temperament" section is an image of compulsion: what "seems impulse . . . turns out to be a certain uniform tune which the revolving barrel . . . must play" (*W*, 3:52; *JMN*, 7:464). The bridging passage, for which I find no journal source, is part of the "turn" in the "Succession" section. That part of the essay begins with a redefinition and renaming of the sovereign state of illusion with which the essay began: "The secret of illusoriness is in the necessity of a succession of moods or objects" (*W*, 3:55). Emerson's return, in this section, to discussion of the partiality of men is transformed by another image of things turning and by the broadening of context that image supports: "Of course it needs the whole society to give the symmetry we seek. The party-colored wheel must revolve very fast to appear white" (*W*, 3:57). The separation, incoherence, and alienation Emerson dramatized early in the essay is a condition of personal life, not a fundamental quality of life even on the level of a society. An image from a May 1843 journal entry dramatizes the transformation of voices which has occurred between the body of the "Temperament" section and the end of "Succession":

Men representative

Like a bird which alights, nowhere, but hops perpetually from bough to bough, seems to me the Power which abides in in no man and in no woman, but for a moment seems to speak from this one & for another moment from that one. [*JMN*, 8:400]

It is the tree, the larger unity Emerson now sees, which allows the image of succession to change from the mechanical action of a compelled music-box barrel to an image which evokes one of the conventional representations of the Holy Spirit. The heading and a cross-reference link this journal entry to another in which Emerson gave a characteristic explanation of this failure of spirit to rest on one bough, an explanation he chose to withhold from "Experience": "[T]he gods will not have their heralds amiable; lest men should love the cup & not the nectar" (*JMN*, 8:403). The dramatic structure of voices in "Experience" did not permit Emerson to include many of the interpretations and explanations his journal entries contain or point to. "Succession," like the other lords of life, is a state of mind or mood, not a concept.

The movement from mood to mood is not a uniform progression from despair to confidence. The voice of "Surface" has escaped from the passive unhappiness of "Illusion" because of both the assertion of will in "Temperament" which rejected the "chuckle of the phrenologist" and the broadening of perspective in "Succession." But despite its willed good cheer, the section is named in a way that evokes the mood in which the essay began. The very long twelfth paragraph of the essay (*W*, 3:61–64) contains a series of apparently casual reversals of mood which suggest why Emerson called the section "Surface" instead of its preliminary name, "the golden mean" (*JMN*, 8:412).[8] The paragraph begins with the passage in which Emerson accepts "the potluck of the day" (from an 1842 journal; *JMN*, 8:321–22), finds his "account in sots and bores," and awakes to "find the old world, wife, babes, and mother . . . and even the dear old devil not far off" (from 1843 and 1842 journal entries; *JMN*, 8:432, 261). The rest of the paragraph is built from expansions of entries in Journal Books Small [Sequence I], entries which suggest the tug between apparently contradictory feelings in this section:

> not too deep
> Do not dive by books beguiled
> Thousand miles in western wild
> If thou wouldst learn the feathered tribes
> On thy orchard edge belong
> All the brags of plume & song
> There is a middle region of life & thought where all wisdom & all poetry & eloquence lie[.]
> All things are superficial & as we take no hold on the deep world but glide ghost like thro' it so does fox & rabbit[,] hawk & muskrat
> Ya
> Atom from atom yawns as far
> As moon from earth or star from star
> [*JMN*, 8:469–70]

While the poem and the first prose sentence are merely conventional, Emerson's expansion of the thought in a journal entry from shortly after Waldo's death expresses the dialectic of the "Surface" section, the perilous strait between "lifeless science" and mere "sensation," "the equator of life, of thought, of spirits, of poetry; a narrow belt" (*JMN*, 8:200). But in the journal there is a different threat. This entry comes immediately before the entry about the "opium instilled into all that is called pain in the world" that provides the framework for the third paragraph in the essay, perhaps the darkest part of the "Illusion" section. On one side of the narrow belt is despair. On the other is what we see in the Books Small passage—superficiality. The rest of the long paragraph in "Surface" follows out this feeling after an associative link that amounts to rhetorical "skating on surfaces." The expansion of the second prose sentence (*JMN*, 8:246) echoes the first paragraph of the essay ("glide ghost like thro [the world]") as well as providing the source for the last two sentences of the long paragraph in "Surface." The poem, repeated on the journal page after this expansion, reinforces the end of the "Surface" passage and the allusion back to the reference to the physical theory of

Ruggiero Boscovich (*W*, 3:48), and the later image in "Subjectiveness" of people as globes, able to touch only at one point (*W*, 3:77). The voice which goes on to say "The mid-world is best," the voice of "Surface," threatens to slip back into the despair of "Illusion" or to slide into mere sensation.

While the voices of "Surprise" and "Reality," largely constructed out of materials from 1842 and 1843 journals, are less dramatic and appear to lead toward a hortatory affirmation of the reality and power of spiritual experience, the voice of "Subjectiveness" interrupts the progression and reimposes the dialectic of "Surface." After the visionary moment of the "new yet unapproachable America I have found in the West" (*W*, 3:71–72; *JMN*, 8:237–38), Emerson explores in "Subjectiveness" the alienating implications of spiritual experience. The long discussion of the impossibility of marriage in the spiritual world—an impossibility that grows out of the fact that the private, subjective self is the only "receiver of Godhead"—is prefaced in the journal with a personal application that turns back toward "Illusion": "Intellect always puts an interval between the subject & the object. Affection would blend the two. For weal or woe I clear myself from the thing I contemplate: I grieve, but am not a grief: I love, but am not a love" (*JMN*, 7:466–67; from 1842). Emerson left unstated in "Illusion" the fundamental explanation of his complaint that grief was not real. In this passage in "Subjectiveness" he gave the explanation but omitted its application to his own emotional life.[9]

It is in the paragraph that ends the "Subjectiveness" section that Emerson dramatized fully the emotional opposition he suggested in the earlier parts of the essay. The man of granite and the man of limestone meet, and it is this meeting which opens the essay to the graceful conclusion in which Emerson's accumulated, balanced voice can finally name the "threads on the loom of time . . . the lords of life" (*W*, 3:83). The blueprint for the paragraph is in the working "scan" Emerson recorded in Lecture Notebook Index Minor:

Yet this good in subjectiveness, that it does not
waste its efforts, or adopt other people's facts.

———

America is an easy-fool

———

Orestes and Apollo (R88) & preoccupied attention (R 109) [*JMN*, 12:546]

In the essay version of the "preoccupied attention" passage, Emerson rejected the demands of those other people whom he had wanted to treat "as if they were real" earlier in the essay: "A preoccupied attention is the only answer to the importunate frivolity of other people; an attention, and to an aim which makes their wants frivolous. This is a divine answer and leaves no appeal and no hard thoughts" (*W*, 3:82). But in the journal source (*JMN*, 8:401), these sentences are part of a commonsensical rejection of the demands of seekers after culture, probably in the German sense of *Kultur*. The journal entry—which includes the anecdote of the road ending "in a squirrel-track" that Emerson used near the beginning of "Surface"—ends, "But this running out into universality, loses the Rhine in the sands" (*JMN*, 8:401). But in the essay a journal rejection of *Kultur* became a rejection of the world for the ideal.

In the rest of the essay paragraph Emerson both validated and under- cut his granitic reversal of the journal sense of the "preoccupied atten- tion" passage through his image of Flaxman's drawing of the *Eumenides* of Aeschylus: "Orestes supplicates Apollo, whilst the Furies sleep on the threshold. The face of the god expresses a shade of regret and compas- sion, but is calm with the conviction of the irreconcilableness of the two spheres. He is born into other politics, into the eternal and beautiful. The man at his feet asks for his interest in turmoils of the earth, into which his nature cannot enter. And the Eumenides there lying express pictorially this disparity. The god is surcharged with his divine destiny" (*W*, 3:82). Within the context of the paragraph, of the "Subjectiveness" section, of the essay up to this point, it seems as if Apollo has replaced Orestes as the true voice of the essay. But there is a reason why readers have been drawn more to the voice that speaks at the beginning of the essay than to the voice of this paragraph. Given what happens next in "Experience," the roles in this tableau change. Emerson turns out to be neither Apollo nor Orestes. The Orestes-voice—what I have called the vein of limestone —is not canceled out by this outcropping of granite. As the allusion to Kehama's curse in the "Illusion" section shows, there is as much pathos in being Apollo as there is in being Orestes.

Even though the Furies are put to sleep for an instant, Emerson did not insist on that instant. In the journal source he added the heading "Art" to this passage (*JMN*, 8:389), but in the essay he interrupted the moment of art toward which his voices had seemed to progress. Immediately after this passage he spoke in the accumulated voice of the conclusion, naming the Furies, the "lords of life." While some critics have regarded Emer- son's acknowledgment in the conclusion of the gap between experiencing and comprehending as a retreat from his earlier, "transcendental" assur- ance, I prefer to see the voice that ends the essay as one that has learned tact. Emerson the artificer had learned not to insist, as a comparison of the end of the essay with its journal source indicates. After what Hyatt Waggoner recognized as Emerson's half-amused *sursum corda*—"up again, old heart!"[10]—Emerson went on to say, "the true romance which the world exists to realize, will be the transformation of genius into practical power" (*W*, 3:86). In the journal, an omitted relative clause and a following sentence complete the assertion and establish a continuity forward to the concerns of *Representative Men*, which Emerson was beginning to shape into a lecture series in 1844:[11] "The true romance not which will be written but which the progress of life & thought will realize, will be the transformation of genius into practical power. The symbol of this is the *working king* like Ulysses, Alfred, Czar Peter" (*JMN*, 9:53).

When, in the long paragraph that constitutes the "Surprise" section of the essay, Emerson said, "I have set my heart on honesty in this chapter" (*W*, 3:69), part of his point involved his awareness that saying too much leads to saying nothing. His tact was a recognition that the imposition of a single meaning upon his experiences would not close the "discrepance" (*W*, 3:85) between the worlds of experience and of thought, a discrepancy he described forcefully in a letter of 30 January 1844 to Margaret Fuller on the second anniversary of Waldo's death:

Does the Power labour, as men do, with the impossibility of perfect explication, that always the hurt is of one kind & the compensation of another. My divine temple which all angels seemed to love to build & which was shattered in a night, I can never rebuild,—and is the facility of entertainment from thought or friendship or affairs, an amends? Rather it seems like a cup of Somnus or of Momus. Yet flames forever the holy light for all eyes, & the nature of things against all appearances & specialities whatever assures us of eternal benefit. But these affirmations are tacit & secular. if [*sic*] spoken, they have a hollow & canting sound; And thus all our being, dear friend, is evermore adjourned. Patience & Patience & Patience! [*L*, 3:239]

With its echoes of both the beginning of the essay ("a cup of Somnus") and its end ("Patience & Patience & Patience"), the letter indicates Emerson's realization that the moods of "Illusion," "Temperament," and the rest are not sequential lessons to be learned and overcome but are "lords" to be named, acknowledged,and accepted.

At the end of the essay Emerson said he wanted to avoid the shrill bitterness of reformers overeager "to realize the world of thought," who "foam at the mouth, . . . hate and deny" (*W*, 3:85). His strategy grew out of a discovery he had made about himself seventeen years before he wrote "Experience." In 1844 he applied to his writing something he had decided was a limitation in a journal entry probably from the fall of 1827: "Robinson Crusoe when in any perplexity was wont to retire to a part of his cave which he called his thinking corner. . . . I have found my ideas very refractory to the usual bye laws of Association. . . . But whilst places are alike to me I make great distinction between states of mind. My days are made up of the irregular succession of a very few different tones of feeling. . . . Among these some are favorites, and some are to me as the Eumenides" (*JMN*, 3:99–100).

"States of mind," "succession," "tones of feeling," and "Eumenides"—these hints about the voices of "Experience" suggest how the Emerson who constructed a self in 1844 converted his earlier sense of helplessness into a source for help. While he wanted us to see the structure of the essay as the casual, "irregular succession of a very few different tones of feeling," study of the history of the essay shows how his modification, selection, and arrangement of journal materials established a scenario of self-construction. At the beginning of the essay he gave play to the voice of Orestes and discovered its limitations. While the middle voice of "Surface" could say things that Orestes could not, it could not account fully for a mental and emotional universe in which Apollo existed. The voice of Apollo could silence the Furies, stay the confusion, but only for a moment. It, too, failed to say all that Emerson knew and in its turn it became a potential Fury. The voices which saw experience as "Illusion," "Temperament," or mere "Succession" were indeed "as the Eumenides." But those "favorite" tones of voice which accepted "Surprise," "Reality," and "Subjectiveness" could not, as in the hortatory conclusions of the "transcendental" essays, be the goal toward which Emerson's artistry worked in "Experience." No single voice could look at and say "experience" to Ralph Waldo Emerson. The succession of voices he found in the journals on his study table in Concord could, however, when tamed and arranged, teach him and teach us to speak up to the limits of what we can say—"Up again, old heart!"

Emerson's Shakespeare

From Scorn to Apothesosis

SANFORD E. MAROVITZ

> . . . How true a twain
> Seemeth this concordant one!
> Love hath reason, reason none,
> If what parts can so remain.
> —Shakspeare, "Phoenix and Turtle Dove"
> (from *Parnassus*)

Apart from his copious references to the first person singular, no one in Emerson's voluminous writings is more often referred to than Shakespeare. Most critical attention concerning Emerson's Shakespeare has focused on his chapter in *Representative Men*, "Shakspeare; or, The Poet," but despite the notoriety of that essay, it is neither the only nor (paradoxically, in light of the title) the most representative evidence of his ambivalent reaction to the Elizabethan. Moreover, because it is not truly representative, it is probably not the most important of his writings on Shakespeare, though it has long been the best known.

In addition to the essay in *Representative Men*, Emerson wrote two early lectures on Shakespeare and a short address that he is presumed to have delivered at a dinner of the Saturday Club in 1864. The published volumes of his journals and notebooks abound with scores of references to Shakespeare and quotations from the plays; in Rusk's edition of the letters, a column and a half in the index are necessary to list all the Shakespearean allusions; and, of course, in the essays and poems Shakespeare's name and those of the characters in his plays embellish many of the pages with their lustral significance and associations. In addition, Emerson pored over two essays on Shakespeare by Jones Very and edited the volume in which they were first published. Shortly afterward, he printed in the *Dial* a paper on Shakespeare that had been written several years before by his brother Charles. Early in the 1850s he maintained a correspondence with Delia Bacon, who was certain that not

Shakespeare but her own ancestor deserved credit for the plays, and Emerson assisted in her attempts to publish her views. At about the same time he wrote a highly laudatory quatrain on Shakespeare, and in the anthology of poetry, *Parnassus*, which he compiled in his autumn years, he included a wide array of selections from the work of his universal bard.

With all of the attention that Emerson paid to Shakespeare for at least half a century, how is it, then, that so little has been given to what he wrote about the subject of his thought, his praise, and at rare times his disapproval? The most comprehensive study, by Robert P. Falk, was published some forty years ago, and although his perceptions were acute and his general conclusions are still tenable, they are necessarily incomplete, drawn as they were before scholars had access to a definitive edition of the journals and early lectures. Furthermore, Falk did not regard his subject from a chronological perspective, and therefore it was not possible for him to perceive a sense of development in Emerson's views or to recognize erratic comments as provoked by specific circumstances rather than by mood, that is, by whether at a given moment Emerson felt more like (in Falk's contrasting terms) a Puritan or a poet.[1] Finally, there are important relevant forces and episodes in Emerson's career that Falk disregarded, such as the likely influence of Charles on his brother's formative views of Shakespeare and perhaps more unexpectedly the dramatic impact upon him of Jones Very in the late 1830s. To appreciate the value of their dynamic emanations, a realization of chronology is imperative.

Also, because in her estimable *Spires of Form* Vivian C. Hopkins indicates that Emerson's aesthetic theory changed less during his lifetime than did his social and political thought,[2] it is probably for that reason that she gives little heed either to chronology or to manifestations of ambivalence in his understanding and appreciation of Shakespeare over a period of many years. Because her study examines Emerson's aesthetic theory rather than his use of particular writers or works, only a few of its pages pertain to his remarks specifically on the Elizabethan playwright.

A clear sense of chronology is also lacking in William M. Wynkoop's more recent *Three Children of the Universe: Emerson's View of Shakespeare, Bacon, and Milton*, in which the author studies Emerson's apprehension of Shakespeare as a "moral type" and devotes little attention to the development of his attitude toward the dramatist, to the personal influences behind that attitude, or to incidental associations between the two writers. Although Wynkoop's complex thesis is too intricate and broad for detailed resumé here, essentially it presents Emerson's

vision of history as three-staged—unitive "Classical," conflictive
(dualistic) "Romantic," and reunified "Modern," which synthesizes and
transcends the conflict of the second stage. Shakespeare represents the
first stage, a stage of innocence in which, as "the Knower," he passively
receives the guidance of the "universal spirit" and thus creates "works
which would reflect by necessity the universal design,"[3] but he lacks the
moral assertiveness that would make him the true poet-priest, "the
Sayer," according to Emerson's idealistic/spiritual view. Although
Wynkoop draws heavily from the lectures and other Emersonian statements on Shakespeare in developing his argument, his moral/
philosophical/historical thesis (in which Bacon and Milton also figure
equally as representative "types") necessitates his minimizing the principal subject of the present essay, that is, the development of Emerson's
appreciation for Shakespeare and changes in his attitude that occurred
over the years.

The antipathy to the theater, which Emerson inherited as part of his
personal puritan legacy, dominated his earliest known assessments of
Shakespeare, and although its force waned considerably soon after his
graduation from Harvard, occasional journal entries as late as the 1850s
clearly signify that it lay dormant in the depths of his consciousness even
then. Before the end of the 1820s, he became excited over reading Coleridge, whose idolatrous attitude toward Shakespeare was soon infective,
abetted as it surely was by the enthusiasm of Emerson's brother Charles.
In the mid-1830s, he delivered a series of lectures of which two were
devoted to Shakespeare; some of the most striking passages of those
lectures were to find their way into that germinal work of American
Romanticism, *Nature*, which was published in the fall of 1836 and carefully read a few days later by Jones Very, who had just earned his
bachelor's degree at Harvard. When he met Very less than two years
later, Emerson was elated; their affiliation would prove to be both fortuit-
ous and calamitous, with little time passing between those two extremes.[4]
In the mid-1840s Emerson lectured on "Representative Men"; the series,
which included "Shakspeare; or, The Poet," was presented in England
later in the decade and published on New Year's Day, 1850. With the
exception of a few occasional journal entries made after that date, Emerson's remaining comments on Shakespeare approach apotheosis, a peculiar anomaly in light of those faintly damning remarks that conclude his
last formal lecture on the Elizabethan poet.

And yet, it is not so anomalous after all if one considers the rich array of favorable comments that preceded them, not only in that lecture itself but more particularly in all of the writing and speaking that Emerson had done through the 1840s. The fact is that throughout his career to that point he had found in the work of Shakespeare virtually everything he believed was essential to poetic art. He recognized Shakespeare as a natural creator with an unmatched gift of universal expression; not only did Shakespeare integrate the material and spiritual, the practical and the ideal, but he also revealed the cheerfulness and artistic sensibility that Jesus lacked; and he epitomized all of human wisdom. It was the essence of Shakespeare that Emerson praised, whereas he objected only to characteristics even at first, external features that seemed offensive but were of an altogether different level of being from the soul out of which the poetry sprang. As Emerson's thought matured, he came to recognize that the value of such externals depends upon the evaluator and the spiritual resources one brings to bear in determining their worth. "Thought makes everything fit for use," he writes in "The Poet," and he includes in this "everything" even the obscene, which he knows has a value greater when apprehended within the moral, aesthetic context of the whole than is apparent only on the surface. Ultimately, Emerson did not have to turn aside from what he had originally considered gross blemishes in the plays, but instead, he could see their intrinsic relation to the organic work of art and give them their due. They, too, belong. But that is something which the eighteen-year-old lad fresh out of Harvard had yet to learn back in 1821.

Little can be said about Emerson's knowledge and appreciation of Shakespeare prior to his college years. A few months after his father's death in the spring of 1811, an edition of Shakespeare from William Emerson's library was sold at auction (*Life*, p. 30), but Waldo, still a child of only eight years at the time, was obviously too young to have made use of it. A decade later, a "Life of Shakspeare" is included in a list of books in the journal under the date 10 June 1821, with no indication of publication data or the author's name (*JMN*, 1:57). Moreover, there is no certainty that Emerson had read the book (*JMN*, 1:55 n), though by this time, only two months prior to his commencement, he was unquestionably familiar with Shakespeare's work. Exactly how familiar, though, one cannot be sure. According to a recollection by William B. Hill, whose father and uncle were Emerson's classmates at Harvard, Emerson allegedly "knew Shakespeare almost by heart" before he had even arrived at college. Kenneth Walter Cameron suggests, however, that the reliability of Hill's information is subject to question in that it came to him from his father, who died when Hill was but a small child.[5] On the other hand, James Elliot Cabot says that Hill acquired the information from his uncle,[6] who remained Emerson's friend "through life" and who also "first saw a copy of Shakespeare's works in full"[7] while visiting Emerson, then a freshman working as messenger boy for President Kirkland. Although Rusk believes it "at least doubtful" that Emerson knew Shakespeare almost by heart at college (*Life*, p. 67), if the letter written by Hill's uncle is accurate, we can be certain that Emerson had in his room a full set of the Elizabethan's writings soon after arriving at Harvard and that—if Hill's recollection is correct—he had been reading them carefully enough and quoting from them often enough to convey the impression that he had committed much of the work to memory. There is nothing, however, that has come to light thus far to confirm Emerson's early by-rote familiarity with Shakespeare; no reference, direct or implicit, to Shakespeare or any of his works appears in his letters until early 1823. Afterward, however, they—and the journals—are spangled with specific allusions and quotations.

Nevertheless, Emerson's attention to Shakespeare as dramatist had clearly been caught by the time he began teaching at his brother William's school for young ladies almost immediately after commencement. Late in 1821 he wrote a series of four "Letters," evidently meant for publication; they deal historically with the drama, from the classical Greek theater through the "stained and rotten web of corruptions" that constitutes the English stage and to the possibilities for the genre in America (21 October 1821, *JMN*, 1:287). Fortunately, either Emerson's own good sense or that of some discriminating editor kept these "Letters" out of print during his lifetime. Betraying the limitations of his heretofore circumscribed world, he contrasts the malignancy to which the British public is allegedly accustomed against "the uncontaminated innocence" of the United States with its "comparative purity" and "youthful people" (*JMN*, 1:287). Not only the theater but Shakespeare himself is condemned for his immorality, which the teen-aged Emerson vilifies with pompousness and passion as "a hideous corruption . . . which made every page offensive" (*JMN*, 1:296). The halo that has been placed around Shakespeare blunts the soul "to the sense of moral turpitude" of the plays, for the observer takes in the immorality unconscious of its offense. "In a reformed theatre Shakspeare should find no place" (*JMN*, 1:296).

And yet, Shakespeare is not altogether condemned, either. Possibly drawing upon Shelley's recently published "Ozymandias" (1817) for his imagery, Emerson acknowledges: "I own I admire the surpassing genius of Shakspeare but I detest his [immorality]. The statue is colossal but its diabolical features poison our admiration for the Genius which concieved [*sic*] and the skilful hand which carved it" (*JMN*, 1:297). It is not unlikely that this moderation was evoked by Emerson's aunt, Mary Moody Emerson, who had written to him possibly at about the time he commenced his studies at Harvard and from whose letter he quotes in his notebook. She writes, too, of her admiration for Shakespeare's strengths and her abhorrence of his sensuality; looking forward to the day that his "deformities" will be expunged, she admits, however: "But to me—to his old admirers nothing could supply his place" (*JMN*, 1:334). In the summer of the following year, Emerson again picked up his pen in his youthful war against theatrical evil and entered his excoriation in the journal; taking a debater's stance, he asserts that "the theatre is the cause as well as the consequence of public vice" and that the "mighty hand of SHAKSPEAR has consented to add another pulse to the rebellious blood," thus fostering public approval of "the poison" emitted by the theater (8 July 1822, *JMN*, 1:154–55).

The rhetorical comments Emerson entered in his journals and notebooks during a period of about nine months constitute the sharpest attack that he would ever make against Shakespeare. Based as they are upon little or probably no personal experience in the theater—certainly none as participant and none recorded as viewer—and upon the traditional puritan disaffection for the stage which was characteristic of Emerson's family and milieu, the denigration is better judged as a starting point at which Emerson made an almost immediate about-face rather than as evidence of a profound and legitimate dislike. Indeed, even before the year of those entries had ended, Emerson was already referring to "the glory of Plato, . . . of Cicero, . . . & of Shakspeare," relating it to the possibilities for an American literature to emerge with continuing westward expansion (21 December 1822, *JMN*, 2:73).

Plentiful allusions in the journals, none of which are condemnatory, entered between 1822 and 1829—the year of his marriage—suggest that whatever affected antipathy Emerson might have felt toward Shakspeare had drained out as the bombast flowed with the ink onto those early pages. "Shakspeare is an outlaw from all systems and would be great in despite of all," he writes parenthetically early in 1823 (*JMN*, 2:109). Two years later, in a long, dazzling passage of January 1825, he emphasizes that "It is not the solitude of place but the solitude of soul which is so inestimable to us," and he affirms that although physical solitude may promote the moral and intellectual life, mortal greatness does not depend upon it, as the lives and works of the worthiest men testify. Using an electric language anticipating Melville's in his letters to Hawthorne, Emerson writes that he praises all which made Newton, Bacon, and Shakespeare great, "and all that subtracted from their respective worth is the very object of my invective, sarcasm, admonition, rebuke, irony, satire, derision, assault. O ye words, I have no breath to utter 'em" (*JMN*, 2:326, 329). Sentences like this and many others on the preceding pages provide graphic evidence in support of Harold Bloom's point that "for Emerson the imagination was linguistic energy."[8]

Although Emerson often alludes to Shakespeare and cites the plays during the 1820s, it was not until nearly the end of the decade that his appreciation for the dramatist would suddenly and genuinely soar, as though injected with a vital shot. The stimulus was Coleridge, whose work Emerson had dipped into from time to time prior to his marriage, but never until afterward read seriously. Ellen became his wife on the last day of September 1829, and in letters to Aunt Mary and to his brothers William and Edward, written in December and the following January, he answered a question (that perhaps had not been asked): "Did not somebody ask me what books I read? . . . Coleridge's Friend—with great interest; Coleridges 'Aids to reflection' with yet deeper."[9] According to Rusk, he had been acquainted with the *Biographia Literaria* since November 1826 (*L*, 1:286 n), and by the time he made his first trip overseas he was able to discourse at length upon it and *The Friend* while touring Edinburgh with Alexander Ireland in August 1833 (*Life*, p. 193).

Considerable attention has necessarily been directed toward the influence of Coleridge in the development of New England transcendentalism, and its pronounced general effect in fostering Emerson's appreciation of Shakespeare may be taken for granted. There surely is no need to go into it here in detail, for Coleridge probably provided Emerson less with new information and critical ideas than with first, a greater incentive to reread Shakespeare more carefully and sympathetically, and second, with a means by which Shakespeare's work could be illuminated and understood in accord with the transcendental philosophy, including the organicism fundamental to its aesthetic. Coleridge and the contemporaneous German critics from whom he drew were equally idolatrous regarding Shakespeare. Is it not likely that Emerson, very much attracted to Coleridgean philosophy, would be strongly affected, also, by this adulation? According to Coleridge in the *Biographia*, Shakespeare may have been "the greatest genius, that perhaps human nature has yet produced, our *myriad-minded* Shakespeare."[10] Before long, Emerson himself would be one of the worshipers. Even more important than the infective idolatry, however, was the correspondence in thought that enabled Emerson to see Shakespeare in terms of his own organic theory of creativity and to recognize the integral relation in Shakespeare of truth with beauty. "No man was ever yet a great poet, without being at the same time a profound philosopher," Coleridge wrote in the *Biographia*; "In Shakespeare's poems the creative power and the intellectual energy wrestle as in a war embrace" (p. 171). Shakespeare's organicism and his being a fountain of "the wisdom of humanity" would become cardinal points in Emerson's early lectures on the dramatist, though they would not be the only ones that he either derived from Coleridge's observations on creativity and the poet or recognized as distinctly echoing his own developing ideas. Though his debt in this respect was probably considerable, it was necessarily limited by Emerson's having access more to Coleridge's relatively general views regarding Shakespeare's method and creative powers than to specific character interpretations or discussions of prosody, imagery, and language in particular plays. (The *Literary Remains* was not published until 1836–39, by which time Emerson's early lectures on Shakespeare had been written and delivered.) Like Coleridge and Lamb, Emerson regarded the plays as better read than seen. Much later in his career, he would confess that at times the story of the drama could so much interfere with his appreciation of the poetry that he found it "safer, therefore, to read the play backwards" (April 1864, *J*, 10:31). This sounds too whimsical to take seriously, however, and it is doubtful that the method would have found much favor with Coleridge had Emerson broached it to him when the two met in 1833.

Perhaps oversimplifying for the sake of brevity, T. M. Raysor proposes that "the most important and valuable aspects of Coleridge's Shakespearean criticism" were "his destructive analysis of the three unities, . . . his studies of Shakespeare's characters, . . . his emphasis upon Shakespeare's art, and . . . the sympathetic mood of his criticism."[11] Though each of these would prove important in varying degrees to Emerson as well, more crucial still would be, as Falk indicates, that in his eyes Shakespeare had come closer than anyone else thus far to the ideal transcendental poet incarnate by "put[ting] himself in harmony with the Universal Mind"[12] and expressing symbolically the essential relations between man and spirit.

For this transcendental view of Shakespeare, however, Emerson may well have been more directly indebted to his brother Charles than to Coleridge or any other individual. Charles was younger than Waldo by nearly six years; he may have had the finer intellect of the two brothers, and he was certainly a better student. He was also sensitive and at times despairing of his possibilities. Of all his brothers, Charles clearly was Waldo's favorite, and the devotion was mutual. Jonathan Bishop holds that Charles was "a kind of alter ego."[13] It would be unwise to speculate at length upon the possibility of their discussing Shakespeare during the 1820s, though there is no reason to suspect that they did not; indeed, although no record of it exists, it is not implausible to assume that Charles helped his brother overleap the puritan barrier and see the essential Shakespeare with universal eyes. But this is conjectural. Far more definite is the manner in which Charles's views on Shakespeare affected Waldo in the early 1830s, after he had begun seriously reading Coleridge and after the death of his "angel," Ellen.

    " 'We know,' Charles says, 'that his [Shakespeare's] record is true' " (28 October 1831, *JMN*, 3:271). Charles had been the only member of the Emerson family present at the ceremony when Waldo married Ellen in the autumn of 1829. The entry in Emerson's journal regarding Charles and Shakespeare was written less than two years later, and already his young bride was dead. Her premature death seemed to bring the two brothers closer than ever, and comments in the journal, particularly those entered after Charles's own unexpected death, suggest that Shakespeare was a subject to which they gave considerable attention in their frequent discourse. By the end of 1831 Waldo and Charles agreed that Shakespeare was singular among men and distinguishable from other poets "by always speaking to the thing itself i.e. after truth, & by always advancing," and they concurred that the sonnets manifest in Shakespeare's genius the "assimilating power of passion that turns all things to its own nature" (27 October 1831, *JMN*, 3:299). These are ideas upon which Charles elaborates in a short essay that was not published until approximately four years after his death, when Waldo edited it and printed it in the first number of the *Dial*, as "Notes from the Journal of a Scholar: Shakspeare."[14]

    Charles's death was for Waldo a shattering loss. Three weeks afterwards, he wrote to Harriet Martineau that he had found in Charles enough company to justify seclusion from all others: "He was my philosopher, my poet, my hero, my Christian. . . . [H]is conversation made Shakspear more conceivable to me; such an adorer of truth that he awed us. . . . I cannot tell you how much I miss him I depended on him so much. . . . Even his particular accomplishments, who shall replace to me? . . . [He was] as in the whole a Vision to me out of heaven and a perpetual argument for the reality & permanence of all that we aspire after" (*L*, 2:25).

Emerson's candor in his journals and letters respecting his great devotion and profound sense of loss at his brother's death suggest that Charles's role as a confidant has been much underestimated. This is especially true regarding Emerson's developing adulation of Shakespeare, which was to cohere in the middle of the decade with his two lectures on the Elizabethan dramatist. The significance of Charles's views on the shaping of Waldo's in these early lectures can best be inferred from the main points of his posthumous *Dial* paper of 1840.

Charles brings out Shakespeare's universality and ability to stimulate empathy with the dramatis personae. Time collapses between readers and plays; present and past merge so that all eras and peoples are unified. "We are no more brief, ignoble creatures; we seize our immortality, and bind together the related parts of our secular being." Yes, *secular* being: Charles emphasizes what he sees as Shakespeare's almost total disregard of Christianity, faith, and religion. "Shakspeare was a proper Pagan. . . . The beauty of holiness, the magnanimity of faith, he never saw. . . . he delighted to get out of the way of Christianity, and not to need to calculate any of its influences." Moreover, Shakespeare did not identify with any of his characters; only his genius did. Hence all was presented clearly, naturally: "his poetry was the very coinage of nature and life," the result of "perfect inspiration . . . which utters the beauty and truth, seen pure and unconfused as they lie in the lap of the Divine Order." Shakespeare, he says, "chanted the eternal laws of morals; but it was as they were facts in the consciousness, and so a part of humanity." Such luminosity occurs only through Shakespeare's depersonalization in writing his dramas, for as personality interferes with the shaping of the prophet's vision, inspiration becomes cloudy, the seer's eye loses its clarity, and the poet's "voice is husky."[15] Here, then, in brief, are essentially the views that Emerson would incorporate with others in the early Shakespeare lectures: the universality of the plays, the complete absence of the playwright from his drama, the presence of pure truth without the incumbrance of religion, the perfect result of natural creativity in terms of both drama and poetry. These are the subjects about which Charles and his brother with the "husky" voice must have conversed at length during those formative years between Ellen's death and mid-decade.[16]

Emerson's abundant references to Shakespeare in the journals of 1832–35 disclose that he was giving increasing attention to the plays and regarding them with a deeper appreciation. Although his Shakespearean observations in the journals for 1834 and 1835 were those upon which he particularly drew in drafting his lectures, as early as mid-1832 his entries manifested the apparent effect of Charles's reading of the dramatic works. "Shakspear's creations indicate no sort of anxiety to be understood," he wrote (16 May 1832, *JMN*, 4:18); then, foreshadowing the language he would apply less reverently in the closing passages of "Shakspeare; or, The Poet" more than a dozen years later, he wrote that the best of the dramatist's characters have "all [been] done in sport with the free daring pencil of a Master of the World. He leaves his children with God." Falk regarded this final sentence as "cryptic," but the context of the entry makes the statement clear: Shakespeare creates his characters and then, as Charles suggests, he stands aside to let them live without hindrance from himself.[17] As readers or observers we admire, empathize, but never fully understand; nor are we expected to. Edward Dowden similarly views the plays; he says that rather than provide philosophical and theological answers to profound enigmas, Shakespeare leaves you "in the solemn presence of a mystery. . . . You remain in the darkness. But you remain in the vital air."[18]

The divinity and mystery which Emerson finds at the center of his most universal poet's work provide the answer even as they provoke the question. The answer, one that would have been very pertinent for Emerson at this point in his career, allows for God and sanctity but not—again as Charles observes—for religion and conventional Christian piety. How different these observations are from those he had penned in superficial fury back in the early 1820s as well as from those he had yet to tack on to the end of his "Representative Men" lecture. Although Shakespeare was not then or ever seen by Emerson as being so perfect as to furnish what he called "the type of a *Man*" (12–16 August 1832, *JMN*, 4:36) rather than that more specifically of a poet, Emerson is nevertheless not at all ambivalent over the essential truth, the high moral value of the plays, as he indicates in quoting from Carlyle's *Life of Schiller* late in 1832: "And thus is Shakspear moral not of set purpose but by 'elevating the soul to a nobler pitch.' So too are all great exciters of man moral" (28–31 October 1832, *JMN*, 4:55). Of course, he realized that readers with prurient inclinations could also find what they sought in the plays, but no longer did he disregard the limpid depths for what he had considered scum on the

surface some ten years before. "There are people who read Shakspear for
his obscenity as the glaucous gull is said to follow the walrus for his
excrement" (22 April 1834, *JMN*, 4:279), but Emerson in the 1830s was
far beyond condemning the plays as decadent theater because the occasional bawdiness might appeal to lascivious tastes. For him, the gross-
ness all but disappeared, thus enabling him to confess: "In Shakspear I
actually shade my eyes as I read for the splendor of the thoughts" (7?
December 1835, *JMN*, 5:112).

It is with this shining vision of Shakespeare in his imagination that
he entered many such laudatory comments regarding the Elizabethan in
his journal for 1835, from which he drew for the two December lectures.
Possibly looking for additional compatible material to incorporate in
them, Emerson wrote to Charles Sprague, a sometime poet of Boston,
requesting a copy of his "Shakspeare Ode," which had been delivered in
1823 at a pageant in that city honoring the dramatist (27 July 1835, *L*,
1:448).[19] Sprague was then working for the Globe Bank in Boston; he
replied with thanks for the request, regretting, however, that he had no
copy of the poem to send and alleging that he had given up writing
poetry.[20] Emerson's letter testifies that he thought well enough of the
"Ode" to request a copy of it twelve years after either hearing it or
reading it in the newspaper; much later he would refer to it as Sprague's
"elegant verse, & on Shakspeare" (18 April 1864, *L*, 5:369).

In addition to the expected laudation that Emerson found in the
poem, two features in particular might have been especially appealing
to him: Sprague's attestation that Shakespeare masterfully represents the
endless variations of man and nature, and his ringing conclusion anticipating the development of Shakespearean art "Deep in the West, as
Independence roves."[21] This chauvinistic theme recalls Emerson's own
germinating thoughts on an American literature, expressed in the journal
in conjunction with Shakespeare's name as early as 1822 (21 December,
JMN, 2:73), and it clearly foreshadows the patriotic closing paragraph of
"The American Scholar" two years later, in which Emerson would declare, "We have listened too long to the courtly muses of Europe."
Although as a writer of odes Sprague will never be confused with Keats,
many worse poems than his have been written on Shakespeare; moreover,
his "Ode" does give voice to the characteristic idolatry of the Elizabethan
dramatist by Americans of the early nineteenth century as well as to the
patriotic call for cultural independence and supremacy that would add to
the fervor promoting "Manifest Destiny" and "Young America" a dec-

ade later. For these reasons, if not for Pindaric greatness, the "Shakspeare Ode" deserves resuscitation—as Emerson's discriminating judgment attests.

The ideas pertaining to Shakespeare that Emerson had been developing over the past several years were assimilated in the two lectures he delivered on the tenth and seventeenth of December in Boston as part of a ten-lecture series on English literature. These lectures are important not only because they enabled Emerson to integrate and generally systematize his thoughts on Shakespeare, but also because they so clearly adumbrate the fundamental ideas that he would be expatiating upon in the immediate future. Some of his most pointed comments, for example, reappear almost verbatim the following year in the "Idealism" chapter of *Nature*. Because these lectures are now readily available (*EL*, 1:287–319) there is no need here to do more than summarize the main points of each.

The two lectures are not even; Emerson develops his major ideas in the first and leaves the second as a kind of catchall for—as he calls them himself—the more miscellaneous matters. One might distinguish broadly and say that whereas the first lecture offers a discussion of Shakespeare's imagination at work, the second more closely approaches a general but not very critical look at the poetry and plays, though it also includes important insights into the dramatist's synthesizing powers that may more properly belong in the first. In developing these lectures, Emerson seems to have "depended chiefly" on Malone's edition (London, 1821), which he checked out of both the Harvard Library and the Boston Athenaeum.[22]

Emerson attempts in Lecture One to "separate the elements of [Shakespeare's] genius" (*EL*, 1:289). He indicates that Shakespeare's imagination, the essential gift of the poet, is greater than that of all other men, and through the use of it, the dramatist reveals nature perfectly as the symbol of spirit; much of this passage is reproduced in *Nature*. Echoing Coleridge,[23] Emerson professes that Shakespeare can subordinate nature more effectively than all other poets and that nature itself becomes "an organ" of the poet's mind (*EL*, 1:292–96). Again drawing largely from Coleridge, specifically from his characterization of the Shakespearean tragic hero (and possibly also in part from Charles W. Upham's recent lecture series on Salem witchcraft), Emerson observes that imagination must be balanced by a philosophical tendency which leads one not only to soar but also to inquire. Without such compensatory action, the imagination is inclined to run out of control, leading to the madness brought on by morbid excess of that faculty.[24] In Shakespeare this balance is maintained through his holistic vision, which, Emerson says, "we call Reason. We speak of it generally as the mind's Eye" (*EL*, 1:296). Another tempering element is Shakespeare's tendency to turn inward, "to explore the grounds of his own being, to compare his own faculties" (*EL*, 1:297). Shakespeare's holism and introspection, then, operating in relation to his imagination, preclude tendencies toward excess in any one faculty, promote intellectual harmony, and lift him into the airy realm of the universal poet. Although all men have access to speculative powers, not all are capable of seeing relations among phenomenal things as Shakespeare can; he has "Common Sense" and discerns worldly associations as lucidly and remarkably as he apprehends Truth. It is this practical side of Shakespeare that gives him affinity with the business world and leads him to write drama (*EL*, 1:301). This insight, too, may have been partially taken from Coleridge, who advises all aspiring young authors to prepare themselves for a trade or profession so as to preclude depending upon their pens for their livelihoods and to achieve, through a satisfactory social and domestic life, the feeling of kinship with ordinary human affairs.[25] According to Emerson, "The action of ordinary life in every sort, the heroic, the wretched, the humorous, yielded [Shakespeare] the aliment he longed for" (*EL*, 1:302). Neither Coleridge nor Emerson finds especial pleasure in the comic elements of Shakespeare,[26] though Emerson occasionally praises Falstaff for his "unrestrained glee" (*EL*, 1:302) in the face of a superior moral force near him that provides reader or viewer with an amusing moral lesson.

Shakespeare's balanced faculties of imagination, intellect, and practical power give him a "hearty sympathy . . . with every pulse and sensation of flesh and blood" and make him a fountainhead of human wisdom. His "wisdom draws men to him. . . . [T]his wondrous Sage takes possession of our heart and mind and instructs and elevates us. He gives us truth, clear, wholesome, and practical" (*EL*, 1:302–3). Shakespeare takes "his stand in that empyrean centre out of which the Divinity speaks" (*EL*, 1:303), and he becomes a touchstone according to which we determine the quality of our own culture and mind. Emerson's closing paragraphs of the first lecture become a eulogy that cloaks his divine Elizabethan dramatist in a mantle of gold.

In the looser and more miscellaneous second lecture, Emerson introduces a theme to which he will return in "Shakspeare; or, The Poet," that is, the extraordinary lack of biographical data for so celebrated a figure. He neither understands it nor attempts to explain it but simply mentions it and passes on. He itemizes several features that he finds of particular value in the plays: the importance of the story (*EL*, 1:307); the lifelike quality of the characters, individualized and yet idealized (*EL*, 1:307, 311); the "wit and eloquence" (*EL*, 1:307); the "splendor of the poetry," in which the "sense of the verse determines its tune" (*EL*, 1:307, 308); the "delicacy of the expression," including a rich, subtle vocabulary that covers all aspects and areas of life appropriately (*EL*, 1:307, 310); and the profundity of thought, especially as revealed in lustrous gemlike passages that are intrinsically almost as valuable as they are in context (*EL*, 1:307, 313). No more time is given to each of these points than necessary to tack it down, but Emerson's comments and his selection of illustrations from the plays and poems leave no doubt of his honest admiration.

The two most important observations made in the second lecture are those dealing with Shakespeare's creative use of the life around him and his borrowing from preceding writers and historians. The plays did not suddenly leap into being, Emerson says, but grew in Shakespeare's mind as he accumulated and assimilated materials from his reading and his life's experience. Emerson, himself a great borrower, finds no fault with this method; indeed, he says, it is "the ordinary course of humanity" that a man takes and uses whatever is excellent and worth preserving (*EL*, 1:317). This is the art of "Composition," *putting together* and revealing relations, that is at the center of artistic creation; and Shakespeare was a master of the "instrument of Synthesis" (*EL*, 1:318). In his working notes for this lecture, Emerson points out that one need only compare Shakespeare's achievements with the originals from which he drew in order to see "the secret of his inexhaustible fertility. It is that all things serve him equally well. He converts dust & stones to gold. . . . He seems to reveal to us at once the immensity of our own wealth, and to deify all men" (*EL*, 1:512). Through his purifying and blending, Shakespeare's innumerable sources gain "a quite new collective power" (*EL*, 1:318) and are transformed into something of his own. Perhaps as Emerson wrote these lines he recalled a couplet in the *Biographia* concerning the fusing of external sources with the generating power of the writer's own imagination; Coleridge recalled: "When Hope grew round me, like the climbing vine, / And fruits, and foliage, not my own, seem'd mine."[27]

That Emerson drew heavily from Coleridge in fashioning his own ideas for these two early lectures is unquestionable; nor would he have denied it. But as Shakespeare borrowed and transformed, giving rise to presentations of his own, so Emerson employed a similar method, enabling him to render a transcendental portrait of the ideal poet for which Shakespeare himself sat as the model. In a sense, Shakespeare was perfect for the part, even aside from the supremacy of his work, for the very dearth of biographical information that could lead one to discern personal affinities between the playwright and his plays precluded such discoveries, thus making him as much an eidolon as a man: "Shakspear will never be made by the study of Shakspear."[28] Shakespeare: the Unknown; the Creator; Master of Relations, of Composition, of Synthesis. Shakespeare; or, *the* Poet. There is not a hint of suggestion in this portrait of the mid-1830s that Emerson would reduce his divine universal poet a decade later and publicize him merely as "master of the revels to mankind" in his next formal lecture on Shakespeare. Before that occurred, however, a self-proclaimed prophet was introduced to Concord—and to him.

Exactly when Jones Very first saw Emerson is impossible now to say. Edwin Gittleman suggests that it may have been at one of the Boston churches when Emerson was supplying the pulpit for the day, or when Emerson was reading his lectures on English literature in that city during the winter of 1836, or, again, he may have heard part or all of another series of lectures that Emerson delivered in Salem, Very's home, shortly afterward.[29] Whenever Very first saw him, it is likely that he was well aware of Emerson's predominant views regarding the relation of man and spirit by the time that *Nature* was published on 9 September 1836, because he is known to have purchased his own copy only a few days later, as though he had been waiting for it to appear. Indeed, having received his degree from Harvard at the end of the previous month and become a student in the Divinity School (albeit an unofficial one) for the coming year, Very had probably heard something to his liking of Emerson while studying in Cambridge. The markings in his copy of *Nature* indicate that he read the little volume with particular care and thoughtfulness, suggesting that he would have a great deal to talk about with Emerson should there be an opportunity for them to meet.

His chance came well over a year later, in April 1838. Elizabeth Peabody, who already had heard of his power as a thinker and speaker, attended the Salem Lyceum when Very lectured there on epic poetry the previous December. She conversed at length with him after the lecture, and both pleased and excited, she immediately convinced Emerson that the young speaker should be scheduled for an appearance in Concord. Emerson concurred, and Very gave the same lecture on 4 April at the

Concord Lyceum, dining with the Emersons afterward. Entries from Very's notebooks imply that during this first meeting with Emerson he poured out his views regarding the nature of man and God as well as the ideas he had been developing on Shakespeare. Emerson was markedly impressed. "Very had affected him in a strange way. How, precisely, he was not sure, but he felt radically different from having spent time with the energetic young man."[30] Gittleman believes it likely that Emerson saw and heard something of himself in Very's remarks, though the ideas were presented differently. In any case, it seems clear that Very left Emerson "emotionally charged by his experience."[31] Especially striking is Gittleman's observation that Very's first two visits generated in Emerson a new hopefulness for America and particularly for the church—if the young enthusiast was representative of incoming divinity students. At the time of these discussions with Very in April, Emerson was preparing his address for the divinity class to graduate from Harvard the following July. According to Gittleman, Very's "dramatic impact" on him at this time evidently "encouraged the rigorous attack upon effete Christianity Emerson was planning."[32] Although a large part of Emerson's excitement may be attributable to Very's finding God in the soul and not through the church or historical Christianity, the dynamic, self-assured, and quite candid student of divinity was by the nature of his speech and manner no less inspiring for his person than for his ideas.

Bookish and attracted to nature as a boy, Very seems to have begun memorizing Shakespeare at about the age of fourteen. Possibly, rereading the plays continually reminded him of his visit to Hamlet's castle at Helsingor in 1823, four years earlier, while a cabin boy on his father's merchant vessel sailing to the North Sea. Very remained long impressed with this youthful experience that ultimately may have helped him identify through Hamlet with Shakespeare.[33] Unquestionably, his attraction to the dramatist was still very strong during his Harvard years as an undergraduate, when he spoke of Shakespeare often and long with Professor Edward Tyrrel Channing, who had measurably impressed Emerson many years earlier. Channing in turn introduced him to Richard Henry Dana, Sr., who was beginning to lecture on Shakespeare "in the manner of Schlegel and Coleridge" around 1834.[34] And, as may be expected, Very did considerable reading about the playwright on his own—Morgann, Hazlitt, Coleridge, the German Romantics (especially A. W. Schlegel), Lamb, and the selections in Nathan Drake's *Memorials of Shakspeare* (1828).

The early nineteenth-century British and German Shakespeare crit-

ics held many points in common, particularly their high praise for the
dramatist which bordered on deification; their recognition of Shakespeare
as at once a child of nature and a perfect reflector, re-creator, of it through
his absolute power of empathy with all things and beings; their perception
of his capacity to probe to the deepest levels of human consciousness; and
their confusion over the dramatist's morality, amorality, or immorality as
manifest in the plays. These and other observations on Shakespeare's
putatively superhuman capabilities are abundantly exemplified among
the diverse contributions included in Drake's *Memorials*[35] and in the
issue of *Blackwood's* that Very is known to have read, containing a long,
anonymous article on the idolatrous reception of Shakespeare in contemporary Germany.[36]

Not surprisingly, then, many direct parallels in thought appear between Very's pronouncements on Shakespeare and those of the British
and German Romantic critics whose works he had been perusing. It may
well be that his mind was moving generally along the same avenues when
he began seriously to read their publications, but the remarkable corre-
spondences between his developing ideas and theirs indicate that he was
more strongly influenced than has generally been recognized by his reading of recent Shakespearean criticism.[37] As he continued to shape his
thoughts on Shakespeare, of course, his prophetic strain became more
imperative and dominating, but the remnants of his earlier reading
nevertheless remain very clear.

If the writings of Coleridge, Lamb, the Schlegels, and others,
cannot be ignored in tracing the roots of Very's Shakespeare essays,
neither can his earlier reading in the philosophy of Bishop Berkeley,
which was no less influential in the development of his "mystical" strain
than in the growth of Emerson's transcendentalism. Cameron points out
that Emerson studied Berkeley at Harvard,[38] and it is most likely that
Very also came to the idealist's philosophy in the curriculum there and
was similarly affected by its fundamental principle: "the cause of ideas is
an incorporeal active substance or spirit."[39] For Emerson this spirit
became the activating force behind the creativity of the "passive Master";[40] for Very the spirit was that of Jesus, whom he believed that—as
poet, mystic, and prophet[41]—he ultimately came to embody. Very
doubtless expected to find the intellectual, philosophical, religious, and
even aesthetic complements of his own germinating ideas when he purchased Emerson's *Nature* and diligently read through it. He found what
he had anticipated, especially in "Idealism," where they all coalesce as
exemplified in Shakespeare, toward whom he had already turned.

Although Very's two Shakespeare essays—"Shakspeare" and "Hamlet"—are rich and suggestive, their principal theses may be briefly summarized. In the first, Very observes that if Shakespeare was kin to humanity, he was also "the unconscious work of God," meaning that as his mind was under God's control, so his *will* was born along with it and could not determine its direction. Shakespeare's mind was "phenomenal and unconscious, and almost as much a passive instrument [of God] as the material world."[42] Very sees Shakespeare as innocent but not virtuous because his innocence was not accompanied by a sense of duty: "True virtue would be *conscious* genius" (p. 55; emphasis mine). When one achieves universality consciously, through his own will, he is virtuous and has the mind of an adult; when one gains universality unconsciously, however, through God's will alone, he shows genius and innocence and has the mind of a child (pp. 55–56). Shakespeare wrote as he did, Very believes, because God gave him the gift of perfect empathy, but he did not infuse his work with moral instruction or with the inspiration to elicit universal love and responsibility from the reader or viewer upon contemplation. Shakespeare's mind, then, was merely a reflector of nature, not a user of it (pp. 68, 74, 76, 77). Nevertheless, the dramatist enables us to see the universal in the particular, and from this we can infer a moral lesson; that is, if we read him rightly, we would learn that loving ourselves should lead us to love others; by becoming most universal, we become most individual, for the two are not in opposition "but different faces of the same thing" (p. 53). Whether or not he drew heavily from the sixth chapter of *Nature* in formulating his own ideas is impossible to know for certain, but the clear parallels in thought and his marginalia in his copy of Emerson's essay strongly imply that he did.

Very's essay on *Hamlet* constitutes a further attempt to apprehend Shakespeare himself, this time through the character he assumes is the dramatist's persona. By identifying with Shakespeare and Hamlet and by understanding them to the depths, Very wishes to grasp the nature of the dramatist, illuminate the man and his work more truly than has ever been done before, *and improve upon* the Elizabethan by revealing his own genius as charged with the moral power of the Holy Spirit. Thus Shakespeare's unconscious and childlike innocence would be transformed into Very's conscious virtue; whereas Shakespeare rejected divine wisdom in favor of creative genius, Very himself has not. With the aid of this gift, which predicates total but conscious surrender of the self to the Holy Spirit, Very believes that he has become the Lord's instrument for divine direct revelation. As Hamlet was the persona of Shakespeare, so is Very the vessel and voicebox of Christ. Shakespeare, Hamlet, and Jesus, then, in a sense reveal themselves through the divinely inspired poet and critic, Jones Very of Salem.

Very's "Hamlet" must have affected Emerson emotionally as well as intellectually, for the loss of Ellen and two brothers was still heavily on his mind, and the essay focuses sharply on the theme of death.[43] Because Shakespeare was so well satisfied with "the simple pleasure of existence," Very proposes, he must have meditated at length about death; "the thought of death touched him in his very centre" (p. 86), and from these thoughts—"the wrestling of his own soul with the great enemy" (p. 86)—came *Hamlet*. Indeed, according to Very, "To be or not to be" is the controlling conflict and idea in the play. "The thoughts of [that] soliloquy are . . . the spirit of the whole. *To be or not to be* is written over its every scene" (p. 100). The same question preoccupied Shakespeare himself and voiced a "mystery which hangs over our being" as well (p. 101).

Very was under confinement as deranged while completing his work on "Hamlet." Not everyone was prepared to see him as the incarnation of the Holy Spirit, especially not the Reverend Charles W. Upham of Salem, who had been Emerson's classmate and fellow debater at Harvard, and who spoke of the transcendentalist's liberal views as atheistic.[44] Emerson read the Shakespeare essay while Very was hospitalized and wrote to Margaret Fuller that it is "a noble production, . . . filled with one thought; but that so deep & true & illustrated so happily & even grandly, that I account it an addition to our really scanty stock of adequate criticism on Shakspear. Such a mind cannot be lost" (28 September 1838, *L*, 2:165). After a month of confinement, Very was released, whereupon almost immediately he visited the Emersons, bringing his essay on *Hamlet* with him. The five-day stay was immensely successful, according to Emerson, who wrote to Elizabeth Peabody shortly after Very left, "I wish the whole world were as mad as he," praising the young poet's profundity and illumination,[45] though admitting that he intended to have the essays copied because he was not certain that he fully understood the first one (30 October 1838, *L*, 2:171)—a surprising confession coming as it did immediately after he had spent five days with the author speaking mainly about the two papers.

Emerson continued to exult over Very's extraordinary views, not least over his Shakespearean criticism. About a week after the poet's successful visit, Emerson reread *Lear* and *Hamlet* "with new wonder & mused much on the great soul whose authentic signs flashed on my sight

in the broad continuous *day light* of these poems." He also pondered over
the greatness of Shakespeare's "wit & immense knowledge of life &
intellectual superiority," regarding *Hamlet* as beyond all other art of all
forms and awed by "the wonderful truth & mastery of . . . these works"
(9 November 1838, *JMN*, 7:140–41). The impact of Very had sent him
back to the plays, which he reread, one might say, with the doors of
perception opened more widely. On the same day, he wrote to Margaret
Fuller again, less certain of Very's mental stability than the quality of the
two essays, which, he says, constitute "pretty great criticism" (9
November 1838, *L*, 2:173). A marvelous journal passage probably entered the following day reveals that he has been thinking suggestively
about Shakespeare as well as rereading the plays, and he confesses that no
matter how often he has felt familiar and saturated with them, each time
he returns they fill him with new wonder and astonishment (10?
November 1838, *JMN*, 7:143). "Shakspeare has for the first time in our
time found adequate criticism if indeed he have yet found it," he writes
assertively in his journal a couple of days later and lists: "Coleridge,
Lamb, [A. W.] Schlegel, Goethe, Very. [*sic*] Herder" (12 November
1838, *JMN*, 7:147). The august company here in which Emerson places
Very as a critic not only indicates the high esteem in which the young poet
is held—at least for the moment—but also suggests the telling effect of
the self-styled prophet upon his Shakespearean insights. Although Margaret Fuller would be little more than noncommittal with her tepid
praise, Alcott confirmed Emerson's endorsement of the essays, acknow-
ledging that they "are remarkable literary productions"; a few days earlier, he had sat up until 3 A.M. reading the "Hamlet" essay and copying at
length from it into his journal.[46]

   Very's star would remain high for Emerson through the beginning of
1839, but as quickly as it rose, so quickly did it fall. Because of Very's
almost intractable position that since the spirit had "dictated" the writings
to him and thus he, Very, could not permit them to be changed, editing
the essays and poems for a small volume in the summer of that year
became for Emerson an ordeal of frustration and drudgery rather than the
simple favor he had expected to perform for a grateful if ardent young
author. By the time the work was over Very seems to have succumbed to
Lidian's matronly charm and dropped altogether out of favor with her
husband. The book was published in September with no reference to
Emerson or acknowledgment of his aid, and the anonymous editor jotted
in his journal late in the month, "Also I hate Early Poems" (28 September
1839, *JMN*, 7:249). Can there be any doubt as to what and whom he

referred? When he reviewed Very's *Essays and Poems* nearly two years later in the July 1841 *Dial*, he praised the sincerity of the "entranced devotion" which gave rise to the sonnets but did not mention the essays that had so markedly impressed him. Despite the powerful vibrations that emanated from him during his few "effective years," as Gittleman denominates Very's short span of glory, Emerson wryly concluded that "when all was over, [he] still remained in the thin porridge or cold tea of Unitarianism" (late 1845, *JMN*, 9:339).[47]

The relationship of Emerson and Very burned brightly during the year or so of its existence, but apart from the initial impact of the prophetic poet and his views, what enduring effect might he have had upon Emerson's appreciation of Shakespeare? More than likely, Very motivated him to reread the plays from a different, more religious perspective, though certainly not from that of a Christian mystic. If one may place much faith in the tenor of his journal entries immediately after his radical experience with Very, Emerson appears to have more clearly associated Shakespeare with biblical figures than he had ordinarily done earlier. This is probably attributable to Very's enthusiasm as a stimulating discussant as well as to the ideas developed in the essays. There was something captivating about the man, something bordering on the hypnotic, and Emerson was by no means the only member of Concord's illuminati to have been smitten. Emerson's journal of this period implies that Very left a residue of religious suggestiveness about Shakespeare; taken in the context of other entries of 1840 which are connotatively related to Very's excesses, they seem to confirm that Emerson's allusions to Shakespeare in conjunction with religious references manifest the major aftereffect of his disillusioning experience with the fanatical poet.

For example, he succinctly and cryptically remarks in an undated notebook entry of the mid-1840s: "There are nations subsisting on one book" (*JMN*, 10:367). But immediately following the entry he refers, through his index code, to an earlier one in the journal of late July 1840 dealing with the problem of an author's presenting himself as universal, which is acceptable, Emerson writes, only if the author is mentally stable. The "perfectly sound nature" alone can present his experience as universal, he observes, but not a "partially sick" one, for only the morbid will accept his experience as true, and all others will find it offensive. The earlier entry, then, clarifies the enigmatic later one. "It is a delicate matter—this offering to stand deputy for the human race, & writing all one's secret history colossally out as philosophy. Very agreeable is it in those who succeed: odious in all others" (July 1840, *JMN*, 7:387). That

Jones Very was almost certainly still in his mind when he made the entry, and undesirably so, is suggested by an item written in the journal while he was in Providence at the end of March the same year, reminding himself—six months after publication—to post copies of "Very's Poems to Carlyle & Wordsworth" (28–29 March 1840, *JMN*, 7:489); that he felt no urgency over the matter is clear, for the books were not sent until more than a year later in May 1841. Equally indicative of his attempt to extirpate Very from his memory by mid-1841 is that when asked for information regarding Shakespeare criticism at about this time, Emerson responded in a letter from Nantasket Beach, Massachusetts, with a full complement of names and titles but no reference whatever to the poet or the essays he had helped publish only two years earlier (14? July 1841, *L*, 2:424–26; see also *L*, 1:xxxiii).[48] As a critic of Shakespeare, Very's day of glory with Emerson had passed.

Nonetheless, though obviously affected adversely by Very's fanaticism, Emerson was motivated to think of Shakespeare more specifically in religious terms than he had prior to 1839. Looking over his earlier writings, for instance, he frets over the odious and laudable elements that he finds coexisting in them side by side; the discrepancies are irksome. "I love facts & so erase this preaching. But also I venerate the Good, the Better & did therefore give it place. Cannot Montaigne & Shakspeare consist with Plato & Jesus?" (29 September–1[?] October 1839, *JMN*, 7:253). At the end of the month he identifies Jesus and Shakespeare as "two men of genius" (31 October 1839, *JMN*, 7:285). In mid-November he observes that Shakespeare "leans on the Bible," which is the "most original book in the world," a "fountain of literature"; nevertheless, he concludes that although the Elizabethan was reverent and devoted to traditional morality, his influence upon us is second to that of the prophets because only a prophet can be independent of the Bible and yet equal to it (17 November 1839, *JMN*, 7:309). Early the next year, he writes of the "poetic raptures" into which we are sent by Shakespeare, Saint Paul, and Plotinus (January 1840, *JMN*, 7:335). In May he notes that "Criticism must be transcendental," that is, must penetrate to the essence of writers; but he complains that few readers go beyond the books, which are usually treated as ends in themselves, to the inspiring spirit that generated them, "behind Dante & Shakspeare, much less behind Moses, Ezekiel, & St. John" (18 May 1840, *JMN*, 7:352). It is not the transcendental reference that should be remarked here, for that theme has been evident in Emerson's Shakespearean views since the 1820s; more important in this context are his specific allusions to biblical figures in conjunction with the Elizabethan poet, whom again he almost deifies by the end of the following year when he asserts that despite the distorting passage of millenia, "only a few are the fixed stars which have no parallax, or none for us; Plato & Jesus & Shakspeare" (21 October 1841, *JMN*, 8:127). At this stage of his career, Emerson seems to have admitted Shakespeare into the realm of "poet-priest," though he was explicitly to deny such a role for the dramatist in the concluding paragraphs of his "Representative Men" lecture. That anomaly, I believe, can be explained by the nature of the lecture itself.

As the opening of the "Representative Men" series approached, the seeds for those lectures, which had been sown in the journals, germinated and grew into crops of observation and insight to be harvested and employed in mid-decade. Meanwhile, late in 1843, Emerson took Elizabeth Hoar and Lidian to see William Charles Macready playing Hamlet in Boston (17 November 1843, *L*, 3:223–24). Escorting these two ladies from Concord to the theater must have been an extraordinary experience, for in his letter telling of it, Emerson follows each of their names with an exclamation point—indeed, at twenty-eight, Elizabeth was attending the theater for the first time in her life. Emerson asked Macready to visit them in Concord, but there is no record that the actor paid him that compliment. In November 1844 James Freeman Clarke recommended that Henry Norman Hudson be scheduled to lecture at the Concord Lyceum the following season because he "lectures on Shakespeare with remarkable power," and Emerson responded favorably, writing that he "had already heard enough to awaken my interest in his course" and that he hoped to hear him (26 November 1844, *L*, 3:267). If he attended Hudson's lecture on *Macbeth* the following New Year's Day, he found the views expounded to be largely compatible with his own—including the organicism, the recognition of Shakespeare's affinity with nature, the adulation, the praise of insight into character, the revelation of higher wisdom, the appreciation of Shakespeare's incomparable conversion of the common English tongue into transcendent poetry, and the representative nature of the poet himself. To be sure, many of the views presented must have seemed very much like his own being read back to him.

Soon after the "Representative Men" course of lectures was announced to open at the end of the year, Emerson entered into a correspondence with Evert Duyckinck, who attempted to negotiate for its publication in Wiley and Putnam's Library of American Books. Duyckinck explained that his "desire for a genuine book" for that series was "like the thirst of the parched traveller in the wilderness" (2 October 1845, *L*, 3:308 n). Emerson responded noncommittally, and despite several later attempts by the New York editor, neither that volume nor any other possible ones then under discussion ever materialized for Wiley and Putnam. At the time Duyckinck initiated the correspondence, the lecture on Shakespeare, scheduled for 25 January, had not yet been written, though Emerson began working seriously on it late in November. Already familiar with considerable Shakespeare scholarship (*L*, 1:xxxiii), he nevertheless borrowed nine volumes of Shakespeare Society publications from Longfellow at that time to help him prepare (2 December 1845, *L*, 3:313, 313 n).

The completed lecture was markedly different from those which he had delivered ten years before. There are some thematic but no textual parallels. Despite the adoration apparent in journal entries of the past few years, his earlier ebullience and sense of wonder over Shakespeare's poetry and plays appear to have abated considerably in the lecture of 1846. The reason for this unexpected aberration is easily discernible if one looks at the series as a whole rather than, as has usually been the case with "Shakspeare; or, The Poet," at that one lecture as a piece complete in itself. Clearly, it is not. Although Emerson's adulation for the poet is still very much present, the overruling purpose of the series *in toto* subordinates even the highest praise. In an almost Hawthornesque revelation, Emerson wishes to expose the ineluctable flaw inherent in every member of the human race, regardless of the genius that makes of some men the great figures they are. Here, then, is the representative man, representative as well in his inevitable human imperfection as in his capacity for inspiration from the Over-Soul, "instantaneous in-streaming causing power," "untaught sallies of the spirit," "instinct," or God—call it what one will. Moreover, in a very personal sense, Emerson identified himself with his representative men through both of these intrinsic elements—the human flaw and the divine breath of soul. Thus he could account for if not altogether resolve those doubts that were building over the meaning and value of his own life and work, uncertainties that would more clearly materialize a half dozen years later in the little poem "Days," which almost seems to have written itself.[49] But for now, early in the winter of 1846, Emerson uses his "Representative Men" series as a vehicle for self assessment and self revelation, almost as Melville would do nearly five years later when he looked into Hawthorne's dark *Mosses* as into a mirror that reflected his own insights and aspirations. This is disclosed near the opening of the first lecture, "The Uses of Great Men," where Emerson makes it explicit: "I can do that by another which I cannot do alone. . . . Other men are lenses through which we read our own minds" (*W*, 4:5).

What quality of mind best characterizes the great man? It is the faculty of seeing relations between man and nature; with mystical suggestiveness, Emerson says, "A man is a centre for nature, running out threads of relation through every thing, fluid and solid, material and elemental. The earth rolls; every clod and stone comes to the meridian: so every organ, function, acid, crystal, grain of dust, has its relation to the/ brain" (*W*, 4:9). The great man, the representative man, can "see connection where the multitude see fragments"; the true scholar, writer, poet, as Emerson explains in "Goethe: or, The Writer," is "an organic agent" (*W*, 4:264). But he is also only human, and instead of divine attributes (apart from the inspiring power of the soul), Shakespeare's "principal merit [is] . . . that he of all men best understands the English language, and can say what he will" (*W*, 4:15). Human greatness will be balanced by human failings. Echoes from Emerson's puritan past resound here, though dimly; with such thoughts, he adumbrates Camus's use of the myth of Sisyphus—the great man throws his shoulder behind the huge rock of humanly imperfection and slowly pushes it up the slope toward immortality only to have it roll back down to its starting point and thus render him but one more frail victim of his inescapable tainted heritage. A somber tinge of melancholy underlies the striking portraits of Emerson's representative men; the author-lecturer seems to be saying, "Yes, to be sure; you and I and Shakespeare alike are to a degree children of God, children of the fire—and children of Adam." How could it be otherwise, then, that "Shakespeare; or, The Poet" would reveal, even emphasize, a human flaw though it be dilated to a major moral weakness far beyond anything derogatory that Emerson had written or said of the Elizabethan since his sophomoric vituperations of 1821 and 1822? Of course, exactly the same method—device, shall we call it?—is no less evident in the other five portraits of the series: each of the great men is sculpted upon a pedestal only to have the pedestal knocked out from under before the sculpture is complete.

Taking this more negative than positive approach to his great men, where climactic attention is given to the shortcomings of his subjects at the end of each lecture rather than emphasis upon the attributes at the beginning, Emerson further tones down his enthusiasm for Shakespeare by devoting an astonishingly small percentage of his text to discussing the playwright's creative powers and writings. I do not wish to belabor this point, but it is not a negligible one to be passed over summarily. Of the thirty-one pages that constitute the printed version in the Centenary Edition, roughly eighteen deal with general and ancillary matters and three denigrate the playwright as "master of the revels to mankind," leaving only about ten pages, or a third of the total, to discuss positively Shakespeare's imagination and work. After generalizing upon the genius of the universal poet in the first few pages, Emerson develops two themes he had introduced ten years earlier: first, Shakespeare as synthesizer of his predecessors' works and his own experience; and second, the dearth of biographical material, which leads him to conclude that the man can be known only through his works—"Shakspeare is the only biographer of Shakspeare" (*W*, 4:208). Moreover, there is nothing really new in his eulogistic central pages, either, where again he highly praises the dramatist's "wisdom of life" and remarkable capacity to transform "the inmost truth of things into music and verse" (*W*, 4:212–13). Shakespeare is "the type of the poet" (but not, notice, the type of the *man*) in that he creates "perfect representation" (*W*, 4:213–14). Emerson's final words of praise before the well-known castigation celebrate the playwright's cheerfulness, without which he could not be a poet (*W*, 4:215–16).

Then the blade falls, and the Elizabethan is condemned for his amorality, his "obscure and profane life," and his dissipation of genius for the sake of "public amusement" (*W*, 4:218). And the lecturer concludes, as if recalling his closing paragraphs in "The Poet" (*W*, 3:37–38), that "The world still wants its poet-priest" (*W*, 4:219). Now, these are hard words, indeed, to be propounded against the same man whom Emerson had described only a few pages earlier as "the type of the poet" and "the best [dramatist] in the world," a writer who "is inconceivably wise." "Shakespeare was puzzling" to Emerson, Rusk supposes (*Life*, p. 376), but in fact he was neither more nor less puzzling than the other five representative men he selected to portray. In light of the controlling purpose of the series and his profuse adulatory comments both immediately before and after the lectures were written, the condemnation simply should not be taken at face value. Emerson used Will Shakespeare the man in this way partly to accommodate the dictates of his puritan heritage—as reinforced by Jones Very—but also and no less important to suit a specific literary purpose. Before and after, he regarded the Elizabethan less as a fellow human being than as a spiritually charged creative force that gave rise to an aggregation of depersonalized plays and poems containing a perfect representation of nature as well as a bottomless fountain of wisdom—and all marvelously expressed.[50]

Moreover, Shakespeare was another face of the mystical "central man," of whom Emerson wrote in his journal in 1846 at some uncertain time after his lecture series had been delivered in Boston; his allusion to the playwright in relating this visionary experience is far more telling than those closing paragraphs of his anomalous lecture: "We shall one day talk with the central man, and see again in the varying play of his features all the features which have characterised our darlings, & stamped themselves in fire on the heart." The "central man" appears as Socrates, then Shakespeare, then Raphael as he talks; then he is Michelangelo, Dante, Jesus—all "great secular personalities [that] were only expressions of his face." One senses the ghostly presence of Charles beside Emerson as these words were written, but the mystic vision subsides, and the journalist is left alone with his dream (1846, *JMN*, 9:395). For Emerson, Shakespeare the secular personality is subordinate to Shakespeare the manifestation of the divine and inscrutable "central man." Apart from a few incidental remarks of the early 1850s suggestive of vague skepticism regarding the value of the theater in appreciating Shakespeare (December 1852, September 1853, *J*, 8:350, 406), whatever Emerson has to say about the dramatist and his work after the "Representative Men" lecture is highly favorable. As might be expected, his affection was strong enough that although a plethora of invitations and a busy lecture schedule kept time short for him during his second tour to England and Scotland in 1847–48, especially as the end of the trip rapidly approached in the summer, he made a special point of visiting Stratford on 13 July; this was "the Emerson day," as it was called by George Eliot,[51] one of several new companions with whom he traveled to Shakespeare's birthplace. Two days later, he was on his way home after nearly a year abroad.

Perhaps the fact that so many people were already familiar with the contents of the "Representative Men" lectures accounts for the favorable reception the book met both in Europe and the United States soon after publication.[52] The journals provide no evidence that Emerson is thinking anew on Shakespeare after that date. Although the Elizabethan often comes to his mind, the thoughts that emerge with his name are largely the old ones presented in different and often strikingly effective garments; nevertheless, it is still Shakespeare's uncanny intellect and wisdom, perceptivity, universality, and capacity for perfect expression, his "all-wise music" (July 1849, *JMN*, 11:134), that astonishes and moves him. Ultimately, he is seen as inscrutable, unmatchable, and therefore alone, as Emerson succinctly reveals with this quatrain, probably of the early

1850s: "I see all human wits / Are measured but a few; / Unmeasured still my Shakspeare sits, / Lone as the blessed Jew."[53]

Very likely, these lines were written at about the time that Emerson's long correspondence with Delia Bacon commenced. Bacon believed that she had found the answer to the problem of Shakespeare's inscrutability, a mystery over which Emerson still puzzled in his journal.[54] She was not the only person in her day—or before and after that—to hold the theory that Bacon rather than Shakespeare was the author of the great plays attributed to the Stratford poet. She had done an enormous amount of research—though she was inclined to overlook what she did not want to see—in order to prove her case, and, believing wholly in her cause, she wrote to Emerson for aid in supporting and promulgating her theory. Emerson's share of the correspondence in 1853 indicates not only a courteous response but also generous encouragement in following out her ideas.[55] He provided her with several introductions in the United States and abroad, including one to Carlyle, who was also cordial and helpful though he found her theory *"quixotic"* and her cause conducive only of "sorrow, toil, and utter disappointment" (9 September 1853, *CEC*, p. 495). Nevertheless, he praised her as admirable in character and promised to do what he could for her.

Bacon wanted to publish her findings quickly in order to convince the world of the misplaced reputation she had uncovered, but Emerson shrewdly advised her to put nothing into print until she had her work completed and could bring it out intact as a book. She insisted, however, and therefore he helped her publish what was expected to be her opening chapter in *Putnam's* as the lead article for January 1856. Initially, the editors had asked her for new segments as she completed them, but once the opening chapter was before the public they refused to publish anything more of the material.[56]

Meanwhile *Putnam's* was returning to her through Emerson three additional chapters which she had already submitted, and he in turn had entrusted them to Sophy Ripley. Unfortunately, on her return to Concord, she misplaced the manuscript packet and lost it irrecoverably. Emerson wrote to Bacon explaining the problem on 23 June 1856. By this time, several years had passed since their correspondence had begun, and the whole project had become so burdensome to him that he could no longer continue his initial encouragement. In fact, he told her flatly that she was too prolix, repetitive, and dependent upon passages that do not adequately support her views. Upset over his sharp missive, the distraught woman wrote to Hawthorne, then consul in Liverpool, who had also been very supportive after meeting her but once in London.[57] Hawthorne's response was both peculiar and unadmiring in its reference to Emerson, who he believed was at least indirectly responsible for the loss of the manuscript and was therefore morally liable for some kind of reimbursement: "Mr. E. ought to feel himself bound to do it, that is, if he were a man like other men; but he is far more than that, and not so much." After the mishap, Emerson's role in Bacon's scholarly adventure ended, though he continued to think well of her as a woman "with genius, but mad"; yet he considered her with Whitman as one of "the sole producers that America has yielded in [the past] ten years" (*Life*, pp. 392–93).

After his controversial episode with Delia Bacon, Emerson evidently gave little consistent thought to Shakespeare's work until April 1864, when he and other members of the Saturday Club decided to celebrate the tricentennial of the playwright's birth with a gala dinner to which special guests would be invited. Charles Sprague, author of the "elegant" "Shakspeare Ode" of 1823, could not accept the invitation which Emerson in great distress had nearly forgotten to send (*L*, 5:369–71). With Holmes and Lowell, he oversaw the arrangements, which led to considerable correspondence, and Emerson himself was to provide the address. The following month he would celebrate his own sixty-first birthday, and his memory was no longer as retentive as it had been in his earlier years. As a result, an amusing hiatus occurs in accounts of that Saturday Club dinner. Although Emerson had prepared his speech, it is not certain that he delivered it. According to Cabot, Emerson arose, looked about tranquilly, and sat down without uttering a word. Cabot did not know, however, that Emerson had prepared an address, assuming that he had been expected to deliver an impromptu talk, which he would ordinarily not willingly do.[58] But, as Rusk notes, no one but him has commented on an alleged lapse by Emerson at that dinner, which would seem to throw Cabot's recollection into doubt. On the other hand, Edward Emerson indicates that although his father himself had jotted on the manuscript a note confirming that his address had been read, the handwriting of that marginal note is that of Emerson as a considerably older man; in light of this observation, Edward suggests that perhaps Cabot was correct, and that Emerson did not speak at the occasion because he had forgotten his notes.[59] In that case, he would have had to provide an extemporaneous talk, after all, and preferred not to do so. Hence the enigma.

Whether delivered or not, the address itself, which Edward notes was considerably longer in manuscript than as printed in the *Works* (*J*,

10:27 n), is pure idolatry. Emerson compresses into a matter of a few
pages the germs of several ideas he has developed at greater length in his
earlier writings, though the brief address is permeated with a mellowness
of genuine appreciation and affection that requires no verbal pyrotechnics
to express. Indeed, the organic imagery with which he praises his divine
Elizabethan poet could not be more evocative or appropriate, considering
the time, place, company, and occasion: "There are periods fruitful of
great men. . . . They are like the great wine years. . . . His birth
marked a great wine year when wonderful grapes ripened in the vintage of
God, . . . and king of men, by this grace of God also, is Shakspeare"
(*W*, 11:452–53). How could this be bettered?

Five years later he gave what was evidently his final public presenta-
tion on Shakespeare when he provided a short introduction and read
favorite passages from the writings as part of a series of "Readings in
English Poetry and Prose" in Boston during the winter of 1869.[60] By this
time, Shakespeare had become for the aging Emerson a touchstone in
advising querying poets how they might assess and improve their own
work. He suggests that they measure their lines against the poet's to see
the tone and sharpness of their own more distinctly and accurately. To
Emma Lazarus, for example, who visited him and whom he came to
know quite well, Emerson responded in 1869 to a request for a critique of
her poetry: "I hate to pick & spy, & only wish to insist that, after reading
Shakspeare for fifteen minutes, you shall read in this MS. a page or two to
see what you can spare" (9 July, *L*, 6:75). Continuing to seek Emerson's
advice, she was offended and bewildered that no sample of her work was
included in *Parnassus*, an anthology of poetry in English which he compiled and published in 1874. But if his seeming disregard caused a breach,
it was eventually healed, and the friendship, if not the discipleship, was at
least partially restored.

Of the hundreds of selections that Emerson chose for *Parnassus*
eighty-nine are taken from Shakespeare, including eight sonnets, "The
Phoenix and the Turtle," and dozens of passages from the plays. Nearly
all the other poets are represented with selections numbering from one to
a score or, in a few cases, more, though only Wordsworth has as many as
half of Shakespeare's number. In his brief preface, Emerson allots only a
few words to the work of his authors, praising Shakespeare as "an exceptional mind in the world" with whom "universal poetry began and ended." Characteristically, he also admires Shakespeare's "absolute con-
cealment . . . in all his miraculous dramas, and even in his love-poems"
in contrast to Wordsworth, he says, who always "childish[ly]" put him-

self forward in his poetry.[61] Emerson's selection of material for *Parnas-*
sus was purely arbitrary; it was based entirely on the way he was personally moved over a long period of time by the poems and passages from
which he drew. One might say that the anthology is an organic one in that
it was compiled from Emerson's copybooks, which grew from lines that
he had admired and copied out over the years. As a result of this year-by-
year growth of his anthology, there is a great deal of Emerson in his
Parnassus, though he included not one of his own poems in it. From the
amount of space he gave Shakespeare, we can well believe that for him by
1874 the dramatist from Stratford had indeed been transubstantiated into
the universal "poet-priest" whose commingled music and wisdom divinely inspired the creative spirit which infused Emerson's whole vital
being.

If Emerson's appreciation of Shakespeare did not change radically
after he turned twenty or twenty-one, it nevertheless progressed through a
series of subtle modulations according to the circumstances of his life at
the time. To be sure, he quickly outgrew his factious indignation over
Shakespeare's "moral turpitude," which he rhetorically displayed in several pages of his journal shortly after earning his baccalaureate. How
familiar he was with Shakespeare's works during this college year is
uncertain; although there is some justification for believing that he had a
good reading knowledge of the plays, his appreciation for them may not
have gone much below the surface. Hence his putative outrage over their
immorality. Probably under the early influence of his sensitive younger
brother Charles, however, Emerson's ersatz scorn rapidly changed to
admiration, and with his reading of Coleridge soon after his marriage, the
admiration itself ripened into the kind of idolatry professed by most of the
important British and German Shakespeareans of the early nineteenth
century. After Ellen's premature death, the likely influence of Charles's
views became still more telling, and by the mid-1830s Shakespeare had
already assumed the transcendental qualities which would lead Emerson
to assess him more as a creative force, both inspired and inspiring, than a
man who had walked the streets of Stratford and London more than two
centuries before. Although Emerson would never disregard the earthy
element of Shakespeare, which he particularly applauded for the bond
that it assured between the ideal poet-priest and humanity, ultimately it
was the transcendental poet, the fire-fed imagination which simultaneously created and reflected nature in all of its manifestations and moods,
that was supreme for him. If Shakespeare himself was unknowable, the

poetry was always there as an endless source of beauty and inspired wisdom.

But Emerson paid little real attention to possible religious implications of Shakespeare until strangely stimulated to do so by Jones Very, whose immediate impact on the transcendental Christian lecturer was as unexpected as it was dynamic. Emerson quickly succumbed to Very's assertions regarding the nature of the relation between man and spirit because at first they seemed very much to extend upon his own views. Very's attempt to interpret Shakespeare more truly than had ever been done before by identifying with him spiritually was also fascinating and brilliant for its possibilities, Emerson believed, and indeed his praise may well have helped rush the audacious poet-prophet toward a quicker climax to his short, explosive career.

Very's spiritual affirmations seem to have left Emerson with an inclination toward thinking more in specifically religious terms when alluding to Shakespeare than he had done previously, a line of thought that may have been instrumental in leading him to the basic thesis of his "Representative Men" lectures, including "Shakspeare; or, The Poet." In this series, Emerson devoted more attention to the representative man's human imperfectibility—not particularly as a result of Original Sin or innate depravity, neither of which Emerson accepted as true—but simply by virtue of his humanness. Hence Shakespeare—like Plato, Swedenborg, Montaigne, Napoleon, and Goethe—could not be idealized, for he, too, was fundamentally flawed. His principal concern, Emerson says in this lecture/essay, was not the dissemination of wisdom or the propagation of moral truth but simple revelry for the sake of amusement alone. In this regard, Emerson's view is directly parallel with that of Very, who professed that Shakespeare lacked the conscience which should have led him consciously to accept the Holy Spirit and utter the truth of Christ through the creation of a higher poetry than had ever before been composed on earth. This is what Very himself had intended to do before he flashed out and became a literary nonentity for the remainder of his long career and life. But Emerson's denunciation of Shakespeare's amorality in this piece is more effective as a device by which the thesis of *Representative Men* is supported than convincing, much less conclusive, in its own right.

After "Shakspeare; or, The Poet," Emerson seldom commented on Shakespeare with even the faintest tones suggestive of disapproval; much more commonly—indeed, almost always—he wrote of the Elizabethan playwright and poet in the most laudatory terms, elevating

him to the highest plane of ideality in his praise. Shakespeare ultimately
becomes a touchstone for the artist as well as for the culture; he becomes a
vision, an ideal, the perfect universal poet, human and divine, open to all
and yet inscrutable. Emerson may have denied him the role of poet-priest
in his most often-cited essay on the dramatist, but virtually everything he
wrote on Shakespeare after its publication in 1850 graphically concedes
that the diadem has been bestowed nonetheless. If Emerson himself was
ultimately satisfied with "a few herbs and apples" from his "pleached
garden," to Shakespeare he granted the rest—"Bread, kingdoms, stars,
and sky that holds them all."[62] In "the supreme genius" of Shakespeare,
truth and beauty, spirit and nature, fused, as seeming contraries merged
in Emerson himself and became one. With this in mind, it is easy to
understand why he was moved to praise "The Phoenix and the Turtle" so
highly in his preface to *Parnassus* and to include the entire text of that
poem in his anthology. To a large extent, it metaphorically represents the
"vanishing dualism"[63] which underlies not only his aesthetic and his
appreciation of Shakespeare but his whole transcendental philosophy:

> Reason, in itself confounded,
> Saw division grow together;
> To themselves yet either-neither,
> Simple was so well compounded:
>
> That it cried, How true a twain
> Seemeth this concordant one!
> Love hath reason, reason none,
> If what parts can so remain.[64]

Perhaps his long devotion to the plays and poems may best be
phrased in terms of an Emersonian equation: *Truth plus Beauty over
Shakespeare equal Apotheosis*. It is a fitting climax to a lifetime's consideration.

The Contemporary Reception of *English Traits*

ROBERT E. BURKHOLDER

There is little doubt that when Emerson first had thoughts of writing a book on England, based largely upon the journal he kept during his second visit there from October 1847 to July 1848, he had no idea that the book would become the most eagerly anticipated and one of the most successful of his publications, and perhaps the most difficult and frustrating work to finish of his entire career. Emerson had conceived the idea for *English Traits* while still in England, and for seven years continued gathering and checking facts in a manner unprecedented in his career, with the possible exception of the "Historical Discourse" (*Life*, pp. 379, 221). It is clear that he initially underestimated both the amount of labor the book would require and the amount of time he would spend away from his study on lecture tours during the early 1850s. It is also a certainty that while he was working on the *Memoirs of Margaret Fuller Ossoli*, he had little spare time for other projects. But when that work was published in February 1852, he was able to devote more time to preparing his book on England. As early as 17 December 1852 Emerson was looking forward to completion of *English Traits*: he wrote his brother William that "my English notes have now assumed the size of a pretty book, which I am eager to complete" (*L*, 4:332). The same desire for completion is apparent in several letters of 1853, including one of 12 October in which he declines Theodore Parker's request to arrange for a revival of the Transcendental Club because "my poor little book is still on my conscience." Emerson adds that "A few good days" are all that are needed to finish the book.[1]

It was two years later, on 9 October 1855, that Emerson sent the first chapter of *English Traits* to Phillips, Sampson, his publisher, promising the rest of the "sixteen or seventeen chapters" soon (*L*, 4:523). However, a winter lecture tour that took him as far west as the Mississippi Valley seriously impeded his completing the book. In January 1856 he was unable to work on the "last sheets which the printers are waiting for" because of the intense cold in Dixon, Illinois, where he was lecturing.[2] At the beginning of June, Emerson was working on "those weary refractory concluding chapters of the little English book," and in a jubilant letter of the twenty-third he announced to William that "My book is ended at last, a week ago."[3] *English Traits* was published on 6 August 1856 (see *JMN*, 14:31).

The question that arises immediately when one considers the problems Emerson had with his "little English book" is whether he was satisfied with the finished product. It can at least be said that quite apart from the book's critical reception, he was pleased with its popular reception. In this context, he wrote to William four days after the publication of *English Traits* to report that despite his forbidding "all their puffing advertisements," 1,700 copies of the book had been sold (*L*, 5:30). Of course, a certain amount of public acceptance also meant a greater financial reward for those seven years of intermittent toil. It was this aspect of the popular success of *English Traits* of which Emerson speaks when he tells William, "The poor book has long been a bore & an obstruction to me; 'tis time it should be something else" (*L*, 5:30).

The promise of success offered by the sales of the first few days was no chimera, and the book did, indeed, become "something else." A month after publication Emerson wrote to William once again, with the news that "The book prospers well enough." By this Emerson means that the initial printing of 3,000 was quickly exhausted and a second printing of 2,000 copies was selling fast (*L*, 5:34). His only reservation seems to be that he had as yet received no money from Phillips, Sampson. This matter was cleared up by the end of September, and the book continued to sell at a rate unfamiliar to Emerson. In tallying sales of his works in Pocket Diary 8, Emerson notes that *English Traits* is in its "seventh 1000" on 5 December 1856 and into its "Eighth 1000" by April 1857 (*JMN*, 14:452).

There are, of course, a number of reasons why *English Traits* achieved so great a popularity. Certainly the change in subject matter, from Emersonian abstractions to an actual country that was not only real but also of great interest to Americans, did not hurt sales; however, there are two reasons for the success of *English Traits* that are less subtle than changes in style or subject matter: Emerson's lectures on England and notices of the work long before it was published. Intentionally or not, he did a great deal of advance work for the success of *English Traits*.

Emerson's lectures on England and the English tended to draw attention to his intention of ultimately publishing his opinions. In fact, one might say that *English Traits* really began with his brief address to the Manchaster Athenæum in November 1847. He returned to America from England on 27 July 1848, and by 5 December he delivered a lecture on "Why England Is England" at the Concord Lyceum. On 7 December he was not only lecturing on England in Newport, Rhode Island, but also receiving the first taste of the criticism his views on that country would eventually receive in book form. According to Ralph L. Rusk, one Rhode Islander, reacting to what he considered more praise of England from Emerson than the country deserved, said, "He laid it on pretty thick, I assure you" (*Life*, p. 379). From 1848 to 1856 Emerson delivered lectures on English topics more than forty times in various parts of the country, from lyceums in New England to St. Louis, Missouri.[4] The notices of these lectures not only informed the public what he was working on but also whetted the popular appetite for more of his views.

In order to demonstrate how the lecture notices ultimately affected the reception of *English Traits*, we might examine a few sample notices from British and American periodicals. In America so much interest had been generated by Emerson's trip to England and the views he brought back that the New York newspapers carried accounts of one of his earliest American lectures on the subject at the Boston Mercantile Library Association on 27 December 1848. Less reviews than summaries of Emerson's main points these newpaper notices caused Emerson the problem of facing audiences that already knew what he was going to say. The lecture notice in the *New-York Daily Tribune* on 6 January 1849 is a case in point. Its purpose is obviously to paraphrase Emerson's entire discourse, as well as to stress that the lecture's main feature was Emerson's "strongly favorable impressions of the English character" (p. 1). As if having his lecture disseminated to the readership of the *Daily Tribune* was not bad enough, N. P. Willis's *New York Home Journal* reprinted the entire notice in the 3 February 1849 number (p. 3). By the time such summaries as these were circulated, the American public expected Emerson's opinions on England to be unqualified praise.

The British, however, did not accede so readily to the idea that what Emerson was saying about them was praise. For example, an article in *Chambers's Edinburgh Journal* on 29 June 1850 claims that Emerson slights the English in one of their "most striking characteristics," their liberality (pp. 415–16). The complaint that Emerson failed to capture a certain prize aspect of English culture or character would become a relatively common cry in the British reviews immediately following the publication of *English Traits*.

These few notices are just a sampling of the large number of commentaries that appeared as Emerson toured the country, but they do give some indication that the critical battleline for *English Traits* would ultimately be geographical. This sort of division is not present, however, in the calls for a book like *English Traits* which began to appear almost the moment Emerson left England. In the 5 August 1848 *Literary World* the Boston correspondent writes that Emerson has recently arrived in Boston, and adds: "The recent struggles in Europe, of which he has been a spectator, will form a fine subject for a new series of Essays or Lectures" (pp. 529–30). Although the lectures Emerson composed had little to do with the European revolutions of 1848, they did give the public the impression that what he had to say about England was worth hearing. In the March 1849 *Holden's Dollar Magazine* the anonymous writer of "Topics of the Month" endorses the ideas expressed in Emerson's lecture on "England" as "well worth heeding" (pp. 187–88), and in the 2 June 1849 number of the *Literary World,* another anonymous commentator favorably contrasts Emerson's views with those of Caroline Kirkland in *Holidays Abroad; or, Europe from the West* (pp. 472–73).[5] The writer expresses a hope that Emerson will ultimately write a book like Kirkland's because "his would be the perfection of Travels, cool, neat, omnisided, manly, and gentlemanly" (p. 472). This is quite a divergence from the view expressed in an earlier comparison of Emerson and Kirkland in the same periodical of 20 January 1849, entitled "England from Two Points of Views," which not only criticizes Emerson's "peculiar feelings and idiosyncrasy" but also complains that Emerson takes "an English view of England," as opposed to Kirkland's inherently American point of view (pp. 50–51).

The anticipation of *English Traits* in England also serves to show that this work had the potential for an extraordinary reception. Noting the apparent death of New England transcendentalism in the *Critic* of 15 July 1853, a commentator points out that only Emerson "survives in the old state of transcendental activity—or passivity." He also notes a rumored change in Emerson's style: "his new work, *Notes on Europe*, is to be of a descriptive rather than of a reflective character. About to be published in this country, previously to appearing in the author's own, it will convey the impressions which we and our French neighbours made upon the serene sage of Concord during the Revolutionary year of 1848" (p. 379). It is impossible to say where this faulty information came from. As we have seen, Emerson was discussing completion of the work as early as late 1852, but he did not actually contact any English publishers in regard to publication in England until September 1855, when he corresponded with both Richard Bentley and George Routledge (*L*, 4:528).

A second anticipatory notice appeared under interesting circumstances in a regular column called "Our Weekly Gossip" in the *Athenæum* for 27 May 1854. In reporting the literary news from America the writer states, "Mr. Emerson's work in England is still in promise. He writes with extreme caution; but he promises to come out with vintages." The writer does, however, believe that Emerson's silence may be partially compensated by the "early utterance of one of his disciples," Mr. H. D. Thoreau (p. 655). The "early utterance" was, of course, *Walden*, but it is difficult to believe that the public and the critics had their desire for Emerson's "little English book" satisfied, even with Thoreau's masterpiece. But because of notices like this, the critical machinery of both continents was primed to expect "vintages" from Emerson in *English Traits*.

Within three months of publication, *English Traits* received more than thirty reviews in British and American literary periodicals and newspapers, and within the next year it would receive at least fourteen more, making it one of Emerson's most noticed books. William Sowder states flatly that "in England it received more reviews in British periodicals than any other work by Emerson."[6] The anticipation created by the lectures and advance notices certainly helped foster a climate in which Emerson's writing was not only discussed by critics but also purchased by the public. In America it is possible that readers who were tired of such belittling accounts of American life and manners by the British as Frances Trollope's *Domestic Manners of the Americans* (1832) looked forward to Emerson's book in the hope that it would be payment in kind. We might also take into account the change Emerson's reputation was undergoing. In his mid-fifties, Emerson was losing the aura of a dangerous radical and rapidly replacing it with that of respected citizen and man of letters. In fact, a writer in *Holden's Dollar Magazine* for June 1849 notes that there was a noticeable change in Emerson's willingness to deal with practical matters, and he ascribes this change to experiences Emerson had among the practical-minded English (pp. 380–82). Ironically the *Holden's* writer may not have been seeing a change at all, but rather Emerson's increasing self-confidence due to his growing acceptance as both lecturer and writer. At least Emerson's letters and journals prove that he never stopped dealing with the practical.

If one can generalize about such diversity of opinion as the reviews of *English Traits* represent, it might be said that on the whole Emerson was treated to kinder reviews in the American press than in the British. It is important to realize that even the American reviews are easily classified by the geographical region from which they originated. The South, for example, had never admired Emerson nor even been just to him. The review of *English Traits* in the October 1856 *Southern Literary Messenger* is no exception. The anonymous reviewer points out that *English Traits* is an improvement over Emerson's previous efforts, but Emerson could improve his work even more, particularly in matters of style: "We have worked to no purpose over 'Representative Men' and cudgelled our brains in vain to unravel the tangled thread of his essays, and we had little hope to find 'English Traits' any clearer to our perception." Ironically, however, the reviewer finds that the English mist and fog of which Emerson complains seems to make his prose clear enough so that there is "moderate assurance that we can comprehend it," despite a reversion by Emerson to his old stylistic "opacity" in his discussions with Carlyle, Coleridge, and Wordsworth. There are other stylistic problems though, an "abruptness" and a lack of logical argument, as well as Emerson's "extravagant" admiration of England and the English (pp. 314–16).

Reviews from Philadelphia were also negative. In the October 1856 *Graham's*, which had a distinctly Southern bias,[7] Emerson fared just as poorly, although one must admit that the reviewer for *Graham's* narrowed his dislike to one aspect of the work, its alleged lack of structural coherence. After extracting large portions of Emerson's first chapter, "First Visit to Europe," the reviewer criticizes Emerson's discussion of meetings in Italy with Horatio Greenough and Walter Savage Landor as "an odd, flighty way of doing things." In fact, this organizational method of Emerson's is used to demonstrate his lack of "desire for convertedness" (pp. 374–76). A reviewer in *Godey's Lady's Book* for November 1856 followed the *Graham's* indictment of Emerson's organization by complaining that *English Traits* is composed of so many "hop-skip-and-jump" sentences that the work is difficult to review; however, this reviewer does manage to find enough "convertedness" in Emerson to imply that he has gone too far in his praise of England (p. 467). Of course, considering the outright condemnations Emerson had received in reviews of previous works, these three negative reviews are comparatively mild. In fact, Emerson was to receive no more severe critical rebuke in America than those presented by *Godey's*, *Graham's*, and the *Southern Literary Messenger*. All other American reviews and reviewers were at the very least willing to admit that there was something good in *English Traits* to redeem Emerson's errors and inconsistencies.

This good fortune was not exactly the case in England. Despite the plausible claim of the writer of an essay on "The Poetry of Wordsworth" for the conservative *Wesleyan-Methodist Magazine* of October 1850 that an indictment of Emerson was also an indictment of the British people because they have "adopted his sentiments, and become accessory after the fact" (p. 1078 n), many of the British critics severely chastized Emerson for what they saw as his upstart views on England. The only unqualified praise Emerson received in Britain appeared in the *Critic* and two organs of liberalism, the *British Controversialist* and the *Leader*. The *Critic* for 15 September 1856 prints a review that praises Emerson for writing an "unpretending" little book that contains "more real wisdom than in the works of all the American travellers put together" (pp. 446–47). A reviewer in the *Leader* for 13 September 1856 goes further in his expression of appreciation by calling *English Traits* "the matured results of a matured and original mind reflecting on the aspects of English Life which came under its observation" (pp. 880–82). This reviewer also believes that any deficiencies in the book are the result of the complexity of the subject matter and have nothing to do with Emerson. The *British Controversialist* for June 1857 prints a review under the pseudonym "L'Ouvrier" that is more general in its praise but no less generous. In the matter of style it is held that Emerson cannot be questioned because "as a great genius, [he] has created a style for himself," and *English Traits* is recommended as a work that cannot fail to provide the reader with "pleasure and profit" (pp. 275–79).

These reviews, however, were the exception in England, where a protectionist strain runs through nearly all the contemporary reviews that found *English Traits* totally or partially lacking. In fact, even a brief notice in the October 1856 *British Controversialist* points out that Emerson is sometimes incorrect, although *English Traits* is generally thought to be a "pretty impartial critique on England and the English" (p. 192). There are, of course, degrees of correctness, but a reviewer in the *New Quarterly Review* (4th Quarter 1856) found that Emerson's book went far beyond error in the presumptions made upon England. The most vehement of all British reviews in its response to *English Traits*, this review nevertheless puts in print a sense of nationalistic anger that seems to lurk beneath the surface of many British considerations of Emerson's book. Since the *New Quarterly Review* was patterned after the more venerable and respected *Quarterly Review*, which was founded in 1809 and intended as a defender of the established order,[8] it is no surprise that the *New Quarterly* would attack Emerson as one who, not long before, was "the prevalent epidemic" who "afflicted the young imagination with a yearning after that obscurity and indefiniteness which . . . soothe the disappointments" (pp. 449–55). At least this is the way Emerson is characterized in an unflattering biographical sketch that prefaces the reviewer's comments on *English Traits*. Initially that work is described as "a series of diatribes upon England and Englishmen, seasoned and served up so as to pique national self-complacency, and swell local conceit in Boston, New York and . . . Montreal" (p. 450). From his general dislike of Emerson's book, the reviewer moves to a discussion of a number of specific complaints against such things as Emerson's egotism and, of course, his liberal views on the English aristrocracy, religion, and universities. The reviewer chooses to admit that all of Emerson's criticisms of these cherished institutions are correct, but he implies that they should not be criticism at all, since the English church was intended to be the church of the gentry and not the poor, and the universities are justifiably hostile to genius. However, the closing comment of the review, even allowing for what precedes it, seems a stronger response than Emerson deserved for writing his "little English book." Angered at Emerson's low opinion of most nineteenth-century British writers, the reviewer expresses what he perceives as "the national English feeling" with this quotation: "If you don't like the country—d——n you—you can leave it!" (p. 455).

Several other British reviews of *English Traits* were only a bit less strong. In a letter to Emerson of 16 September 1856, Carlyle wryly comments that an Irish newspaper, the *Nation*, noticed a "*medicinal* intention" in Emerson's book, but "God knows there was hardly ever such a Hospital of Lepers" (*L*, 5:33). In one of the earliest reviews of *English Traits*, in the *Athenæum* of 6 September 1856, an anonymous reviewer complains that the book "will be remembered—if remembered at all—as a work wanting in substance and genuineness" (pp. 1109–11). This reviewer, like his colleague in the *New Quarterly*, takes exception to Emerson's apparent underestimation of England and particularly to Emerson's claim that England has reached its pinnacle of power and has begun to decline. In November 1856, a review in another conservative periodical, the *National Magazine*, condemns Emerson's work for exactly the reason discussed at length in the *Athenæum* of 6 September: that Emerson's prophecy of English decline is the result of his "ignorance of what is or is not English" (pp. 39–40). The *Evangelical Respository* of March 1857 states that Emerson has much to learn and suggests that his book might more appropriately be titled "*Mr. Emerson's Table-Talk concerning the English"* (pp. 233–34). Reviews like these inevitably served as a challenge to the more moderate reviewers. They generally responded with more balanced critiques of *English Traits* that, while refusing to ignore problems in the book, were more than fair in discussing its value.

For example, the *Press* of 13 September 1856 published a review that addressed directly the critics who had panned *English Traits*: "We do not share in the dissatisfaction which some critics have expressed with the latest production of Mr. Emerson." Despite taking offense at Emerson's negative statements on the English universities and religion, this reviewer is willing to defend *English Traits* on the ground that Emerson more than counterbalances his criticism with "unqualified eulogy" (pp. 879–80). Likewise, a reviewer in the 6 September *Literary Gazette* finds Emerson "not well qualified" for writing on the topics of the aristrocracy, religion, and universities, but he nevertheless claims to be "much pleased" with Emerson's book (pp. 657–58). Later, in the *Saturday Review* of 4 October 1856, Charles Kingsley, a minister of the Church of England but also a committed social reformer, claims that Emerson's fairness to those institutions of which the English are justly proud is one of the most positive aspects of *English Traits*. Kingsley's recommendation of the book, however, is made with a sense of surprise, because he frankly admits that he expected little from a man who not only held questionable views but was also guilty of eulogizing the "prose run mad" of Walt Whitman (pp. 509–10).

Another ground for defense of Emerson's work by the British reviewers of *English Traits* was his originality. Although there was some debate on both sides of the Atlantic as to whether Emerson was truly an original thinker or merely a writer gifted enough to dress up rather ordinary ideas in language that made them interesting,[9] several reviewers believed that the apparent novelty of many ideas in *English Traits* more than compensated for the flaws. Those flaws were noticed by a reviewer in the *Spectator* for 13 September 1856, who considers Emerson's perpetuation of "popular errors" about English character as the major problem in *English Traits*. He cites, for example, Emerson's statement concerning the outright ownership of the wife by the husband in English marriages, which, it is claimed, has not only never been the case but is illegal. However, this reviewer's verdict on *English Traits* is that it is an example of "an original-minded man" writing favorably about a country with which he has much in common, but from which he is sufficiently removed to be objective (p. 981). Emerson's originality in *English Traits* receives ever greater praise in a review published in the *Examiner* for 20 September 1856. Here Emerson is celebrated as "one of the most original men of our day," but in the matter of truth, the reviewer warns his readers to be wary of the difference between what is "well said" and what is "truly said" (p. 599). Like the reviewer in the *Spectator*, this critic implies a genuine concern for what he perceives as being, at best, a misinterpretation of English culture and character. In fact, the intent of most of these mixed reviews is summed up in a one-sentence notice of *English Traits* that appeared in the October 1856 *National Review*: "Often epigrammatic, sometimes fanciful, but every where readable" (p. 496).[10]

Atypical in the strength of its criticism of Emerson and its favorable opinion of *English Traits* is a lengthy review in the January 1857 *London Quarterly Review*, which roundly condemns Emerson in its opening pages but then warms to find *English Traits* a worthwhile publication. A Methodist periodical founded in 1853, the *London Quarterly* generally carried only brief reviews that were colored by its main function as an instrument of religious propaganda.[11] Such coloring is the most conspicuous feature of this reviewer's low opinion of Emerson, who is described as having the leisure to be "familiar with the greatest intellects of every age," but who, nevertheless, remains "ignorant as darkness itself, his mind is a perfect blank." The criticism is based upon the reviewer's perception that Emerson has "missed sight of Christianity" and is lost in the fog of his own speculation with the "mightiest influence in the life of humanity blotted-out." Such opinions as this are reminiscent of the emotion typical of negative reviews of Emerson's work in the late 1830s and early 1840s, but such emotion is extremely rare by 1856. As if to demonstrate the confusion experienced by detractors of Emerson after reading *English Traits*, the reviewer for the *London Quarterly* even finds it "difficult not to admit" the truth of Emerson's comments on religion in England. The apparent contradiction of denouncing Emerson's want of religion on the one hand and then agreeing with his observations of religion in England on the other does not seem to occur to this reviewer, who, like the critics in the *Press*, *Literary Gazette*, and *Saturday Review*, ultimately considers Emerson's "impartiality" as the greatest of *English Traits*' many "distinguishing excellencies" (pp. 381–406).

Undoubtedly the most influential, as well as comprehensive, review of *English Traits* in Britain was that which appeared in the highly respected *Westminster Review* in October 1856. Here the reviewer presents an even-handed discussion of *English Traits* which, unlike many other reviews of Emerson, concentrates exclusively upon the work at hand. The tone of the entire review may be characterized by these introductory remarks: "Mr. Emerson has given us a book from which we may learn many things; much about ourselves, about what we have, and about what we have not; and, still more, from which we may learn that the nobleness of spirit which gives praise as well as blame where it is due, may be relied on as existing across the Atlantic." This tone of respect is dominant, even in discussions of what the reviewer considers Emerson's flaws. One of the reviewer's complaints deals with Emerson's style. Critics often complained of Emerson's epigrammatic style as being responsible for making his prose incoherent, but this reviewer points out that such a style is necessarily artificial and, if carried to the extreme, can be unsatisfying: "Reading his book is like eating potted meat; it is very good, very creditable to cook, and a little of it goes a long way, but it is not exactly the genuine beef." A second problem is illustrated in Emerson's chapter on "Race," where he propounds what this reviewer calls "the jelly theory of races," which, simply stated, holds that the more complex a civilization the higher the culture. Such theories, it is believed, demonstrate that Emerson's poetical temperament and fertile imagination make him susceptible to false analogies. More specific criticism is brought against what is believed to be Emerson's misunderstanding of the English church and his idea that the English mind degenerated once it was introduced to the philosophy of Locke. In all cases, however, the strictures against Emerson are balanced by the reviewer's opinion that "there is much more to admire than to find fault with," and rather than ordering Emerson to leave England if he does not like it, this reviewer claims that "Englishmen cannot complain of any want of courtesy, or any deficiency of insight" on the part of Emerson in *English Traits* (pp. 494–514).

If the British reviewers found it necessary to attack or defend Emerson for his insults to England, the reaction was the reverse in America. Many American reviewers held to the opinion of that Rhode Islander who felt that in his praise of England, Emerson "laid it on pretty thick." For example, H. N. Turner in the Cincinnati-based *Ladies' Repository* for April 1857 criticizes Emerson for looking too much "on the sunny side of the English nature and nation, feeling altogether graciously inclined toward those who come to meet him at railway stations, and feast him, and toast him, and make set speeches at him" (pp. 237–39). The implication, of course, is that anyone who is being made a lion of will be rather shortsighted when it comes to the defects in those who are doing the lionizing. The reviewer believes that the English are the greediest people in the world and that Emerson was, for all intents and purposes, pampered into believing otherwise. This view is closely related to Parke Godwin's criticism, published in the October 1856 *Putnam's*, that because of Emerson's contact with only the English middle and upper classes he was prevented from hearing "the great heart of the people" (pp. 407–15) and a review by Andrew Preston Peabody in the influential *North American Review* of October 1856, claiming that *English Traits* "ignores pauperism, ignorance, and crime, aristocratic pretension and plebian sycophancy, sinecure laziness and under-paid labor,—in fine, all the inequalities of condition, realized right, and availing privilege" inherent in the British moral and social systems (pp. 503–10). An anonymous reviewer in the 12 August 1856 *Boston Post* also finds *English Traits* wanting in Emerson's lack of discussion of the inequities among the English poor and the excesses of the wealthy: "It has regard to very few, comparatively, of the people of England, and it rather judges of the whole nation by what has been said and done by generations of the privileged classes" (p. 4).

American envy or dislike of the British was manifested in other ways in reviews of *English Traits*. A reviewer for the *New-York Daily Tribune* of 16 August agrees with Emerson's criticism of the British social system (p. 6), which neither Godwin, Peabody, nor the *Boston Post* reviewer thought strong enough, and the *National Era* for October 1856 seems to relish the idea that Emerson demonstrates that vaunted English common sense has reduced that nation to a position behind most other civilized countries in philosophy (p. 162). Most original of all, however, was the tactic used by an anonymous reviewer in the September 1856 *Harvard Magazine* to suggest that the "spirit of justice that pervades every page [of *English Traits*] is a quality the English would do well to adopt in their strictures upon our country" (pp. 297–302). But no matter how it was expressed, both British and American reviewers did not hesitate to infuse nationalism into their reviews.

We have seen that nationalism in American reviews often manifested itself in criticism that Emerson either went too far in his praise or not far enough in his criticism of England. It is not surprising, then, to note also that American reviewers singled out for praise aspects of *English Traits* that might actually be considered American traits. One of the significant strengths of Emerson's work, according to an anonymous reviewer in the *Quarterly Journal* of the American Unitarian Association for 1 October 1856, is the "tone of Yankee common-sense shrewdness" that will surprise those readers who considered Emerson "only as a mystic" (p. 100). This comment is certainly a forerunner of that made by James Russell Lowell in his review of *The Conduct of Life* in the February 1861 *Atlantic Monthly*, when, in attempting to explain the conundrum of Emerson's popularity in New England, he asks: "Is it not that he out-Yankees us all?" (pp. 254–55).

While slightly less graphic, other reviewers also emphasized what might be considered typically American aspects of Emerson's prose. The reviewer for the *Harvard Magazine* thinks *English Traits* particularly attractive because of its "manliness and independence" (p. 297), as if to say that Emerson was unaffected and unintimidated by the wealth and power of the British. Even the *Knickerbocker*, which had originally discovered too profound a German influence on Emerson and his school, published a review in its December 1856 number that stresses the ruggedness of *English Traits*. The book is said to be "as invigorating as a horseback ride" or a walk on an October morning and is recommended to the reader for its "strength and manly self-reliance" (pp. 630–31).[12] This critical ploy of praising the peculiarly American aspects of Emerson's style is, of course, related to the advancement of the cause of literary nationalism in America, but it is also part of the growing recognition among American critics that Emerson was becoming an American of international reputation who, ultimately, could contribute to the respectability of American letters. Therefore, from the early criticism of Emerson as an imitator of Carlyle and the Germans, his reputation grew to the point where the "Editor's Table" in the March 1858 *Harper's Monthly* could proclaim with pride that "Emerson is more read in England than Carlyle" (p. 554).

As previously mentioned, the question of style was as important in considerations of *English Traits* as it was in discussions of Emerson's earlier works, only here the critics were faced with deciding whether Emerson's style had changed significantly. The majority of American reviewers did note a new clarity, but there was still some negative criticism. For example, the *Christian Review* for October 1856 notes that even though *English Traits* was written in Emerson's "peculiar manner," nothing by him to date "has so much delighted us" (p. 625). A reviewer in the October 1856 *Harper's Monthly* was even more specific and negative in basing his final judgment of *English Traits'* worth on Emerson's style: "It will not command universal assent, and its inconsecutive, aphoristic style, makes it liable to misconstruction." This view is a significant part of this critic's thesis that despite Emerson's choice of the "most solid realities" of England as his subject, *English Traits* treats those realities with "the same qualities which characterize his previous compositions." "Qualities," however, is used to mean both the good and bad aspects of Emerson's work. As well as power of observation, fidelity of description, insight into human motives, and felicity of expression, the *Harper's* reviewer notices Emerson's usual "fanciful analogies," "rash generalizations," "and a total absence of consecutive order and development" (pp. 694–96).

Other reviewers did not agree that Emerson was rehashing old stylistic problems in *English Traits*. The reviewer in the *Harvard Magazine*, for instance, anticipates such a charge by stating that "obscurity of style, a fault of which Emerson is often accused, cannot be urged against him here, however just the accusation may be with regard to his previous writings" (p. 297). This idea was also expressed in the *Boston Post* of 12 August 1856, whose reviewer claims that *English Traits* "is intelligibly written, and in this respect is far superior to most of his [Emerson's] previous productions" (p. 4.)

The brief notice in the *Quarterly Journal* of the American Unitarian Association commends *English Traits* as having a "rare felicity of language" and compares Emerson's style to that of Sir Thomas Browne (p. 100). In the November 1856 *New Englander*, Noah Porter, Jr., theorizes that in *English Traits* Emerson has adopted the style "of the quaint old travellers and humorists" whose "extravagance and simplicity, the wit and the wisdom" are congenial to Emerson's particular genius (pp. 573–92). F. D. Huntington, writing in the September 1856 *Monthly Religious Magazine and Independent Journal*, praises Emerson for "a very direct, straightforward style." Huntington finds in *English Traits* an Emerson who shows "something more of common-sense reflection and practical observation than is generally looked for in him by those who know him least." These kind words are tempered, however, by Huntington's acknowledgment that *English Traits* contains "occasional exaggerations, paradoxes, one-sided opinions, and criticisms too unqualified for justice" (p. 214). The April 1857 *Ladies' Repository* claims that reading an Emerson work that could be understood is a pleasure, and the *Christian Examiner* for September 1856 states that Emerson's circle of readers will be enlarged because *English Traits* is "more local and less abstract than most of his former writings" (pp. 309–10).

Since its publication of Francis Bowen's scathing attack on Emerson's *Nature* specifically and transcendentalism in general in January 1837, the *Examiner*'s position had been liberalized to the point where the reviewer can note his reservations about Emerson's "literary and per-

sonal judgements" in *English Traits* and still praise "his sober
waggeries, his closely packed amplifications, his aphorisms of smiling
penetration" (p. 310).[13] Even the totally negative review in the October
1856 *Southern Literary Messenger* is willing to grant that Emerson
achieves a new clarity of style in *English Traits*, although the implication
seems to be that Emerson's style only seems clear in contrast to the mist
and fog of London.

Others, however, were not quite so willing to excuse Emerson from
what had previously been perceived as transgressions. A number of the
Central Presbyterian Magazine published in the autumn of 1856 even
goes so far as to state that when Emerson abandons the subject of religion
he is capable of being "intelligible, interesting, and sometimes instructive." While this review was alone in its speculation that Emerson's much
discussed clarity of style in *English Traits* was due to his abandonment of
religion as his principal subject, other reviewers disagreed with the religious opinions expressed by Emerson in *English Traits*. In the *New
Englander*, Noah Porter, Jr., objects to Emerson's observation that con-
versing with an Englishman on the subject of his religion is like talking to
a box turtle. Porter believes that Emerson "is not accurately informed"
on the subject of religion in England, and he considers Emerson typically
presumptuous in assuming that the "Englishman has no reasons for his
Christian faith" (p. 586). The complaint of Andrew Preston Peabody in
the October 1856 *North American Review* is reminiscent of earlier criticism of Emerson's religious views in its denunciation of the "intense
subjectivism" that ultimately "neutralizes moral distinctions, eliminates
duty and accountability, obliterates religion, and excludes the conception
of a personal and self-conscious Deity" (p. 505). According to this
reviewer, the indifference that is a product of such a subjective philosophy is discernible in *English Traits* whenever Emerson touches upon
religion.

Reviewers on both sides of the Atlantic also took exception to
Emerson's belief that contemporary English literature could boast no
great writers. For instance, the reviewer for the *Christian Examiner*
thinks that few could agree with Emerson's low assessment of the work of
Pope, Scott, Southey, and Landor. The 6 September *Literary Gazette*
merely states that Emerson's comments on English literature "are not so
attractive as might have been anticipated" (p. 658), and the January 1857
London Quarterly review cites some of Emerson's opinions on literature
as being "hasty and unworthy" (p. 401). The most important reaction to

Emerson's impressions of England's literary men, however, appeared in pamphlet form before the end of November 1856.

During his first trip to Europe in 1833, Emerson visited Florence and was there introduced to Walter Savage Landor by the American sculptor Horatio Greenough. Apparently Emerson was rather disappointed with Landor, for in a letter to his brother, Charles, Emerson records his impressions of Landor immediately following a discussion over breakfast: "He does not quite show the same calibre in conversation as in his books.—It is a mean thing that literary men, philosophers, cannot work themselves clear of this ambition to appear men of the world. As if every dandy did nt understand his business better than they. I hope better things of Carlyle who has lashed the same folly" (*L*, 1:383). The key phrase in this description of Landor is "men of the world," because when Emerson records his impressions of Landor in the "First Visit to England" chapter of *English Traits*, he pictures him as something of an aesthetic dogmatist, who pontificates on subjects ranging from sculpture and painting to plants and great men (*W*, 5:6–10). Emerson writes that Landor was "decided in his opinions," that he was perhaps overfond of the Greeks as artists and historians, and "He pestered me with Southey; but who is Southey?" Emerson also states that in his breakfast meeting Landor "glorified" Chesterfield more than he deserved and undervalued Burke and Socrates. Landor also selected and named three of the greatest men in a manner that suggested a "pomologist" selecting the best pears for an orchard. Emerson is careful, however, to balance these criticisms with his belief that Landor is undervalued in England, and that the scholar must return to Landor again and again, because of his "elegant sentences," "for wisdom, wit, and indignation that are unforgettable."

Edward Waldo Emerson theorizes that Emerson included this criticism because he did not expect his book to be popular in England, and he knew there were few Americans who would protest such criticism of an English author (*W*, 5:326). Whatever the reason, we have seen that *English Traits* was popular enough in Britain to create much critical interest, and one of the most interested Britons was Landor.

Landor's *Letter from W. S. Landor to R. W. Emerson* is perhaps most remarkable for the restraint shown by Landor in defending himself against Emerson's opinions.[14] In fact, much of the twenty-two page letter is devoted to a justification of the views he advanced twenty-three years before, explaining his taste in sculpture and history and praising Southey's *Curse of Kehama*, but there are also diatribes against the perverseness of Carlyle and democracy, which Landor claims to abhor. There is also a defense of contemporary British writers. Perhaps the best way to characterize the entire episode is in the words of a contemporary reviewer who, in a review of Landor's *Letter* in the 29 November 1856 *Athenæum*, says: "Mr. Emerson, as our readers know, lately touched Mr. Landor with his lance. The hurt was not serious—a mere touch-and-go that scarce drew blood—but a prick rouses the war-horse, and the literary veteran leaps into the arena, brandishing his weapon, and ready to break a spear with his adversary, and make sport for the literary Philistines." Nevertheless, this reviewer is willing to admit that Landor's reply, unjustified or not, is "excellent sport" and some of Landor's best prose (pp. 1460–61).

Beyond the disputes, like that with Landor, that arose with the publication of *English Traits*, it is apparent that this work marked a significant turn, not only in Emerson's critical reception but also in the acceptance of his work by the public. The relatively small number of reviews that reproached Emerson's religious views demonstrates that what had been extremely controversial in the 1830s and 1840s was now considered so only by the most zealously conservative. Discussions of the American quality of Emerson's prose tended to emphasize that he was rapidly becoming important in advancing the cause of literary nationalism. Most important, however, was the sense created by *English Traits* that Emerson had abandoned some of his old mysticism and was becoming more practical and concrete. Such an attitude certainly must have helped in creating an audience for Emerson's next major publication, with its practical-sounding title, *The Conduct of Life*.

"The Adirondacs" and Technology

Ronald A. Sudol

Since Emerson's reputation as a poet rests most securely on remarkable single lines—sometimes in verse, often in prose—and on a handful of short poems, it is not surprising that a relatively long poem of 342 lines like "The Adirondacs" (*W*, 9:182–94) is not more often read and admired. What the reader expects, and initially confronts, are prosodic monotony, tedious cataloging of narrative and scenic details, and insistent affirmations of transcendental unity. Yet, the poem is without detractors, and two recent students of Emerson's poetry have found merit in "The Adirondacs." Hyatt H. Waggoner, admiring its "flawlessly conventional blank verse," considers it "an interesting, too little appreciated work, valuable for the quality of the mind we hear speaking to us in a voice at once cultivated and colloquial, an assured, easy, confident voice, equally at home with the distinguished campers and the traditional verse form."[1] R. A. Yoder finds in it "good-natured narrative and digression [imitating] the repose of nature in a subdued wisdom."[2]

One source of interest in the poem is its form—though written in twenty verse paragraphs it is also designated "A Journal" in the subtitle. As such, the narrator is Emerson himself, and the story he tells in blank verse is both historical record and autobiography, related as well to essays, addresses, journals, and notes as to poems. This middle ground in the spectrum of rhetorical forms that "The Adirondacs" occupies might be a fruitful starting point for a reading aimed at describing its nature and assessing Emerson's achievement. If, as is sometimes thought, his best poetry appears in his prose, it is because his gift for language finds its most vital outlet in the more rhetorical, less artistic, forms—chiefly in public addresses and essays, where his quotable phrases are shaped by purpose, situation, and intended audience. "The Adirondacs," dedicated to his "Fellow-Travellers," has such a public frame of reference, but it is also a distilled and versified personal journal recording an episode in its author's intellectual and spiritual growth. In this merger of public poem and personal journal Emerson presents himself as renewed not so much by vacationing in the Adirondack wilderness as by learning of the completion of the transatlantic cable. The wilderness vacation provided a fertile setting for this news even as the verse journal subsequently provided the public framework for revealing the impact of the cable upon the poet's spiritual renovation.

Emerson eagerly accepted the invitation of several prominent members of the Saturday Club to join in a trip to the Adirondack Mountains for two or three weeks in August 1858. He was fifty-five, and in letters prior to the trip he looked forward to leisurely dissipation, though certainly philosophical and scientific discourse could be expected to occupy much of the leisure time of this party of ten prominent men of affairs.[3] Indeed, their ten guides dubbed it "Philosophers' Camp." William J. Stillman's painting of the group in their camp depicts Emerson as the chief philosopher, occupying the center but aloof and separated from the naturalists, sportsmen, and guides.[4] In celebration of the centennial of the Adirondack trip Paul F. Jamieson retraced the route from Lake George through a complicated system of waterways and carries to Follansby Pond and pointed out some of Emerson's errors—getting the names of mountains wrong, mistaking upstream for downstream and north for south.[5] But Emerson's incompetent woodsmanship, apart from furnishing good-natured amusement, provides the context in which the news of the cable acquires significance, for in the communicative vitality of that electric link between the old and new worlds Emerson reaffirms his own competence as a philosophical messenger.

In the dedication to his fellow travelers, Emerson declares that if he "drew / Their several portraits," the reader would agree that Chaucer and Boccacio "had no such worthy crew," but the verse portraits did not become part of the published poem.[6] If he had focused such attention on the individuals in the party, bringing "The Adirondacs" closer to the Chaucerian model, the resulting generality and comprehensiveness would be a distraction from the more personal odyssey that the poem reveals. The ten scholars are treated as a single entity from which the narrator occasionally emerges, especially during the climactic event. As the ten boats, a scholar and guide in each, move toward the remote destination, "We made our distance wider, boat from boat, / As each would hear the oracle alone." In this deliberate search for oracular voices in the privacy and isolation of the wilderness what Emerson finally hears is not the oracle but news of the cable, his Adirondack sojourn having provided an accommodating setting in which to accept the evolution of human technology. When Emerson claims to be going up the Pere Raquette River, when actually he is going down, he is at least metaphorically correct. Heading toward the source, he eventually finds it in the old world brought to the new, the east to the west by way of the cable.

The first six verse paragraphs follow the party from Lake Champlain to the establishment of the camp at Follansby Pond. Emerson is awed by the unexplored status of this particular wilderness; many of the mountains are "without muse or name," the campers wield "the first axe these echoes ever heard," and they search for the rumored Lake Probability "Long sought, not found." He seems eager to include whatever naturalistic detail he learns along the way:

> The wood was sovran with centennial trees,—
> Oak, cedar, maple, poplar, beech and fir,
> Linden and spruce. In strict society
> Three conifers, white, pitch and Norway pine,
> Five-leaved, three-leaved and two-leaved, grew thereby.
> Our patron pine was fifteen feet in girth,
> The maple eight, beneath its shapely tower.

Fortunately, such botany lessons and strict measurements are not characteristic of "The Adirondacs" as a whole. Emerson is better as an observer than as a conveyor of information:

> Evening drew on; stars peeped through maple-boughs,
> Which o'erhung, like a cloud, our camping fire.
> Decayed millenial trunks, like moonlight flecks,
> Lit with phosphoric crumbs the forest floor.

Simplicity, directness, clarity—for these characteristics the verse-journal form may be given at least partial credit.

The scholar-campers are quickly acclimated by nature and fancy themselves Sioux Indians or boys, not missing their soft beds and heavy duties:

> No door-bell heralded a visitor,
> No courier waits, no letter came or went,
> Nothing was ploughed, or reaped, or bought, or sold;
> The frost might glitter, it would blight no crop,
> The falling rain would spoil no holiday.

Though the campers escape the anxieties of the civilization left behind, the line about there being no courier and no letter is proleptic of the courier who later brings civilization's latest triumph into the wilderness.

One of the themes of the poem is the contribution of work to the human community. The important community roles of the campers are temporarily obliterated when they are made "freemen of the forest laws." In contrast, the guides, who are described in paragraphs seven through ten, bend to vital tasks, their skills overcoming the barriers imposed by the wilderness and exposing the daydream of the scholars:

> Look to yourselves, ye polished gentlemen!
> No city airs or arts pass current here.
> Your rank is all reversed; let men of cloth
> Bow to the stalwart churls in overalls:
> *They* are the doctors of the wilderness,
> And we the low-prized laymen.

As if the polished gentlemen were not humbled enough by the practical competence of the guides, Emerson relates his own tale of ineptitude—trying to shoot a deer from a boat by the light of a jack lantern, aiming "at a square mist," and not only missing but failing even to scare the "astonished" buck.

Once he has paid the guides their respectful due, Emerson elevates the visiting scholars to new status in the eleventh and twelfth paragraphs. The guides have perfected the skills of survival, but the scholars bring alternative varieties of perception, scientific curiosity, and a craving for aesthetic pleasure. The scientists dissect the deer, weigh the trout's brain, identify and classify the flora. Emerson and the others more inclined toward the spiritual dimension of their experience simply enjoy nature's "redundant horn":

> Above, the eagle flew, the osprey screamed,
> The raven croaked, owls hooted, the woodpecker
> Loud hammered, and the heron rose in the swamp.
> As water poured through hollows of the hills
> To feed this wealth of lakes and rivulets,
> So Nature shed all beauty lavishly.

Feeling like lords of the realm and "associates of the sylvan gods" they condemn the "timorous ways" and "big trifles" of the "distant town" and resolve to build a lodge to which they will return with their sons who may learn to be "more adroit" than they.

The poem progresses by means of a series of dramatic modulations. The campers' initial boyish wonder is modified by the guides' practical competence. That in turn is modified by the various modes of perception applied by the representatives of civilized culture. In the next two paragraphs, their sense of being lords of the realm is modified by the "comic misery" of primitive food, hard beds, and relentless insects. Emerson does not allow himself to get too serious about their feeling like "dwellers of the zodiac," and much of the charm of the poem lies in its straightforward acknowledgment of the hardships of camping out. Emerson makes the best of the insects by affirming that they defend "our leafy tabernacle / From bold intrusion of the travelling crowd." But the philosophers are determined intruders and "learn to scatter with a smudge, / Or baffle by a veil, or slight by scorn" the midge, mosquito, and fly.

In the fifteenth verse-paragraph Emerson again modulates the mood, this time by turning inward:

> For who can tell what sudde privacies
> Were sought and found, amid the hue and cry
> Of scholars furloughed from their tasks and let
> Into this Oreads' fended Paradise.

Nature has provided spiritual lessons, but there is a "mystical hint" that wakes "a new sense / Inviting to new knowledge, one with old." This intellectual restlessness is represented by a petulant warbler, an endless seeker after a "bluer light" and "purer sky." And, in the next section, the sky changes, and the pensive mood is overtaken by

> A melancholy better than all mirth.
> Comes the sweet sadness at the retrospect,
> Or at the foresight of obscurer years?

For the first time in the poem Emerson acknowledges mutability: "Suns haste to set, that so remoter lights / Beckon the wanderer to his vaster home."

The elegiac urge that "no day of life may lack romance" is satisfied, for the next day is one to be marked with a "vermilion pencil." Two of the campers bring news from the outside world:

> One held a printed journal waving high
> Caught from a late-arriving traveller,
> Big with great news, and shouted the report
> For which the world had waited, now firm fact,
> Of the wire-cable laid beneath the sea,
> And landed on our coast, and pulsating
> With ductile fire. Loud, exulting cries
> From boat to boat, and to the echoes round,
> Greet the glad miracle.

The delivery of the news reverses the progress of human communication—from cable, to newspaper, to messenger, to exultant voices shouted from boat to boat. The wilderness may invite new knowledge and purify thought, but the cable gives it a "new-found path" supplementing "all trodden ways" and matching "God's equator with a zone of art." And that is Emerson's role: although no woodsman, classifier, or scientist, he is an artful communicator. In 1858 the slavery question and the impending civil war provided urgent need for the cable as Emerson envisioned it. Its messages would

> . . . lift man's public action to a height
> Worthy the enormous cloud of witnesses,
> When linked hemispheres attest his deed.

That year's cable failed, but when a better cable succeeded in 1866, Emerson made a similar observation in his journal: "Besides, the suggestion of an event so exceptional and astounding in the history of human arts is that this instant and pitiless publicity now to be given to every public act must force on the actors a new sensibility to the opinion of mankind, and restrain folly and meanness" (*J*, 10:155–56).[7] His reliance on the moral uses of the new technology anticipates a persistent problem in the age of instant electronic access to world events and answers Thoreau's objection that Maine may have nothing to say to Texas. The appropriate human dimension of technology is discovered by examining the human dimension of the wilderness, for the cable is but lightning mastered, and "cedar grove and cliff and lake should know / This feat of wit, this triumph of mankind."

But even in this triumph Emerson senses "a shade of discontent" that

> . . . corporate sons of trade,
> Perversely borrowing from the shop the tools
> Of science, not from philosophers,
> Had won the brightest laurel of all time.

What starts as a conflict of hand and head—one swift, the other slow, one Prometheus, the other Jove—becomes cooperation and unity like the spirit that binds the campers and their guides in the wilderness. A "free race with front sublime" is needed to "lift humanity," a task too grand for Indians or guides.

> We flee away from cities, but we bring
> The best of cities with us, these learned classifiers,

> Men knowing what they seek, armed eyes of experts.
> We praise the guide, we praise the forest life:
> But will we sacrifice our dear-bought lore
> Of books and arts and trained experiment,
> Or count the Sioux a match for Agassiz?
> Oh no, not we!

What he discovers in his confrontation with the wilderness takes the form of a vigorous and uncompromising defense of progressive culture. If entrepreneurial charlatans provided the cable, what does it matter? The apparent mastery of culture and technology over nature is not only mastery but renewal:

> Mind wakes a new-born giant from her sleep.
> Twirl the old wheels! Time takes fresh start again,
> On for a thousand years of genius more.

After striking camp on a cool August day, Emerson notes that nature

> Permitted on her infinite repose
> Almost a smile to steal to cheer her sons,
> As if one riddle of the Sphinx were guessed.

"Who telleth one of my meanings, / Is master of all I am" asserts the "universal dame" in the earlier poem "The Sphinx," enjoining us to take our "quest through nature." Emerson's quest, recorded in the more colloquial, relaxed, and pleasurable later poem-journal, reaffirms the supremacy of the human spirit and directs his autumnal energies toward the work of communicating that grand assertion.

Emerson as Teacher

MERTON M. SEALTS, JR.

"To every serious mind," Ralph Waldo Emerson liked to say, "Providence sends from time to time five or six or seven teachers" (*W*, 10:101).[1] Emerson was a graduate of Harvard College, in the class of 1821, but there was not a single Harvard professor on the private list of personal benefactors he drew up in 1836, when he was thirty-three (*JMN*, 5:160). And though Emerson was no professor himself, many other men and women of the nineteenth century, in all walks of life and with varying amounts of schooling, looked on him as their teacher and benefactor, known to them either through his published writings or by his appearance on local lecture platforms.

Considering Emerson in the role of teacher is not the customary approach to this "man without a handle," as the elder Henry James once addressed him.[2] Indeed, the problem of what to *call* Emerson has bothered critics and historians ever since his death in 1882. Matthew Arnold, when he came to lecture in America soon afterward, spoke of Emerson as one of the great "voices" heard in England during his youth and affirmed that "snatches of Emerson's strain" had continued to haunt his memory ever since. But though he warmly praised this "friend and aider of those who would live in the spirit" and singled out his *Essays* as "the most important work" written in English prose during the nineteenth century, Arnold found himself finally unable to categorize Emerson or to celebrate his achievement as that of either "a great poet," "a great writer," or even "a great philosophy-maker."[3]

Arnold's difficulty has persisted down to our own day: we too are uncertain how to classify Emerson, how to deal with his poetry, or even in what course or department to consider his *Essays*. As Arnold recognized, they are not exactly *philosophy*. Indeed, few professional philosophers later than William James and George Santayana have looked in a kindly way on Emerson, any more than professional historians of recent years have been hospitable to Henry Adams. Like

Teufelsdröckh in his friend Carlyle's *Sartor Resartus*, Emerson was a "Professor of Things in General"—*Allerley Wissenschaft*[4]—and was rightly suspicious of all compartmentalizing and departmentalizing. Indeed, he looked on specialization as necessary enough, but as a kind of necessary evil, or evil necessity. In an age of increasing specialization his American scholar should be "Man Thinking," speaking for Man to men—as a generalist rather than a specialist or narrow advocate; we might well say that the substance of the Scholar's discourse would be the substance of a liberal education. The Scholar as teacher, having access to what Emerson calls "this original unit, this fountain of power," is one who can help others to "possess" themselves—the phrase turns up again in Emerson and also in Arnold—by returning to the same fountain, the common source accessible to every one of us (*CW*, 1:53).

Here is a clue not only to Arnold's response to Emerson but to Emerson's own admiration for Milton. "Better than any other," he said in an early lecture of 1835, Milton "discharged the office of every great man, namely, to raise the idea of Man"—capital *M*—"in the minds of his contemporaries and of posterity." Milton was thus a master teacher of true humanism, "foremost of all men . . . in the power *to inspire*" (*EL*, 1:148–49), and for Emerson the great business of books and teachers alike was "to inspire" rather than merely to instruct (*CW*, 1:56). "Truly speaking," he said at Harvard in 1838, "it is not instruction, but provocation, that I can receive from another soul" (*CW*, 1:80). The teacher may inspire or provoke; in the last analysis the student, responding actively and not passively, must finally *learn* for himself.

The occasion for Emerson's remark about "provocation" was a memorable one in his early career. He had been invited to address the graduating class at Harvard Divinity School, not by the reverend professors on the faculty but by some of the senior students themselves—young men who had been visiting Concord to talk theology with this sometime clergyman, a Harvard product who had resigned his own pulpit six years before. What Emerson said in his address at Cambridge was provocative enough to shock old-guard Unitarians, men who looked on his liberal ideas about preaching and teaching as "the latest form of infidelity";[5] it would be thirty years before he was again invited to speak at Harvard. Having in effect left the ministry, Emerson would have welcomed a professorship, as he freely admitted in his journal—if not at Harvard then perhaps in one of the "country colleges" like Dartmouth where he sometimes spoke; it would serve as a base of operations, he thought, and challenge him with a stated task (*JMN*, 10:28).[6] But no such post was offered him, and in the absence of other opportunities he continued lecturing and writing, not to enrolled students in college classrooms but to a whole generation of general listeners and readers at home and abroad, inspiring and provoking an ever-widening audience as his reputation steadily grew. Like all teachers of power, moreover, he attracted a broad spectrum of students, not all of whom liked what they read and heard or stayed to finish the course.

In Cambridge and Concord, Emerson was able to teach directly— face to face. "What are you doing now?" he asked young Henry Thoreau of Concord in 1837. "Do you keep a journal?" Thoreau's response was prompt: "So I make my first entry to-day."[7] A Brooklyn newspaper editor, Walt Whitman, first knew Emerson indirectly, through his books: "I was simmering, simmering, simmering," said Whitman of the years before *Leaves of Grass*; "Emerson brought me to a boil."[8] But though Emerson heated up some students like Thoreau and Whitman, others who sampled his offerings were cooled off or turned off. Nathaniel Hawthorne, his neighbor in Concord, was never sympathetic to Emerson's teachings; he wrote with amusement of how the village was "infested" by the "variety of queer, strangely dressed, oddly behaved mortals" who pursued Emerson to his home.[9] Herman Melville, whose New York friends had warned him against Emerson's supposed obscurity, was pleasantly surprised on hearing Emerson lecture in Boston in 1849; "they told me that that night he was unusually plain," he explained. For years to come, both in private jottings and in published works, Melville alternately praised and damned "this Plato who talks thro' his nose."[10] Had Emerson "not been there both to stimulate and exasperate Herman Melville," Perry Miller once remarked, "*Moby-Dick* would have emerged as only another sea-story."[11] Miller no doubt exaggerated, but his basic point was well taken: Emerson could indeed both inspire and provoke—in every sense of both words. "*Emerson was their cow, but not all liked the milk.*" So ran a caption in *Time* magazine some years ago under a panel of photographs: Hawthorne, Thoreau, Whitman, and Melville, in that order, with Emerson gazing benignantly from one side.[12]

It was not only literary figures of the day who responded to Emerson. "His works, other men found, were in many respects diaries of their own which they had not kept," as Professor Lyon Richardson has finely said.[13] A good example is Rutherford B. Hayes, lawyer, soldier, congressman, thrice-elected governor of Ohio, and later president of the United States. As a young attorney in Cincinnati, Hayes helped to arrange for Emerson's first lectures there in 1850. Emerson remained his favorite author; in Hayes's judgment he had "the best mind of our time and race."[14] As Emerson continued distilling his lectures into published essays and his readers in distant places grew increasingly eager to see and hear him, like Hayes in Ohio, his field of operations as itinerant teacher inevitably expanded. By the 1850s he was in steady demand as a lecturer, not only along the eastern seaboard as far south as Baltimore but across the Atlantic to England and Scotland in 1847–48 and also beyond the Hudson into what was then "the West." The vogue of the popular lecturer and the growth of the lyceum movement in the United States during the second quarter of the nineteenth century reflected the prevalent desire for self-improvement and the widespread interest in adult education that accompanied westward expansion and growing national prosperity. By the 1860s Emerson was making annual western tours: to Ohio, Indiana, and Illinois; to Michigan and Wisconsin; and eventually across the Mississippi to Iowa and Minnesota. In 1868 James Russell Lowell called him "the most steadily attractive lecturer in America."[15]

Emerson traveled West by train, stage, carriage, and boat, often under the most trying conditions; during one cold winter he crossed the frozen Mississippi four times on foot. When he made his first trip to Ohio in 1850 for his engagement in Cincinnati, he was en route by Lake Erie steamer to Sandusky when the vessel caught fire off Cleveland, where it made port safely in time for local Emersonians to assemble for an unscheduled lecture he was persuaded to give.[16] The lecture in Cleveland was free; by the 1860s the going rate for a one-night stand in the larger western cities had risen to $50. Thus Emerson's contemporary Thomas Starr King, when asked what he lectured for, answered: "FAME—Fifty and My Expenses."[17] Emerson himself wrote of lecturing in the West as an annual wager: " 'I'll bet you fifty dollars a day that you will not leave your library, and wade and ride and run and suffer all manner of indignities and stand up for an hour each night reading in a hall'; and I answered, 'I'll bet I will.' I do it and win the $900" (*J*, 10:91–92).[18] Early in January of 1856, after a week of temperatures "varying from 20 to 30 degrees below zero," he observed that the climate and people of the West "are a new test for the wares of a man of letters. . . . At the lyceum, the stout Illinoian, after a short trial, walks out of the hall. The Committee tell you that the people want a hearty laugh, and [those] who give them that, are heard with joy. . . . These are the new conditions to which I must conform. . . . And Shakspeare, or Franklin, or Aesop coming to Illinois, would say, I must give my wisdom a comic form, instead of tragics or elegiacs" (*JMN*, 14:27–28). Emerson's words seem prophetic of Mark Twain, who in the late 1850s, as Samuel L. Clemens of Missouri, was learning to be a riverboat pilot on the Mississippi, his other vocation as lecturer and writer being still some years before him.

In the course of a long career Emerson filled nearly fifteen hundred lecture engagements in twenty-two states and Canada plus his lectures in England and Scotland. Some cities and towns brought him back repeatedly. He spoke on many subjects, from popular science, biography, and literature in the early 1830s to an address on Carlyle in 1881, the year before his death. During the 1850s, when he appeared most often, he was giving more than fifty lectures every winter; in the 1860s both his platform reputation and his fees reached their highest peak. Apart from local newspaper reviews, which varied widely in tone, some of the best testimony about what it was like to hear Emerson speak comes from younger contemporaries who attended his lectures repeatedly from their student days into middle age—men of letters such as Lowell, George William Curtis, and E. P. Whipple. With such younger listeners in the early years, if not with their elders or the authorities of Harvard, Emerson was immediately popular; for Lowell and his generation he became "our favorite teacher."[19] An older man once told Curtis that though *he* couldn't understand "Mr. Emerson," "my daughters do."[20] Emerson himself quickly recognized the difference in generations. He remembered a question his uncle Samuel Ripley had asked him years before, when as a boy of thirteen he had done his first actual teaching in his uncle's school: "How is it, Ralph, that all the boys dislike you & quarrel with you, whilst the grown people are fond of you?" "Now am I thirty six," Emerson reflected in the year after the Divinity School affair, "and the fact is reversed,—the old people suspect & dislike me, & the young love me" (*JMN*, 7:253).

What the young people liked and understood in their teacher was less the explicit message than the spirit of the man who spoke it; as Lowell explained, "We do not go to hear what Emerson says so much as to hear Emerson."[21] Certainly they did not go for cheap popularization or sidewinding oratory, though both were common enough at a time when public speakers customarily performed with all stops out. Emerson never spoke extemporaneously or even from notes; he invariably read from a prepared manuscript, though he had a disconcerting habit of shuffling his pages about while he was talking. His delivery was simple and even conversational; when speaking he was "apt to hesitate in the course of a sentence," according to the senior Oliver Wendell Holmes, as though "picking his way through his vocabulary, to get at the best expression of his thought."[22] "There was no rhetoric, no gesture. . . no dramatic familiarity and action," said Curtis, "but the manner was self-respectful and courteous to the audience, and the tone supremely just and sincere."[23]

Moncure Conway agreed: Emerson depended not on "tricks of any kind" but rather on "clearness of thought and simplicity of statement."[24] Henry James the elder emphasized his modesty and grace on the platform, recalling

his deferential entrance upon the scene, his look of inquiry at the desk and the chair, his resolute rummaging among his embarrassed papers, the air of sudden recollection with which he would plunge into his pockets for what he must have known had never been put there, for his uncertainty and irresolution as he rose to speak, his deep, relieved inspiration as he got well from under the burning-glass of his auditors' eyes, and addressed himself at length to their docile ears instead. . . . And then when he looked over the heads of his audience into the dim mysterious distance, and his weird monotone began to reverberate in your bosom's depths, and his words flowed on, now with a river's volume, grand, majestic, free, and anon diminished themselves to the fitful cadence of a brook . . . and you saw the clear eye eloquent with nature's purity, and beheld the musing countenance turned within, as it were, and hearkening to the rumour of a far-off but on-coming world: how intensely personal, how exquisitely characteristic, it all was![25]

Audiences everywhere were particularly struck with Emerson's voice, which Holmes described as "never loud, never shrill, but singularly penetrating."[26] It had "a strange power," said E. P. Whipple, "which affected me more than any other voice I ever heard on the stage or on the platform."[27] But however entranced by Emerson's way of speaking, few of his auditors followed everything they had listened to or even agreed with what they thought he had said. Hawthorne's son Julian recalls leaving the lecture room in Concord one evening when he overheard "Prescott, the grocer, say to Jonas Hastings, the shoemaker, 'Did you get that about the Oversoul?' . . . Jonas . . . shook his head: 'No use wondering what he means; we know he's giving us the best there is.' "[28] At the other end of the spectrum there was downright hostility, particularly when Emerson ventured outside New England. In Wisconsin, for example, the *Kenosha Democrat* stigmatized him in 1860 as "an infidel—an abolitionist—a monarchist—all these, though he talk as musically as any dying swan."[29] Some unenthusiastic listeners, like the "stout Illinoian" Emerson himself mentioned, simply walked out of the hall. Those who stayed enjoyed Emerson's quiet humor, more characteristic of his lectures than of his published essays. They especially liked the illustrative anecdotes "that sparkled for a moment upon the surface of his talk," as Curtis remarked; "and some sat inspired with unknown resolves, soaring upon lofty hopes."[30] By the 1860s, when he had become something of an institution, Lowell felt that younger members of the audience were taking him for granted, failing to realize what they owed to him; their elders, Lowell said, recognized "how much the country's intellectual emancipation was due to the stimulus of his teaching and example."[31] Curtis, who was a successful lecturer himself, put the same idea somewhat differently. Emerson, he said, "was never exactly popular, but always gave a tone and flavor to the whole lyceum course. . . . 'We can have him once in three or four seasons,' said the committees. But really they had him all the time without knowing it. He was the philosopher Proteus, and he spoke through all the more popular mouths. . . . They were . . . the middle-men between him and the public. They watered the nectar, and made it easy to drink."[32]

Like all teachers, especially those who teach other teachers, Emerson thus reached students even at second or third hand. "A teacher affects eternity," said Henry Adams; "he can never tell where his influence stops."[33] The thought is disturbing, since "when?" and "how?" and "by what channels?" and "to what effect?" are questions difficult to answer on any chart or evaluation, however well intentioned. Doubtless Emerson himself, who thought a discourse should have some edge to it, was not too troubled when the response of listeners and readers was not unanimously favorable, though the outburst occasioned by the Divinity School Address proved more than he had quite bargained for. Religious conservatives then and now have protested against his liberal theology. When he lectured in Scotland in 1848 he was accused of being a pantheist.[34] At Columbus, Ohio, in 1867, a local Presbyterian minister preached against his appearance there, saying that "he had not expected to live to see the time when a Presbyterian pulpit would be disgraced by Ralph Waldo Emerson lecturing from it."[35] Among twentieth-century critics, Yvor Winters called Emerson and the transcendentalists "moral parasites upon a Christian doctrine which they were endeavoring to destroy,"[36] and Randall Stewart stigmatized him as "the arch-heretic of American literature."[37] On the other extreme, the obvious vestiges of clericalism in Emerson have always offended the secular-minded. D. H. Lawrence, for example, admired "Emerson's real courage," but disliked the limitations of his idealism. In Lawrence's words, "all those gorgeous inrushes of exaltation and spiritual energy which made Emerson a great man, now make us sick,"[38] and some contemporary readers agree.

There has been a similar difference of opinion about Emerson's political and social views, which have also offended the extreme left and the extreme right of two centuries. In the 1840s he inclined toward the principles of what he called "the movement party" (*W*, 3:263) rather than toward the conservatism of "the establishment" (*CW*, 1:190, 195), but he was never a partisan in the conventional sense. His increasing antipathy to slavery led him to support Free-Soil candidates and later to gravitate toward the new Republican party, though for a long time he resisted identification with the Abolitionist movement. But believing as he did that slavery was flatly wrong and seeing its evil increasingly compounded by abridgment of the right of free speech and coercion of Northern freemen as well as of Southern slaves, he ultimately found himself endorsing even John Brown's use of violence in retaliation. And so during the 1850s the peace-loving teacher became a militant activist, remaining so for the duration of the Civil War. If his moral activism seems inconsistent with his vocational role, it was not altogether out of character for a man who had insisted in his first published book that "The moral law lies at the centre of nature and radiates to the circumference" (*CW*, 1:26). To condone slavery was unnatural and immoral, a denial of human worth and dignity and freedom; he *must* stand up and be counted with the opposition. "I divide men as aspirants & desperants," he once told Holmes. "A scholar need not be cynical to feel that the vast multitude are almost on all fours; that the rich always vote after their fears; that cities churches colleges all go for the quadruped interest, and it is against this coalition that the pathetically small minority of disengaged or thinking men stand for the ideal right, for man as he should be, & . . . for the right of every other as for his own" (*L*, 5:17).

However one may judge Emerson's reluctant foray into public affairs,[39] this prolonged engagement with moral issues at considerable cost to his own peace and prosperity illustrates what he liked to call "the scholar's courage" (*JMN*, 10:28), a form of his cardinal principle of self-reliance. In David Riesman's phrase, he was an *inner-directed* man, living from within. What he regarded as "the moral law of human nature" he had enunciated as early as 1833, when he was thirty: "A man contains all that is needful to his government within himself. He is made a law unto himself. All real good or evil that can befal him must be from himself. He only can do himself any good or any harm. . . . The purpose of life seems to be to acquaint a man with himself. . . . The highest revelation is that God is in every man" (*JMN*, 4:84).

On this moral and religious basis Emerson deplored imitation of any model however fine and refused conformity to all wholly external patterns, rituals, creeds, sects, parties, precedents, curricula, or institutions of any kind, including churches, colleges, and governments. The law he followed, though wholly internal, was rigorous; "If any one imagines that this law is lax," as he said in "Self-Reliance," "let him keep its commandment one day" (*CW*, 2:42). When a man can look within and "read God directly," as "The American Scholar" has it, the hour is too precious for secondhand readings (*CW*, 1:57). On this same basis, looking back with a measure of detachment on the Divinity School controversy—that "storm in our washbowl," as he called it (*CEC*, p. 196), he could write in 1840 that "In all my lectures I have taught one doctrine, namely, the infinitude of the private man. This, the people accept readily enough, & even with loud commendation, as long as I call the lecture, Art; or Politics; or Literature; or the Household; but the moment I call it Religion,—they are shocked, though it be only the application of the same truth which they receive everywhere else, to a new class of facts" (*JMN*, 7:342).

The "one doctrine" that Emerson specifies lay at the vital center of his teaching over a lifetime, whether the subject addressed was religion, morality, or teaching itself. His conception of "the private man" was essentially religious, idealistic, and optimistic. Where "desperants" such as his Puritan forebears and his less sanguine contemporaries stressed the finite limitations of humanity, as in the fiction of Hawthorne and Melville, his own abiding impulse, like that of Thoreau and Whitman, was to emphasize mankind's infinite potential, though the experience of his middle years brought him to an increasing realization of the limiting power of circumstance. By temperament Emerson was an idealist, an "aspirant." But as his journals reveal, he was forever being reminded of that "yawning gulf" that stretches "between the ambition of man and his power of performance," and it is this disparity between desire and capacity that for him "makes the tragedy of all souls" (*W*, 4:183), a tragedy all too frequently compounded by distorted aims and wasted forces.

If the purpose of life, as Emerson thought, was "to acquaint a man with himself," the purpose of a teacher should be to foster one's full realization, in every sense, of his or her own worth and potential. This is the burden of the lectures, addresses, and essays in which Emerson touches in some way on learning and teaching: the Address on Education and "The American Scholar" of 1837, the Divinity School Address and "Literary Ethics" of 1838, the lecture on "Education" of 1840, and such essays of 1841 and 1844 as "Self-Reliance," "Spiritual Laws," "The Over-Soul," "Intellect," and "The Poet," this last with its Emersonian emphasis on the human need for self-expression—"It is in me, and shall out" (*W*, 3:40)—that not only brought Walt Whitman to a boil but also anticipated the teachings of John Dewey. Emerson's thinking about education, being of a piece with his general ideas, was essentially religious in character, though it has obvious secular implications and applications. To educate means *to draw out*; Emerson complained that "We do not believe in a power of Education. We do not think we can call out God in man and we do not try" (*EL*, 3:290). His own basic objective, to "call out God in man," was not inherently different from that of the builders of medieval universities or nineteenth-century church-related colleges. Like them, he believed that religion and learning spring from a common source. He delighted to celebrate that source, that "original unit" and "fountain of power," as he called it in "The American Scholar," common to all individuals and linking them both with "Man"—again, capital *M*—and also with nature.

Every human being, Emerson believed, stands "in need of expression," students and teachers included: "In love, in art, in avarice, in politics, in labor, in games, we study to utter our painful secret" (*W*, 3:5). It is no different in teaching, though what a teacher expresses, he felt, is less what he *knows* than what he *is*. For him there were two kinds of teachers: those who "speak *from within*," and therefore teach with firsthand knowledge and authority; and those who speak only "*from without*, as spectators merely," on the basis of secondhand evidence (*W*, 2:170). For him, only the former—Emerson's "true scholars"—deserve the name of teacher. Like Alfred North Whitehead in our own century, Emerson protested against dead knowledge—what Whitehead in *The Aims of Education* (1929) would call "inert ideas."[40] "Life, authentic life, you must have," Emerson insisted, "or you can teach nothing" (*JMN*, 7:27).[41] If life and power are present within, they will manifest themselves outwardly, whether by our conscious intention or otherwise. "That which we are, we shall teach," he wrote, "not voluntarily but involuntarily. . . . Character teaches over our head" (*CW*, 2:169). "If a teacher have any opinion which he wishes to conceal, his pupils will become as fully indoctrinated into that as into any which he publishes"

(*CW*, 2:85). Again: "The man may teach by doing, and not otherwise. If he can communicate himself he can teach, but not by words. He teaches who gives, and he learns who receives" (*CW*, 2:88).

Since for Emerson a student's self-realization meant self-reliance, he reminded himself of "the cardinal virtue of a teacher" exemplified by Socrates: "to protect the pupil from his own influence" (*JMN*, 10:471). Neither teachers nor parents, he cautioned, should try to make duplicates of themselves. " 'Get off that child!' he said in a lecture; 'One is enough.' "[42] His friend Moncure Conway, writing of Emerson's powerful stimulation of a variety of writers differing in both their aim and their style, rightly observed that "they who came to his fontless baptism were never made Emersonians."[43] His words would have pleased Emerson himself, who in his later years remarked in his journal, "I have been writing and speaking what were once called novelties, for twenty-five or thirty years, and have not now one disciple. Why? Not that what I said was not true; not that it has not found intelligent receivers; but because it did not go from any wish in me to bring men to me, but to themselves. I delight in driving them from me. . . . This is my boast that I have no school follower. I should account it a measure of the impurity of insight, if it did not create independence" (*J*, 9:188–89).

Independence, self-reliance, self-knowledge, self-expression, self-fulfillment—these were the "novelties" that Emerson taught as writer and lecturer, whatever his subjects and courses. The lesson was heard and repeated. "I would not have any one adopt *my* mode of living on any account," wrote one of his alumni, Henry Thoreau, in *Walden*. "I desire that there may be as many different persons in the world as possible; but I would have each one be very careful to find out and pursue *his own* way."[44] "Not I, not any one else can travel that road for you," Walt Whitman responded in *Leaves of Grass*, "You must travel it for yourself."[45] Even Melville chimed in, though with a note of warning, in *Moby-Dick*: "the only mode in which you can derive even a tolerable idea of [the whale's] living contour, is by going a whaling yourself; but by so doing, you run no small risk of being eternally stove and sunk by him."[46] So Emerson, by recurrent challenge and by cumulative example, provoked and inspired and *educated* his students—and in turn his students' students—to walk on their own feet, to work with their own hands, to speak their own minds, just as every great teacher invariably does. Indeed he is no teacher unless, like Emerson, he truly creates independence.

Notes
Index

Notes

Preface

1. The high standards of excellence set by Ralph L. Rusk in his edition of Emerson's letters in 1939 have been followed in subsequent editions of Emerson's early lectures (1959–72), journals and miscellaneous notebooks (1960–present), correspondence with Carlyle (1964), and published writings (1971–present).
2. Future scholars should be well served by Eleanor M. Tilton's edition of Emerson's letters, the publication of Emerson's additional journals and notebooks under the direction of Ralph H. Orth, the editing of Emerson's lectures continued by James H. Justus and Wallace E. Williams, the continued publication of Emerson's works under the direction of Joseph Slater and Douglas Wilson, the descriptive bibliography of Emerson's writings by Joel Myerson, and the annotated secondary bibliography of writings about Emerson by Robert E. Burkholder and Myerson.

The Moonless Night: Emerson's Crisis of Health, 1825–1827

1. Oliver Wendell Holmes, *Ralph Waldo Emerson* (Boston: Houghton, Mifflin, 1884), p. 53.
2. See her manuscript letters at the Houghton Library, Harvard University. For a discussion of Mary Moody Emerson's life and influence on her nephew's literary style, see my "Emerson and the Angel of Midnight: The Legacy of Mary Moody Emerson," *Mothering the Mind: Twelve Studies of Writers and Their Silent Partners*, ed. Ruth Perry and Martine Brownley (Athens: Univ. of Georgia Press, forthcoming). See also my "Emerson and 'The Magician': An Early Prose Fantasy," *American Transcendental Quarterly*, no. 31 (Summer 1976), supplement, pp. 13–18, which deals with Mary's role in her nephew's life and his tale "Uilsa"; some aspects of this article are revalued in my 1982 essay. A more extensive discussion of their relationship will appear in the book I am writing on "The Roots of Prophecy: Emerson's Early Life and Writings."
3. James Thacher, *American Modern Practice: Or a Simple Method of Prevention and Cure of Diseases* (Boston: E. Read, 1817), pp. 436–37.
4. David Greene Haskins, *Ralph Waldo Emerson: His Maternal Ancestors* (Boston: Cupples, Upham, 1887), p. 71.

5. James Elliot Cabot, *A Memoir of Ralph Waldo Emerson* (Boston: Houghton, Mifflin, 1887), 1:35.
6. This was a recurrent issue in many letters to her nephews; see, for example, bMS Am 1280.226.816, Houghton Library, Harvard University.
7. On 3 January 1817, Reynolds wrote to his former teacher, John Collins Warren: "Mr. Cooper has also taken Mr. Travers into partnership with him in his surgical lectures. He has been giving us a full course of lectures on ye diseases of the eye, of which he has a very extensive opportunity of becoming acquainted with, at the London Eye Infirmary. These render the courses more valuable than they were before" (see J. Collins Warren, "Surgery in London at the Beginning of the Nineteenth Century," *Boston Medical and Surgical Journal* 162 no. 23 [9 June 1910]: 767–73 [p. 23 in the offprint pamphlet]).
8. Alvin A. Hubbell, *The Development of Ophthalmology in America: 1800 to 1870* (Chicago: Keener, 1908), p. 70.
9. I am indebted to Mr. Charles Snyder, Curator of Rare Books, Librarian of the Massachusetts Eye and Ear Infirmary, and the author of a manuscript study of Reynolds, for sharing his knowledge with me.
10. Travers's book describes only two types of intraocular surgery: cataract removal and the artifical pupil or iridectomy. A record from a later period at the leading infirmary where Travers had practiced still divided all eye surgery into the two operations for cataract and the artificial pupil. Other intraocular procedures began to develop after 1844 (see Benjamin Travers, *A Synopsis of Diseases of the Eye*, 3d ed. [London: Longmans, 1824], pp. 318–88; E. Treacher Collins, *The History of the Moorfields Hospital* [London: Lewis, 1929], p. 74).
11. George Frick, *A Treatise on the Diseases of the Eye . . . Including the Doctrine and Practice of Surgeons*, ed. Richard Welbank (London: J. Anderson, 1826), pp. 63–71; J. V. Solomon, *Tension of the Eyeball: Glaucoma* (London: Churchill, 1865), quoted in Daniel M. Albert and Nancy Robinson, "James Wardrop: A Brief Review of His Life and Contributions," *Transactions of the Ophthalmological Societies of the United Kingdom* 94 (1974): 907.
12. James Wardrop, "On the Effects of Evacuating the Aqueous Humor in Inflammation of the Eyes, and in Some Diseases of the Cornea," *Medico-Chirurgical Transactions* 4 (1813): 142–87; see also his "Account of the Rheumatic Inflammation of the Eye with Observations on the Treatment of the Disease," *Medico-Chirurgical Transactions* 10 (1819): 1–5.
13. Albert and Robinson, "James Wardrop," p. 896.
14. Wardrop, "Evacuating the Aqueous Humor," pp. 145–46, 153–54, 162–87.
15. Drs. McGregor and Mueller alone had successfully employed the procedure twenty-three and eighteen times, respectively (*A Treatise on the Diseases of the Eye* [London: J. Churchill, 1833], pp. 237–38, 280–82). An older authority who still preferred bleeding as sufficient remedy was William Mackenzie, *A Practical Treatise on the Diseases of the Eye* (Boston, 1833), pp. 337–42.
16. Wardrop, "Evacuating the Aqueous Humor," p. 158; Wardrop, "Account of the Rhuematic Inflammation," pp. 11, 12.
17. C. Snyder, personal communication.
18. *The American Encyclopedia and Dictionary of Ophthalmology* (Chicago:

Cleveland Press, 1919) gives *ophthalmia rheumatica* only as an archaic sublisting of the disused "rheumatism"; *ophthalmia rheumatica* does not appear in the *National Medical Dictionary* (1890) or in the *Dictionary of Medical Science* (1895), although both include rheumatism.

19. Wardrop, "Account of the Rheumatic Inflammation," pp. 6, 7, 8.
20. Edward Reynolds, *Hints to Students on the Use of the Eyes* (Edinburgh: Clark, 1835), pp. 27, 28.
21. I am grateful to Donald Stern, M.D., of the Harvard Medical School, for reading the manuscript and for discussion of this and other points.
22. Frederick Harold Theodore and Abraham Schlossman, *Ocular Allergy* (Baltimore: Williams and Wilkins, 1958), pp. 13, 327.
23. Michael J. Hogan and Lorenz E. Zimmerman, *Ophthalmic Pathology: An Atlas and Textbook*, 2d ed. (Philadelphia: Saunders, 1962), pp. 373–74; Paul B. Beeson and Walsh McDermott, *Textbook of Medicine*, 14th ed. (Philadelphia: Saunders, 1975), pp. 371–73; Theodore and Schlossman, *Ocular Allergy*, pp. 15, 340. Information on rheumatic fever comes from personal communication with Dr. Martin Wohl.
24. Hogan and Zimmerman, *Ophthalmic Pathology*, pp. 373–74.
25. Theodore and Schlossman, *Ocular Allergy*, p. 341.
26. Ellen Tucker Emerson, in MS Am 1280.227, Houghton Library, Harvard University; *JMN*, 4:228; and *Life*, p. 162 n.
27. Theodore B. Bayles, "Psychogenic Factors in Rheumatic Diseases," *Arthritis and Allied Conditions*, ed. Joseph L. Hollander and D. J. McCarty, 8th ed. (Philadelphia: Lea and Febinger, 1972), pp. 230 et passim.
28. A differential diagnosis suggested by Dr. Martin Wohl is ankylosing spondylitis, a form of arthritis which begins normally in the lower back or sacroiliac, attacks mainly young men, may, like tuberculosis, go into remission, and is also like tuberculosis in being associated with uveitis. Ankylosing spondylitis, however, also produces fusion of the joints, and we have no evidence of that or of back trouble. See also *Tuberculosis: A Treatise by American Authors on Its Etiology, Frequency, Semeiology, Diagnosis, Prognosis, Prevention and Treatment*, ed. Arnold C. Klebs (New York: Appleton, 1909), pp. 735, 745. For the "striking" tendency of joint tuberculosis to cure itself, see William Osler, *Principles and Practice of Medicine* (New York: Appleton, 1892), pp. 194, 246; W. Watson Cheyne, *Tuberculous Diseases of Bones and Joints*, 2d ed. (London: Oxford Univ. Press, 1911), pp. 120–22, 146, 169. Cheyne also stresses the body's tendency to resist this disease. See also N. Stenn, *Tuberculosis of Bones and Joints*, 3d ed. (London: Oxford Univ. Press, 1932), pp. 2–3, 53, 55, 61, 72, 74–75, 102; Glenn M. Clark, "Tuberculous Arthritis," *Arthritis*, ed. Hollander and McCarty, pp. 1242–54; Metro A. Ogryzlo, "Ankylosing Spondylitis," *Arthritis*, ed. Hollander and McCarty, pp. 699–723. I am indebted to Dr. Martin Wohl of the Harvard University Health Services, Dr. Mark D. Altschule, president of the Boston Medical Library, Professor Barbara G. Rosenkrantz of the Departments of Public Health and the History of Science of Harvard University, and Dr. Donald Stern for valuable discussions, and to Drs. Rosenkrantz and Stern for also reading the manuscript. Any errors of course are my own.

29. Holmes, *Emerson*, p. 53.
30. *The Works of Oliver Wendell Holmes* (Boston: Houghton, Mifflin, n.d.), 9:294.
31. Personal communication with Mark D. Altschule, M.D.
32. Samuel George Morton, *Illustrations of Pulmonary Consumption* (Philadelphia: Key & Biddle, 1834), p. 10; see also *Tuberculosis*, ed. Klebs, p. 807.
33. Nor of twentieth-century medicine either. Dr. Lewis Moorman diagnosed Emerson as tuberculous in a medical article in 1945, referring in turn to similiar findings by Arthur C. Jacobson in 1926. Moorman, whose article was not noticed by literary scholars, did not discuss the relation of tuberculosis to Emerson's other diseases or problems, and damaged his case by a naïve equation of his "genius" with what he called the ecstatic workings of the toxins of the tubercle bacillus. I would note, however, that every medical practitioner with whom I have consulted concurs with the diagnosis of tuberculosis offered here (Moorman, "Tuberculosis and Genius," *Bulletin of the History of Medicine* 18 [Nov. 1945]: 361–70; Jacobson, *Genius: Some Revaluations* [New York: Greenberg, 1926]).
34. Morton, *Pulmonary Consumption*, pp. 47–48, 145, 167–68; Thacher, *American Modern Practice*, p. 432; Francis Hopkins Ramadge, *Consumption Curable* (London: Longman, 1834), pp. 1–2, chaps. 3–4.
35. Osler, *Principles and Practice of Medicine*, p. 249.
36. Thacher, *American Modern Practice*, p. 423.
37. Morton, *Pulmonary Consumption*, p. 88.
38. Osler, *Principles and Practice of Medicine*, p. 204.
39. P. C. A. Louis, *Researches on Phthisis*, 2d ed., trans. W. H. Walshe (London, 1844), p. 472. The first edition was dated 1825.
40. Ramadge, *Consumption Curable*, pp. 86 ff; Thacher, *American Modern Practice*, pp. 436–37.
41. Morton, *Pulmonary Consumption*, pp. 164, 45–50.
42. Ibid., pp. 55–56.
43. Ramadge, *Consumption Curable*, pp. vi, 22–26.
44. Morton, *Pulmonary Consumption*, p. 64.
45. Edward Smith, *Consumption* (London: Walton & Maberly, 1862), p. 285.
46. W. W. Hall, *Consumption* (New York: Redfield, 1857), p. 41.
47. Morton, *Pulmonary Consumption*, p. 46.
48. Personal communication with Professor B. G. Rosenkrantz; I am indebted also to Professor Taylor Stoehr for a helpful discussion of Waldo's relation to William.
49. *Tuberculosis*, ed. Klebs, p. 409.
50. Emerson's interest in Hume is best traced in the running commentary and debate between himself and his aunt which appears in the manuscript letters of Mary Moody Emerson at the Houghton Library, Harvard University, in the 1909–14 edition of the *Journals*, which contains significant letters not reprinted by Rusk in the 1939 *Letters*, and in his frequent comments on Hume in *JMN*, vols. 1–3 et passim.
51. See Evelyn Barish, "The Birth of Merlin: Emerson, Magic, and Death," *CUNY English Studies I* (New York: AMS Press, forthcoming).
52. Letter to Overbeck, 12 Nov. 1887, quoted by Karl Jaspers, *Nietzsche: An*

Introduction to the Understanding of His Philosophical Activity, trans. C. F. Wallraff and F. J. Schmitz (Tucson: Univ. of Arizona Press, 1965), pp. 112–13.

53. Research for this paper was assisted by grants from the National Endowment for the Humanities and the Research Foundation of the City University of New York.

"Christ Crucified": Christology, Identity, and Emerson's Sermon No. 5

1. In the 1820s Emerson emphasizes moral growth by learning from and participating in history. Often during this period, however, as Emerson seeks to define heroism and his own personality, he depicts the viciousness of tyrants and mobs who threaten the existence of the saint and the rebel. Gustaaf Van Cromphout shows that in the 1830s Emerson's "hero" is, in the "positive" sense, "antithetical" to society and thus discovers/makes history; in the 1840s, as hero and society become more compatible, "Emerson's Representative Men do not share his earlier heroes' independence from history." See "Emerson and the Dialectics of History," *PMLA* 91 (Jan. 1976): 55, 57–58.

2. Lewis P. Simpson presents the development of Emerson's thought against a backdrop of "poverty, illness, and death" and of "agonizing doubts about his personality," in "The Crisis of Alienation in Emerson's Early Thought," *Emerson's Relevance Today*, ed. Eric W. Carlson and J. Lasley Dameron (Hartford: Transcendental Books, 1971), p. 36. Joel Porte has recently interpreted Emerson's search to become a "great man" in Eriksonian terms in *Representative Man: Ralph Waldo Emerson in His Time* (New York: Oxford Univ. Press, 1979).

3. The classic essay is Henry Nash Smith, "Emerson's Problem of Vocation: A Note on 'The American Scholar,' " *New England Quarterly* 12 (Mar. 1939): 52–67.

4. Emerson's lifelong reluctance to give up completely on Christianity can be traced to the fact that, as David Robinson points out, "He had largely identified Christianity with morality in his early years." See "Emerson's Natural Theology and the Paris Naturalists," *Journal of the History of Ideas* 41 (Jan.–Mar. 1980): 75.

5. *Literary Transcendentalism: Style and Vision in the American Renaissance* (Ithaca: Cornell Univ. Press, 1973), chap. 4.

6. In view of Emerson's preoccupations with the threatening "mob" and his failure to win renown, Richard Lebeaux's observations on the young Thoreau apply in some degree to young Emerson's vision of militant Christianity: "Thoreau's 'military nature' may partly be attributed to his need to keep at a distance those many people by whom he felt threatened"; "military imagery gave Thoreau an opportunity to express hostility and aggressiveness, and to feel that he was 'manly' " (*Young Man Thoreau* [Amherst: Univ. of Massachusetts Press, 1977], p. 122).

7. Emerson's southern journey constituted a kind of Eriksonian "moratorium," an interval that permitted delay of further preaching duties and a chance to

reflect on the tangle of personal, theological, and vocational issues that fill the early journals. Richard Lebeaux argues that the postponement of commitment to a variety of American institutions and values was particularly appealing to the transcendentalists. For the "moratorium" afforded Thoreau by the two-years' stay at Walden Pond, see *Young Man Thoreau*. See also Lebeaux's "Emerson's Young Adulthood: From Patienthood to Patiencehood," *ESQ: A Journal of the American Renaissance* 25 (4th Quarter 1979): 203–10.

8. Quotation from Sermon No. 5, bMS Am 1280.215, is by permission of the Houghton Library, Harvard University. I have referred to manuscript pages by numbering sequentially from the first leaf recto, ignoring the numerals written earlier in a hand other than Emerson's.

9. Emerson's method of composing Sermon No. 5 yields added glimpses of autobiographical and theological significance. The editors of vol. 3 of *JMN* observe that "although Emerson wrote down many an idea for a sermon in his journals, as time went on he wrote the sermons independently," and that the sermons are "different versions of his journals—structured, more formal, prepared for a live audience, but still the embodiment of what he was thinking from day to day" (p. ix). Sermon No. 5 includes two long journal entries and a short one composed over a seven-month period; the longer passages were carefully revised and significantly expanded when adapted to the sermon. The remaining two-thirds of the sermon was written just before it was first delivered. The composition suggests, then, a fusion of relatively spontaneous journal entries and substantial "independent" material in the final product.

10. Emerson's condescending criticism of middle-class values of improvement, progress, and materialism, while it ostensibly yearns for a kind of Calvinist moral toughness, suggests by its generality the kind of vague sentimentalism Ann Douglas shows evolved in the nineteenth century in a ministry bereft of real power and needing to redefine its sphere of authority. See *The Feminization of American Culture* (New York: Alfred A. Knopf, 1977).

11. *Literary Transcendentalism*, p. 109.

12. *William Ellery Channing: Unitarian Christianity and Other Essays*, ed. Irving H. Bartlett (New York: Bobbs-Merrill, 1957), p. 74.

13. Because Emerson had "committed" himself to a respectable career, one cannot strictly term the period of his ministry a "moratorium." But it is wrong to view the period of Emerson's ministry as a time of self-repression. While Emerson never rested easy with his vocation, Unitarian theology was flexible enough that he never had to really commit himself to firm doctrinal positions; it is significant that before he opted for the freedom of the European trip in December 1832, he forced the issue of the Lord's Supper on a congregation willing to compromise to avoid contention (*Life*, pp. 160–61).

   In ways crucial to his later vision and artistic power, the ministry, as no other occupation could have, afforded Emerson the chance to define his values and self-image and to discover his voice. Indeed, Emerson's version of transcendentalism *evolved* from his experience as a minister within the tradition of New England Puritanism. See my "Emerson and Antinomianism: The Legacy of the Sermons," *American Literature* 50 (Nov. 1978): 369–97.

14. Channing's Jesus also "looked forward to the accomplishment of his design"; "this calm, unshaken anticipation of distant and unbounded triumphs are

remarkable traits, throwing a tender and solemn grandeur over our Lord, and wholly inexplicable by human principles or by the circumstances in which he was placed" (*Unitarian Christianity and Other Essays*, p. 75).

15. Joel Porte rightly calls attention to the "severity" of expression in this journal entry, a severity "perhaps surprising" to the reader acquainted only with the great essays (*Representative Man*, p. 169). Sermon No. 5, however, is ultimately less important as a revelation of Emerson's gloomy private assessment of human nature than for the triumphant depiction of Jesus, with whose final victory Emerson clearly identifies.

16. David Porter comments on the importance of personae in Emerson's sermons and later, in *Emerson and Literary Change* (Cambridge, Mass.: Harvard Univ. Press, 1978), pp. 189–205.

17. Arthur C. McGiffert, Jr., edits Sermon No. 76, "The Authority of Jesus," in *YES* (pp. 90–98), and cites a variety of references to Jesus in other Emerson sermons (pp. 233–35).

18. *Representative Man*, p. 76.

19. David Robinson has kindly provided me with a typescript chapter of his book-length study which fully traces the ways in which Emerson absorbed Jesus into broader patterns of "moral inspiration" and "self-culture." I want to thank Professor Robinson for his help with this paper.

20. Carol Johnston discusses the address as a jeremiad in "The Underlying Structure of the Divinity School Address: Emerson as Jeremiah," *Studies in the American Renaissance 1980*, ed. Joel Myerson (Boston: Twayne, 1980), pp. 41–49.

Emerson's Foreground

1. See Conrad Wright, *The Beginnings of Unitarianism in America* (Boston: Starr King Press, 1955), pp. 8–14.

2. Wright, *Unitarianism*, pp. 57–58.

3. See Alexander Kern, "The Rise of Transcendentalism" in *Transitions in American Literary History*, ed. Harry Hayden Clark (Durham, N.C.: Duke Univ. Press, 1953), pp. 252–53.

4. "Jonathan Edwards to Emerson," *New England Quarterly* 13 (Dec. 1940): 600.

5. *JMN*, 1:207; see also Sheldon W. Liebman, "Emerson's Transformation in the 1820's," *American Literature* 40 (May 1968): 133–54.

6. *The Transcendentalists: An Anthology*, ed. Perry Miller (Cambridge, Mass.: Harvard Univ. Press, 1950), pp. 23, 25.

7. *Representative Man: Ralph Waldo Emerson in His Time* (New York: Oxford Univ. Press, 1979), pp. 125–26.

8. Liebman, "Emerson's Transformation in the 1820's," p. 133.

9. Joy Bayless, *Rufus Wilmot Griswold; Poe's Literary Executor* (Nashville, Tenn.: Vanderbilt Univ. Press, 1943), p. 66.

10. "The Head," *EL*, 2:256. Variations of this passage occur in *JMN*, 5:112, and the essay "Intellect."

11. Gay Wilson Allen, "A Look at Emerson and Science" in *Literature and*

Ideas in America; Essays in Memory of Harry Hayden Clark, ed. Robert Falk (Athens: Ohio Univ. Press, 1975), p. 69.

12. "The stars awaken a certain reverance" (*Nature*); "I once heard a preacher who sorely tempted me to say, I would go to church no more" (Divinity School Address).

13. *JMN*, 4:95. The final clause was later amended to read: "but the language put together into a most significant & universal book."

14. See also Allen, "A New Look at Emerson and Science," p. 70.

15. Frederic Ives Carpenter, *Emerson and Asia* (Cambridge, Mass.: Harvard Univ. Press, 1930), pp. 44–45.

16. Porte, *Representative Man*, p. 315.

17. *Waldo Emerson: A Biography* (New York: Viking, 1981), p. 258.

18. Horace Traubel, *With Walt Whitman in Camden, November 1, 1888–January 20, 1889* (New York: Mitchell, Kennerley, 1914), p. 453.

Emerson on "Making" in Literature
His Problem of Professionalism, 1836–1841

1. On *Nature*, see Richard P. Adams, "Emerson and the Organic Metaphor," *PMLA* 69 (Mar. 1954): 121–22. On "first philosophies," cf. *JMN*, 5:57. For two early examples of Emerson's philosophizing, see *JMN*, 2:294–306, 413, 420.

2. *Life*; Whicher, *Freedom and Fate: An Inner Life of Ralph Waldo Emerson* (Philadelphia: Univ. of Pennsylvania Press, 1953), esp. chaps. 2–4; Smith, "Emerson's Problem of Vocation," *New England Quarterly* 12 (Mar. 1939): 52–67.

3. Feidelson, *Symbolism and American Literature* (Chicago: Univ. of Chicago Press, 1953), p. 150. Two later studies of Emerson's literary theories are Jonathan Bishop, *Emerson on the Soul* (Cambridge, Mass.: Harvard Univ. Press, 1964), esp. pt. 3; and Lawrence Buell, *Literary Transcendentalism: Style and Vision in the American Renaissance* (Ithaca, N.Y.: Cornell Univ. Press, 1973), esp. chaps. 2, 5. I am indebted to both these books.

4. See *JMN*, 4:355, and *CW*, 1:10.

5. Bluestein, "Emerson's Epiphanies," *New England Quarterly* 39 (December 1966): 450–51, 447.

6. See, for example, *JMN*, 7:93, 206, 210, 327, 505.

The Method of Nature *and Emerson's Period of Crisis*

1. Emerson records sending the essay to press on 1 Jan. 1841 (*JMN*, 7:411), apparently meeting a self-imposed deadline as a letter to Carlyle of 30 Aug. 1840 suggests: "Hope for me that I shall get a book ready to send you by New Years Day" (*CEC*, p. 278). He had hoped to write the book much earlier. Over a year before this, on 16 Apr. 1839, he had written Bronson Alcott that "I have been writing a little and rearranging old papers more, and by and by, I hope to get a shapely book of Genesis" (*L*, 2:194). On 4 July, he reported to Carlyle

that he had "three essays nearly done, and who knows but in the autumn I shall have a book?" (*CEC*, p. 243). But in Aug. 1839, in the course of a letter to William Emerson alluding to financial problems, he writes that "I see plainly I shall have no choice about lecturing again next winter" (*L*, 2:218). These lectures eventually became the series entitled "The Present Age." More details can be found in Linda Allardt's discussion of the composition of *Essays* (*JMN*, 12:xxv–viii). Allardt notes that as early as May 1835, Emerson had asked himself, "Where are your Essays?" and discussed "the law of Compensation" and "the sublimity of Self-Reliance" (*JMN*, 5:40).

2. In late June 1840, Emerson laid plans for an essay on "Nature" by noting, "I think I must do these eyes of mine the justice to write a new Chapter on Nature" (*JMN*, 7:374). "Nature" also appears in a list of topics for *Essays* apparently drawn up in June or July 1840 (*JMN*, 7:498). But in a letter of 22 Mar. 1841 to William Emerson, he explains its absence from the finished book: "It is curtailed of its original proportions by the loss of a chapter on Nature at the end of the volume, which for some passages which I could not finish to my mind I unwillingly left out. Should we ever come to the honors of a second edition, it shall come then, though I wanted it for a balance to this chapter of Art" (*L*, 2:387).

3. Richard Lee Francis, "The Evolution of Emerson's Second 'Nature,' " *American Transcendental Quarterly*, no. 21 (Winter 1974), pp. 33–35. Francis's essay traces the process by which Emerson came to complete "Nature" in *Essays: Second Series*, with reference to the place of *The Method of Nature* in this process.

4. In later remarks on the essay, Spiller says that it "contains some of his best passages but is confused and unconvincing"; see "The Four Faces of Emerson," in *Four Makers of the American Mind: Emerson, Thoreau, Whitman, and Melville*, ed. Thomas Edward Crawley (Durham, N.C.: Duke Univ. Press, 1976), p. 16. Carlyle complained of the essay's abstractness, calling for "some *concretion* of these beautiful *abstracta*" (*CEC*, p. 312). William H. Gilman and J. E. Parsons remark briefly on the essay's "placidity" in comparison with "the tragic awareness and skeptical strength of 'Experience' " (*JMN*, 8:ix).

5. Emerson retired to Nantasket Beach in July 1841 to finish the oration, but during the writing he confessed a resigned disappointment to Lidian in a letter of 15 July: "I see at least how such materials as I have will work into an oration although I have not had any of those visitations of the high Muse which make a few moments of every life memorable & one which would have given me the golden seed of a new Discourse that should have defied all my old readings & writings & been a new plant a new flower in me as in the world" (*L*, 2:427). On its reception see Edwin Percy Whipple, *Recollections of Eminent Men* (Boston: Houghton, Mifflin, 1890), pp. 145–47, in which Whipple records Emerson's own recollection that the address "was heard with cold, silent, unresponsive attention, in which there seemed to be a continuous unuttered rebuke and protest" (p. 146). See also Arthur J. Roberts, "Emerson's Visits to Waterville College," *Colby Mercury* 5 (1 April 1934): 41–45, for further details on the address.

6. Whipple, *Recollections*, p. 146. But compare this recollection with Emerson's

letter to Lidian written during the composition of the address, quoted in n. 5 above.

7. According to Spiller, "The summer of 1841 was apparently the nadir of his spirits" ("The Four Faces of Emerson," p. 16). See also, Francis, who notes Emerson's turn to the oration during "the troublesome time after the Divinity School Address" ("The Evolution of Emerson's Second 'Nature,' " p. 33).

8. For Emerson's scientific thinking, see the following: Harry Hayden Clark, "Emerson and Science," *Philological Quarterly* 10 (July 1931): 225–60; Joseph Warren Beach, *The Concept of Nature in Nineteenth-Century English Poetry* (New York: Macmillan, 1936), pp. 336–43; Sherman Paul, *Emerson's Angle of Vision* (Cambridge, Mass.: Harvard Univ. Press, 1952), pp. 208–20; Jonathan Bishop, *Emerson on the Soul* (Cambridge, Mass.: Harvard Univ. Press, 1964), pp. 45–59; Gay Wilson Allen, "A New Look at Emerson and Science," *Literature and Ideas in America: Essays in Honor of Harry Hayden Clark*, ed. Robert Falk (Athens: Ohio Univ. Press, 1975), pp. 58–78; and David Robinson, "Emerson's Natural Theology and the Paris Naturalists: Toward a 'Theory of Animated Nature,' " *Journal of the History of Ideas* 41 (Jan.–Mar. 1980): 69–88.

9. Leonard N. Neufeldt, "The Law of Permutation—Emerson's Mode," *American Transcendental Quarterly*, no. 21 (Winter 1974), pp. 20–30.

10. Brian Harding, "Metamorphic Imagery in Emerson's Later Essays," *American Transcendental Quarterly*, no. 31 (Summer 1976), supplement, pp. 18–21; and Daniel B. Shea, "Emerson and the American Metamorphosis," *Emerson: Prophecy, Metamorphosis, and Influence*, ed. David Levin (New York: Columbia Univ. Press, 1975), pp. 29–56.

11. Stephen E. Whicher, *Freedom and Fate: An Inner Life of Ralph Waldo Emerson* (Philadelphia: Univ. of Pennsylvania Press, 1953), p. 94.

12. This is particularly true of the essay "Circles": see Whicher, *Freedom and Fate*, pp. 94–105; and David Robinson, "Emerson and the Challenge of the Future: The Paradox of the Unachieved in 'Circles,' " *Philological Quarterly* 57 (Spring 1978): 243–53.

13. The discussion in this section is based on my work on Emerson now in progress entitled "Apostle of Culture: Emerson as Preacher and Lecturer."

14. Conrad Wright, *The Liberal Christians: Essays on American Unitarian History* (Boston: Beacon, 1970), p. 5.

15. Clark, "Emerson and Science," pp. 226–27.

16. This was Achille Murat. For a description of Emerson's meeting him see *Life*, pp. 121–22.

17. Emerson, "[Belief in God innate]," manuscript sermon bMs Am 1280.215 (23), Houghton Library, Harvard University. Quoted by permission of the Houghton Library.

18. Emerson, "[Conscience, a proof of God]," manuscript sermon bMs Am 1280.215 (21), Houghton Library, Harvard University. Quoted by permission of the Houghton Library.

19. For discussions of Emerson's visit to the Jardin des Plantes, see *Life*, pp. 187–89; Jonathan Bishop, *Emerson on the Soul* (Cambridge, Mass.: Harvard Univ. Press, 1964), pp. 54–55; and Robinson, "Emerson's Natural Theology and the Paris Naturalists."

20. Whicher calls "Circles" "the most unsettled and unsettling" of the pieces in *Essays: First Series* and discusses the "fresh consciousness of impermanence" in Emerson's thought (*Freedom and Fate*, p. 94).

21. This key term in Emerson's formulation of his vocation has been discussed by Merton M. Sealts, Jr., in "Emerson on the Scholar, 1833–1837," *PMLA* 85 (Mar. 1970): 185–95, and "Emerson on the Scholar, 1838: A Study of 'Literary Ethics,' " *Literature and Ideas in America,* pp. 40–57.

22. See also the entry of 12 Feb. 1841, in which Emerson laments the constant fret and hurry of life, complaining that "Every rational thing gets still postponed and is at last slurred & ill done or huddled out of sight & memory" (*JMN*, 7:421).

23. The tension between vision and expression is a prominent theme in "Circles." Emerson's thought as a whole has been approached from a similar dichotomy, power versus form, in Jeffrey Duncan, *The Power and Form of Emerson's Thought* (Charlottesville: Univ. Press of Virginia, 1973).

24. Although Emerson did fight a private struggle over the cost of being an artist, one other immediate source of this idea is a conversation with Thoreau of 10 Nov. 1838, in which Emerson was forced to confess to Thoreau "that this was the tragedy of Art that the Artist was at the expense of the Man" (*JMN*, 7:144).

25. Nichol's *View of the Architecture of the Heavens* (1840; 2d ed., New York: Dayton & Newman, 1842) combined diagrams, factual information, and theologically tinged speculation to serve as an introduction to astronomy for the lay reader.

26. Emerson received the invitation from John L. Moses on 22 Mar. 1841; see *L*, 2:390 n, 392.

27. The full story of Emerson's place in antebellum reform movements remains to be told, and in my opinion, previous discussions of this side of his thought have exaggerated his cautious conservatism. See particularly the comments of Arthur M. Schlesinger, Jr., in *The Age of Jackson* (Boston: Little, Brown, 1950), pp. 384–86. I have found Sherman Paul's discussion of his hopes for a Concord community most helpful (*Emerson's Angle of Vision*, pp. 183–93). Emerson's sense of vocation will be essential to understanding this side of his thought, as Henry Nash Smith recognized in "Emerson's Problem of Vocation: A Note on 'The American Scholar,' " *New England Quarterly* 12 (Mar. 1939): 52–67. Sealts's work on the "scholar" in Emerson's thought (see n. 21 above) will help to clarify this issue of vocation.

28. Emerson's reference to "the portentous year of Mizar and Alcor" is a response to Nichol's discussion of the long period required for the star Mizar to revolve around Alcor (190,000 years). Nichol uses this fact to stress the comparative smallness of time periods on earth (pp. 57–58).

29. Emerson mentions reading Plotinus in an entry of 20 Jan. 1841 (*JMN*, 7:413) and quotes Plotinus and Plato in an undated entry, presumably later in the spring (*JMN*, 7:547). The language of an important entry in May 1841 strongly suggests the influence of Plotinus's doctrine of emanation (*JMN*, 7:449), and is used in *The Method of Nature* (*CW*, 1:124). Emerson also mentions reading Plato while at Nantasket Beach as he composed the address (*L*, 2:421).

30. This association of the circle and divinity is most explicit in "Circles": "St. Augustine described the nature of God as a circle whose centre was everywhere

and its circumference nowhere" (*CW*, 2:179). See also Sherman Paul's discussion of Emerson's use of circle imagery, *Emerson's Angle of Vision*, pp. 98–99.

31. This passage is followed in the text by Emerson's reworking of his journal entry of Apr. 1841 (*JMN*, 7:427), which deals with man as nature's failed experiment.

32. Emerson's adaptation of sermon form in his literary work has been discussed in Lawrence Buell, *Literary Transcendentalism: Style and Vision in the American Renaissance* (Ithaca, N.Y.: Cornell Univ. Press, 1973), pp. 102–39. Emerson's list of applications here is a very good example of what Buell elsewhere labeled the technique of the "buried outline"; see "Reading Emerson for the Structures: The Coherence of the Essays," *Quarterly Journal of Speech* 58 (Feb. 1972): 58–69. It should be noted that Emerson does not label this series as a series until he introduces his third application, love: "But there are other examples of this total and supreme influence, besides Nature and the conscience" (*CW*, 1:133).

33. For discussions of the Puritan debate over preparation for salvation, see Perry Miller, " 'Preparation for Salvation' in Seventeenth-Century New England," *Nature's Nation* (Cambridge, Mass.: Harvard Univ. Press, 1967), pp. 50–77; Norman Pettit, *The Heart Prepared: Grace and Conversion in Puritan Spiritual Life* (New Haven, Conn.: Yale Univ. Press, 1966), pp. 86–124; and James W. Jones, *The Shattered Synthesis: New England Puritanism before the Great Awakening* (New Haven, Conn.: Yale Univ. Press, 1973), pp. 6–10.

34. I would like to acknowledge support from the National Endowment for the Humanities, the College of Liberal Arts and General Research Programs at Oregon State University, and the Center for Advanced Study in the Behavioral Sciences, Stanford, California.

The Poet and Experience: Essays: Second Series

1. Karl Barth, *Dogmatics in Outline* (New York: Harper & Row, 1959), p. 59.
2. For another view of metamorphosis in Emerson's art, see Daniel B. Shea, "Emerson and the American Metamorphosis," *Emerson: Prophecy, Metamorphosis, and Influence*, ed. David Levin (New York: Columbia Univ. Press, 1975), pp. 29–56.

Emerson's Eumenides: Textual Evidence and the Interpretation of "Experience"

1. David Porter argues for this position in *Emerson and Literary Change* (Cambridge, Mass.: Harvard Univ. Press, 1978), pp. 7–29.
2. Consult the individual forewords to volumes of the *JMN* and the headnotes to each journal for discussions of dating.
3. Journal passages are quoted in a clear-text form, omitting cancellations and incorporating additions.
4. Study of Emerson's use of sources requires use of two categories in the *JMN*

indexes—"Experience" under "Emerson, Ralph Waldo; WORKS," and "Life" under "Emerson, Ralph Waldo; INDEX HEADINGS AND TOPICS." The subtopics of the essay also provide suggestive passages parallel to those he used in the essay.

5. *Representative Man: Ralph Waldo Emerson in His Time* (New York: Oxford Univ. Press, 1979), p. 182.
6. Cf. Porte's mention of Keats's "Ode to a Nightingale," *Representative Man*, p. 179, and Porter's allusion in *Emerson and Literary Change* to Coleridge's "Dejection: An Ode," p. 119.
7. See the first "Character" essay (*W*, 3:96) for another use of this entry.
8. The identification of the journal title with "Surface" comes from Emerson's reference in the outline to the passage which ends the "Surface" section in the essay (see *W*, 3:66; *JMN*, 8:317).
9. See Lawrence Buell's discussion of Emerson's use of the "buried outline" and "careless list" in "Reading Emerson for the Structures: The Coherence of the Essays," *Quarterly Journal of Speech* 58 (Feb. 1972): 60.
10. *American Poets: From the Puritans to the Present* (Boston: Houghton Mifflin, 1968), p. 113.
11. Note also the link back to Emerson's conception of the centrality of action in the scholar's life in "The American Scholar."

Emerson's Shakespeare: From Scorn to Apotheosis

1. Falk, "Emerson and Shakespeare," *PMLA* 56 (June 1941): 543.
2. Vivian C. Hopkins, *Spires of Form: A Study of Emerson's Aesthetic Theory* (Cambridge, Mass.: Harvard Univ. Press, 1951), p. 5.
3. William M. Wynkoop, *Three Children of the Universe: Emerson's View of Shakespeare, Bacon, and Milton* (The Hague: Mouton, 1966), p. 28.
4. Over the years a clear pattern emerges in Emerson's spelling of Shakespeare's name. In the earliest journals he spells it with a final *e*, but by the mid-1830s he has dropped it. The final *e* is usually added again after his reading of Jones Very's essays in 1838, and alternate usage is evident until mid-1839. After that, with only one exception (in the following January), the final *e* remains. Although Edwin Gittleman (see n. 29, below) indicates that Very's Shakespeare and *Hamlet* manuscripts are not extant, from his spelling in the *Essays and Poems* (1839)—and it is not likely that Emerson would have altered Very's spelling—it appears that Very consistently used the final *e* in writing the name. If so, this suggests that Emerson may well have been so strongly impressed with Very's remarks that he changed his spelling of Shakespeare's name to conform with that of the younger man.
5. Cameron, *Emerson the Essayist* (Raleigh, N.C.: Thistle Press, 1945), p. 459 n.
6. Cabot, *A Memoir of Ralph Waldo Emerson* (Boston: Houghton, Mifflin, 1887), 1:59.
7. Ibid., 1:62.
8. Bloom, "The Freshness of Transformation: Emerson's Dialectics of Influence," in *Emerson: Prophecy, Metamorphosis, and Influence*, ed. David

Levin (New York: Columbia Univ. Press, 1975), p. 139; Bloom's emphasis on "*was*" deleted.

9. Quoted in Cabot, *Memoir*, 1:161; *L*, 1:291.
10. Coleridge, *Biographia Literaria* (London: J. M. Dent, 1906), p. 167.
11. Coleridge, *Shakespearean Criticism*, ed. Thomas Middleton Raysor, 2d ed. (London: J. M. Dent, 1960), 1:xviii–xxi.
12. Falk, "Emerson and Shakespeare," p. 534. From Wynkoop's point of view, however, Emerson ultimately placed Milton rather than Shakespeare in this position, as "the Sayer."
13. Bishop, *Emerson on the Soul* (Cambridge: Harvard Univ. Press, 1964), p. 175.
14. *Dial* 1 (July 1840): 14–16.
15. Charles Emerson, "Shakspeare," p. 15. Could it have been Charles's use of the adjective "husky" thus which led Waldo to belittle his own poetic talents with the same word when writing to Lydia Jackson that his "singing to be sure is very 'husky' " (1 Feb. 1835, *L*, 1:435)? Note that Emerson put the word within quotation marks.
16. Emerson seems to have inherited Charles's edition of Shakespeare (*L*, 5:432–33 n; also see Rusk's "Introduction," *L*, 1:xxxiii).
17. Falk, "Emerson and Shakespeare," p. 539; Charles Emerson, "Shakespeare," p. 16.
18. Dowden, quoted in Edward A. Armstrong, *Shakespeare's Imagination: A Study of the Psychology of Association and Inspiration* (Lincoln: Univ. of Nebraska Press, 1963), p. 153 n.
19. The reprinting of Sprague's "Shakspeare Ode" in a supplement to the *Boston Transcript* of 23 Apr. 1864 may well be attributable to a request from Emerson; see 18 Apr. 1864, *L*, 5:369, and below.
20. However, several collected editions of Sprague's works (1841, 1850, etc.) belie this statement.
21. Sprague, "Shakspeare Ode," stanzas 5–8 and closing stanza.
22. Editors' "Introduction" to "Shakspear," *EL*, 1:287. Long after these lectures were written, however, Emerson indicated in a letter that the edition he had been using for some forty years was that of Isaac Reed, *The Dramatic Works of William Shakespeare* (London, 1821), based on the text of Samuel Johnson and George Steevens. This is the edition he apparently inherited from his brother Charles, whose signature appears in it, dated July 1822 (*L*, 5:432, 432–33 n). See also Thomas A. Perry, "Emerson, the Historical Frame, and Shakespeare," *Modern Language Quarterly* 9 (Dec. 1948): 446.
23. Whicher and Spiller indicate that Emerson was at this time "under the spell of Coleridge's philosophy" and that the lectures show "a close reading of *The Friend* and other volumes" (*EL*, 1:207). See also Cameron, *Emerson the Essayist*, pp. 196–97.
24. Coleridge, *Shakespearean Criticism*, 1:34.
25. Coleridge, *Biographia*, pp. 119–20, 123–24.
26. Coleridge, *Shakespearean Criticism*, 1:xxx–xxxi, 69, 69 n. See also *W*, 8:394–95.
27. Coleridge, *Biographia*, p. 262.

28. 9 ? Aug. 1837, *JMN*, 5:357. The quotation reappears in "Self-Reliance," *W*, 2:83.
29. Edwin Gittleman, *Jones Very: The Effective Years, 1833–1840* (New York: Columbia Univ. Press, 1967), pp. 121–22. Apart from primary materials, my basic source of information on Jones Very has been Gittleman's rich and rewarding study. His book has been of immeasurable value to me throughout this section of my essay.
30. Gittleman, *Jones Very*, p. 164.
31. Ibid., p. 165.
32. Ibid., pp. 165–66.
33. Ibid., p. 148.
34. Ibid., p. 25.
35. *Memorials of Shakspeare; or, Sketches of His Character and Genius by Various Writers*, ed. Nathan Drake (London: Henry Colburn, 1828).
36. "Shakspeare in Germany. Part I: Shakespeare's Tragedies—Hamlet," *Blackwood's Edinburgh Magazine* 37 (Feb. 1835): 236–55.
37. For example, see Warner B. Berthoff, "Jones Very: New England Mystic," *Boston Public Library Quarterly* 2 (Jan. 1950): 68–69, and S. Schoenbaum, *Shakespeare's Lives* (New York: Oxford Univ. Press, 1970), p. 252.
38. Cameron, *Emerson the Essayist*, pp. 69, 69 n, 74–75, 74 n. Rusk notes the strength of Berkeley's early influence on Emerson in *L*, 1:lvi–lvii.
39. Quoted in Cameron, *Emerson the Essayist*, p. 71.
40. Emerson, "The Problem," *W*, 9:8.
41. The word "prophet" is used here in accord with Abraham J. Heschel's descriptions and characterizations throughout *The Prophets* (Philadelphia: Jewish Publication Society of America, 1962); e.g., see pp. 6–7, 18, 22, 155, 188, 205, 217–218, 222, et passim.
42. Very, "Shakspeare," *Essays and Poems* (Boston: Little, Brown, 1839), p. 41; subsequent page references to this volume will be cited parenthetically in the text.
43. For example, see 5 ? Sept. 1838 in *JMN*, 7:65: "Is there another Shakspeare? Is there another Ellen?" What a revelation appears in these two brief questions! Such a juxtaposition must have sprung from the very core of Emerson's being.
44. Cameron, *Emerson the Essayist*, pp. 431–32, 437, 441. Upham would later be instrumental in having Hawthorne removed from his office in the Salem Custom House; see Randall Stewart, *Nathaniel Hawthorne* (New Haven, Conn.: Yale Univ. Press, 1948), pp. 86–89.
45. Very's mystical notion of personal identification with Christ would not have struck Emerson as being preposterous or heretical. He had felt similarly himself a few years earlier, when he remarked in the privacy of his journal: "I would fly in the face of every cockered prejudice, feudal or vulgar, & speak as Christ of their good & evil" (12 Aug. 1832, *JMN*, 4:35–36). Going public with such pronouncements, however, as Very did, was another matter.
46. Quoted in Gittleman, *Jones Very*, pp. 295, 296.
47. See also Carlos Baker, "Emerson and Jones Very," *New England Quarterly* 7 (Mar. 1934): 96–99.

48. Wynkoop considers this letter to be one of the most valuable of Emerson's epistolary comments on Shakespeare, though he overlooks the significance of its including no reference to Very among the Shakespearean critics listed (p. 38). In fact, although he devotes several pages to parallels of thought between Emerson and Very (pp. 85–91), he does not consider the possibility of influence from the young fanatic upon his benefactor. Yet, ironically, if his analysis of Emerson's thought is correct, it further substantiates my own view that Very's dynamic presence in Emerson's life for less than a year in the late 1830s had a pronounced though not necessarily permanent effect on the older man's appreciation of Shakespeare.

   According to Wynkoop, Emerson's recognition of Shakespeare's limited moral assertiveness and ambition was explicit in the "Representative Men" lecture but only implicit in the earlier two (see p. 38). By far, most of the supporting statements that he has extracted from Emerson's writings in support of his theory were written after the break with Very in 1839. Moreover, he suggests, Emerson was possibly influenced at about this time by Samuel Johnson's observation that Shakespeare "sacrifices virtue to convenience, and is so much more careful to please than to instruct that he seems to write without any moral purpose" (quoted on p. 78). He notes that Emerson may have been alluding to this striking passage (from the preface to Johnson's edition of Shakespeare), which adumbrates his own conclusion to "Shakespeare; or, The Poet," when he commented favorably upon "something in Johnson's Preface" in a letter to Margaret Fuller late in 1838 (9 Nov., *L*, 2:173). This letter was written only ten days after Very's highly successful stay with the Emersons, during which Shakespeare was a major topic of discussion. Very had read Johnson, of course (see Very, "Hamlet," p. 88), and it is not at all unlikely that he reminded Emerson of the point made in that preface, a major point of his own. Emerson's reference to Johnson's preface, his delight and astonishment over Very's ideas, and the subtle reshaping of his own understanding of Shakespeare at this time as if in accord with the young mystic's more rigorous moralism, are too remarkably in tune to have occurred simultaneously by mere chance.

49. Editor's note to "Days," *W*, 9:479.

50. Frederic Ives Carpenter contends that Emerson considered Shakespeare "to be *the* perfect poet in spite of his profane life," and that he "valued both Dante and Milton far below Shakespeare" (*Emerson Handbook* [New York: Hendricks House, 1953], p. 218).

51. Letter to Sara Sophia Hennell, 14 July 1848, in *The George Eliot Letters*, ed. Gordon S. Haight (New Haven, Conn.: Yale Univ. Press, 1954–55), 1:271.

52. Editor's notes to *Representative Men*, *W*, 4:299.

53. *W*, 9:296; see also the editor's notes, *W*, 9:497. In November 1852, Emerson entered in his journal: " 'T is said that the age ends with the poet or successful man who knots up into himself the genius or idea of his nation; and that when the Jews have at last flowered perfectly into Jesus, there is the end of the nation" (*J*, 8:345). The image of Christ as the Jews in ultimate and perfect flower corresponds directly to his vision of Christ in the quatrain.

54. See Jan. 1853, *J*, 8:360.

55. The correspondence is published in Theodore Bacon, *Delia Bacon: A Biographical Sketch* (Boston: Houghton, Mifflin, 1888).
56. Bacon, *Delia Bacon*, pp. 93–94, 163.
57. Bacon, *Delia Bacon*, p. 213. Part of Hawthorne's association with Delia Bacon is given in *Our Old Home* (1970), vol. 5 of *The Centenary Edition of the Works of Nathaniel Hawthorne*, ed. William Charvat et al., 13 vols. to date (Columbus: Ohio State Univ. Press, 1962–), pp. 90–119. Randall Stewart indicates, however, that Hawthorne was more generous toward her than he himself acknowledged; see *Nathaniel Hawthorne*, p. 168 n.
58. Cabot, *Memoir*, 2:621–22.
59. Editor's note to "Shakspeare," *W*, 11:633.
60. See Wynkoop, *Three Children of the Universe*, p. 38 n; (abot, *Memoir*, 2:299).
61. *Parnassus* (Boston: Houghton, Osgood, 1874), pp. v, vii.
62. "Days," *W*, 9:228.
63. Quoted from Paul Elmer More in Falk, "Emerson and Shakespeare," p. 534.
64. *Parnassus*, p. 124.

The Contemporary Reception of English Traits

1. *L*, 4:390; for related letters, see Emerson to Anna Jameson and to Richard Fuller, *L*, 4:352, 384.
2. See Emerson's letters to his wife Lidian, 3 Jan. and 13–14 Jan. 1856, *L*, 5:4, 7.
3. See Emerson's letters to his brother William, 2 June and 23 June 1856, *L*, 5:23, 24.
4. William Charvat, *A Chronological List of Emerson's American Lecture Engagements* (New York: New York Public Library, 1961), pp. 23–31.
5. (New York: Charles Scribner, 1849).
6. *Emerson's Impact on the British Isles and Canada* (Charlottesville: Univ. Press of Virginia, 1966), p. 47.
7. Just three years before, *Graham's* printed an unfavorable review of *Uncle Tom's Cabin* which caused such a furor that George R. Graham was forced to reply to his displeased readers in the Mar. 1853 number of his journal. Graham later claimed that the review of Stowe ultimately drove him out of business (see Frank Luther Mott, *A History of American Magazines 1850–1865* [Cambridge, Mass.: Harvard Univ. Press, 1957 (1938)], p. 553).
8. Walter Graham, *English Literary Periodicals* (New York: Thomas Nelson, 1930), pp. 241–48, esp. p. 245, where Graham cites the conservative *New Quarterly Review*'s "reputation for unfairness and vituperation."
9. See, e.g., the *Westminster Review* 64 (Oct. 1856): 497, where the reviewer states that "We seem to have heard every sentence before, and yet find every sentence new. We know it all, and yet we like to read it."
10. One other mixed review appeared in the *Dublin University Magazine* 48 (Nov. 1856): 569–79.
11. Graham, *English Literary Periodicals*, p. 257.
12. The *Knickerbocker* also reprinted the review from the *North American Review* 83 (Oct. 1856): 503–10.

13. For a discussion of a liberalization of the *Christian Examiner,* see Mott, *History of American Magazines*, pp. 288–89.
14. (Bath: E. Williams, 1856).

"The Adirondacs" and Technology

1. *Emerson as Poet* (Princeton, N.J.: Princeton Univ. Press, 1974), p. 76.
2. *Emerson and the Orphic Poet in America* (Berkeley: Univ. of California Press, 1978), pp. 119–20.
3. *L*, 3:414, 4:499, 5:110, 111, 114, 115. The other members of the party were Louis Agassiz, Dr. Amos Binney, Ebenezer Rockwood Hoar, John Holmes, Estes Howe, James Russell Lowell, William J. Stillman, Horatio Woodman, and Jeffries Wyman. Stillman's account of the trip is in his *The Autobiography of a Journalist* (Boston: Houghton, Mifflin, 1901), 1:248–67.
4. Stillman's painting is reproduced in Edward Waldo Emerson, *The Early Years of the Saturday Club, 1855–1870* (Boston: Houghton Mifflin, 1918), following p. 170.
5. "Emerson in the Adirondacks," *New York History* 39 (July 1958): 215–37.
6. See Emerson, *Saturday Club*. The book includes some of Emerson's "Attempts to sketch in verse some of the company" by means of the younger Emerson's "siftings from various trial-lines": Woodman (p. 125), Stillman (pp. 175–76), Howe (p. 283), and Wyman (p. 125).
7. See Kenneth Walter Cameron, "Emerson, Thoreau, and the Atlantic Cable," *Emerson Society Quarterly*, no. 26 (1st Quarter 1962), pp. 45–86.

Emerson as Teacher

1. See also *JMN*, 10:300–301, and "Culture," *W*, 6:147.
2. Henry James to Emerson, 3 Oct. 1843, in Ralph Barton Perry, *The Thought and Character of William James*, 2 vols. (Boston: Little, Brown, 1935). 1:51.
3. See Matthew Arnold, "Emerson," in *Discourses in America* (London: Macmillan, 1885), pp. 138–207.
4. Thomas Carlyle, *Sartor Resartus: The Life and Opinions of Herr Teufelsdröckh*, ed. Charles Frederick Harrold (Garden City, N.Y.: Doubleday, Doran, 1937), p. 18.
5. See Andrews Norton, "A Discourse on the Latest Form of Infidelity," an address delivered before a meeting of the alumni of the Harvard Divinity School on 19 July 1839 and subsequently printed as a pamphlet. The address is excerpted in *The Transcendentalists: An Anthology*, ed Perry Miller (Cambridge, Mass.: Harvard Univ. Press, 1950), pp. 210–13, along with other documents in the controversy which Emerson's address of 1838 provoked.
6. "Why has never the poorest country college offered me a professorship of rhetoric? I think I could have taught an orator, though I am none" (*J*, 9:413). Moncure Daniel Conway, *Emerson at Home and Abroad* (Boston: James R. Osgood, 1882), p. 55, reports that Emerson once told him that when he

graduated from Harvard "his ambition was to be a professor of rhetoric and elocution."

7. *The Journal of Henry D. Thoreau*, ed. Bradford Torrey and Francis H. Allen, 14 vols. (Boston: Houghton Mifflin, 1906), 1:19.

8. Whitman, in conversation with John Townsend Trowbridge in 1860, in Trowbridge, *My Own Story* (Boston: Houghton, Mifflin, 1903), p. 367.

9. Nathaniel Hawthorne, "The Old Manse," in *Mosses from an Old Manse* (Columbus: Ohio State Univ. Press, 1974), p. 31.

10. Melville to Evert Duyckinck, Boston, 3 Mar. 1849, in *The Letters of Herman Melville*, ed. Merrell R. Davis and William H. Gilman (New Haven, Conn.: Yale Univ. Press, 1960), p. 79.

11. Perry Miller, Introduction to *The Golden Age of American Literature* (New York: George Braziller, 1959), p. 12.

12. Review of F. O. Matthiessen, *American Renaissance: Art and Expression in the Age of Emerson and Whitman*, *Time*, 2 June 1941, p. 84.

13. Lyon N. Richardson, "What Rutherford B. Hayes Liked in Emerson," *American Literature* 17 (Mar. 1945): 28.

14. Letter of 5 Dec. 1889, quoted from *Diary and Letters of Rutherford B. Hayes*, ed. Charles Richard Williams, in Richardson, "What Hayes Liked in Emerson," p. 23.

15. James Russell Lowell, "Emerson the Lecturer," in *My Study Windows* (Boston: James R. Osgood, 1871), p. 375.

16. See David Mead, *Yankee Eloquence in the Middle West: The Ohio Lyceum 1850–1870* (East Lansing: Michigan State College Press, 1951), pp. 24–27.

17. Carl Bode, *The American Lyceum: Town Meeting of the Mind* (New York: Oxford Univ. Press, 1956), p. 201.

18. See Eleanor Bryce Scott, "Emerson Wins the Nine Hundred Dollars," *American Literature* 17 (Mar. 1945): 78–85, which illustrates Emerson's western experiences with an account of his reception in Rock Island, Ill. on New Year's Day, 1856.

19. Lowell, "Emerson the Lecturer," p. 375.

20. George William Curtis, "Emerson Lecturing," *From the Easy Chair* (New York: Harpers, 1892), p. 22.

21. Lowell, "Emerson the Lecturer," p. 378.

22. Oliver Wendell Holmes, *Ralph Waldo Emerson* (Boston: Houghton, Mifflin, 1884), pp. 363–64.

23. Curtis, "Emerson Lecturing," p. 26.

24. Conway, *Emerson at Home and Abroad*, p. 55.

25. Henry James, Sr., "Emerson," *Atlantic Monthly* 94 (Dec. 1904): 741 (written ca. 1868).

26. Holmes, *Ralph Waldo Emerson*, p. 363. Holmes also remarks that "the music of his speech pleased those who found his thought too subtle for their dull wits to follow" (p. 376).

27. Edwin Percy Whipple, "Some Recollections of Ralph Waldo Emerson," *Harper's Magazine* 65 (Sept. 1882): 580.

28. *The Memoirs of Julian Hawthorne*, ed. Edith Garrigues Hawthorne (New York: Macmillan, 1938), p. 99.

29. Quoted in C. E. Shorer, "Emerson and the Wisconsin Lyceum," *American Literature* 24 (Jan. 1953): 468.
30. Curtis, "Emerson Lecturing," p. 22.
31. Lowell, "Emerson the Lecturer," p. 382.
32. Curtis, "Emerson Lecturing," pp. 23–24.
33. Henry Adams, *The Education of Henry Adams* (Boston: Houghton Mifflin, 1961), p. 300.
34. His lectures in Edinburgh occasioned a pamphlet entitled *Emerson's Orations to the Modern Athenians; or, Pantheism* (*Life*, p. 338).
35. Mead, *Yankee Eloquence in the Middle West*, p. 60.
36. Yvor Winters, "The Significance of *The Bridge*, by Hart Crane," in *In Defense of Reason* (New York: Swallow Press and William Morrow, 1947), p. 587.
37. Randall Stewart, *American Literature and Christian Doctrine* (Baton Rouge: Louisiana State Univ. Press, 1958), p. 55.
38. D. H. Lawrence, "Model Americans" [review of Stuart P. Sherman's *Americans*], *Dial* 74 (May 1923): 507.
39. I have discussed this subject in "The American Scholar and Public Issues: The Case of Emerson," *Ariel: A Review of International English Literature* 7 (July 1976): 109–21.
40. Emerson made his distinction concerning teachers as early as 1830, when in a sermon he commented on the "wide difference between the power of two teachers," one of whom speaks "*living* truth" while the other presents "dead truth, . . . passively taken . . . like a lump of indigestible matter in his animal system, separate and of no nourishment or use. It is, compared with the same truth quickened in another mind, like a fact in a child's lesson in geography, as it lies unconnected and useless in his memory, compared with the same fact as it enters into the knowledge of the surveyor or the shipmaster" (*YES*, pp. 92–93). The parallel with Whitehead's "inert ideas" is striking.
41. The teacher's "capital secret," Emerson liked to say, is "to convert life into truth" (*EL*, 2:202; *CW*, 1:86). On the relation between life and truth, see also *JMN*, 5:324, and *CW*, 1:55.
42. Conway, *Emerson at Home and Abroad*, p. 298; cf. "Education" (1840), *EL*, 3:295.
43. Conway, *Emerson at Home and Abroad*, p. 297.
44. Henry David Thoreau, *Walden*, ed. J. Lyndon Shanley (Princeton, N.J.: Princeton Univ. Press, 1971), p. 71.
45. Walt Whitman, "Song of Myself," lines 1210–11, in *Leaves of Grass: Comprehensive Reader's Edition*, ed. Harold W. Blodgett and Sculley Bradley (New York: New York Univ. Press, 1965), p. 83. "The best part of Emersonianism," Whitman wrote later in an essay on "Emerson's Books, (The Shadows of Them.)," is that "it breeds the giant that destroys itself. Who wants to be any man's mere follower? lurks behind every page. No teacher ever taught, that has so provided for his pupil's setting up independently—no truer evolutionist." See Whitman, *Prose Works 1892*, ed. Floyd Stovall, 2 vols. (New York: New York Univ. Press, 1964), 2:517–18.
46. Herman Melville, *Moby-Dick*, ed. Harrison Hayford and Hershel Parker (New York: W. W. Norton, 1967), p. 228.

Index